CONTENTS

THE
TEXTILE INSTITUTE

10 Blackfriars Street   Manchester M3 5DR

President: J. Boulton, M.Sc.Tech., F.R.I.C., F.T.I., F.S.D.C.

Acting General Secretary: P. W. Carlene, B.Sc., Ph.D., F.R.I.C., F.T.I., F.S.D.C.

Dates of Presentation of Papers at Annual Conference

Papers 1–7: Thursday, May 13th, 1976

Papers 8–13: Friday, May 14th, 1976

Papers 14–16: Saturday, May 15th, 1976

1—COMMERCIAL DEVELOPMENTS IN OPEN-END SPINNING

By P. R. LORD

Any non-conventional system takes a finite time before it can be fully developed to take into account the requirements of the ultimate consumer. The communication difficulties between successive markets (between machine and finished fabric) can lead to machine overcapacity caused by early overbuying and negative market reaction. This limits machine sales, which in turn tends to inhibit further development. Open-end spinning in the U.S.A. seems to have followed that pattern, and the future is a major question that is as yet unresolved.

Part of the difficulty has been the lack of realization of the technical differences between open-end-spun and ring-spun yarn. Intensive searches are being made for suitable end-uses, and the late start is part of the communication lag responsible for some of the difficulty. This paper discusses the economic and technical backgrounds to the observed oscillation in interest in open-end spinning. Analogies are drawn with texturing, and it is estimated that open-end spinning will establish itself firmly in a sector of the market towards the end of the current decade.

1. INTRODUCTION

Open-end spinning is at a stage at which it is of value to take stock, evaluate progress, and consider the future.

In common with the introduction of other successful and formerly unconventional systems, there are phases of (i) inception, (ii) research aimed at machinery development, (iii) development of commercial machinery, (iv) merchandising the machinery, (v) development of the textile product, (vi) merchandising the textile product, and (vii) up-dating of the machine (which tends to start the design-process cycle again). Naturally, there is overlap between the various phases, there are research and development by outside parties, and there is a possibility of concurrent development within several phases.

The motivation behind the initiation of the design process (i.e., the inception phase) arises because of pressure to reduce manufacturing costs in terms of money and labour *or* to produce a product with an improved sales appeal relative to other materials on the market *or* both. The pressure is frequently applied because of the success of a competitive product; for example, textured yarns gained a substantial market share, and a breakthrough in staple-fibre-yarn technology was required to maintain a competitive position. In this respect, it is interesting to note that the first great texturing developments were aimed at product improvement rather than cost-saving, whereas open-end spinning seems to have been aimed at cost-saving.

It can be shown (Appendix I) that there has to be a balance between the user-investment costs on the one hand and (labour + power) costs on the other. To achieve the objectives of designing a new machine, it is unavoidable that the machine maker invest large sums of money, which have to be reflected in the machine price and thus the user-investment costs. For minimum yarn cost, this necessitates a higher production speed, and any radically new design therefore involves a step change in productivity over existing machinery.

To ensure success, the textile product must at least be satisfactory to the user, regardless of cost. Thus it is of importance to ensure that the yarn is salable and that the users of the yarn are satisfied with its performance.

Unanswered questions arise as to whose responsibility it is to determine this and how the necessary information can be fed back to the machinery maker in the shortest possible time.

A further ingredient of success is to achieve a sufficiently low level of cost of the textile product. Numerous factors are involved, such as the costs of money, space, power, labour, raw materials, and competitive products, and many of these vary with the geographical locale and the general economic climate.

This paper will deal with some of these ideas as they apply to open-end spinning in the hope of obtaining a reasonably accurate forecast of the future of open-end spinning. A brief survey of texturing will be included to provide a few benchmarks.

2.   CONSTRAINTS ON THE INTRODUCTION OF NEW YARN-MAKING MACHINERY

The development and introduction of a new type of machine are hedged in by limitations of diverse sorts. In the long run, the machine (or process) will be judged indirectly by the ultimate consumer of the textile product. The ultimate judge is rarely a textile expert, and he or she tends to judge the final fabric on the basis of cost, quality, and aesthetic value in various proportions; the intermediate products are of little interest except in so far as they affect the stated attributes of the fabric. Thus, the machinery maker has to get feedback from each of the markets (Fig. 1) before he can be assured of success. It is insufficient to produce a mechanically perfect machine that produces inferior yarn or leads to the production of inferior fabric.

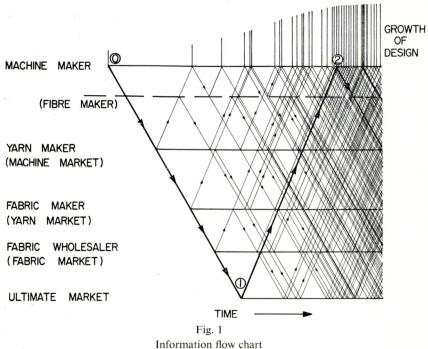

Fig. 1

Information flow chart

The machinery maker rarely has direct contact with the ultimate judge. He often sells to a yarn maker, who then supplies a fabric maker, who may or may not merchandise the final product. Each marketing stage involves delays and a loss in the quality of information, with the result that the stock of experience builds up slowly at first. The frontal wave of information is shown by the path 012 in Fig. 1, and it will be seen that the complete information required cannot be obtained before point 2. After this, the information-feedback rate is high and, if properly used, should permit correct design judgements to be made. The information system tends to have a high inertia, and the delayed-signal-transmission system gives the strong possibility of oscillation in the whole series of markets. Reluctance to buy on the part of the yarn makers tends to lead to a barrage of propaganda from the machinery makers. Once a few brave companies buy the equipment, the general reluctance is greatly diminished out of fear of loss of position due to the competition. At this time, a wave of machine-buying results, irrespective of the fact that insufficient data have been received back from the markets. The result is temporary overcapacity, and, if the market feedback is adverse, the problem becomes serious; the price of the textile product falls, the profit margins shrink or disappear, and there is a halt in machine-buying. Design alterations in both the machinery and the textile product may improve the position, but the scepticism of the market has to be overcome again; this is probably a crucial stage in the development process.

The rate of selling high-cost machinery is dependent to some extent on the availability of capital and labour. When money is tight owing to adverse economic conditions, sales are much less likely than in easier times. The economic cycles are well known, especially in textiles, and need not be dwelt upon. However, there are some other consequences of the economic cycles that may not be so well known. When times are bad, textile workers are often among the first to be laid off because the public reacts by cutting down on luxuries (and many of these have high textile content); this is demonstrated by the fall-off in fibre usage before the economy as a whole declines (Fig. 2). Naturally, this creates discontent, and it becomes increasingly difficult to persuade workers (especially those of high quality) to return when things improve; furthermore, foreign competition tends to depress wages (Fig. 6), and this compounds the difficulty. Thus, when the cycle swings the other way, labour shortages become acute, and there is a search for labour-saving machinery. Concurrent with this, the general affluence in these good times tends to blunt the discrimination of the textile buyer, and the quality of the textile product seems to matter less; capital is also more freely available. Thus a surge of machine sales might be expected with a booming economy. The timing of the introduction of radically new types of equipment can be seen to be very important.

A further factor is the cost and nature of the raw materials to be fed to the machine. If the machine requires an expensive diet of fibre, the yarn is likely to be expensive too, and the major aim of the machine designer has to be to produce a superior fabric. If the machine can digest low-cost fibre and yet produce adequate yarn, there is an obvious economic gain. However, a sudden demand upon a low-cost fibre can cause the price to rise so that the 'obvious' gain may only be temporary. Furthermore, if the low cost of the fibre is associated with losses in running efficiency at any stage between fibre and finished fabric, then an apparent saving may turn out to be a net loss.

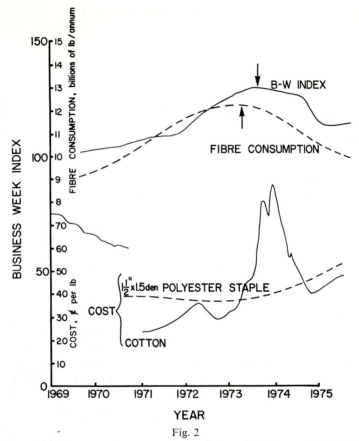

Fig. 2

Trends in fibre cost and consumption in relation to the *Business Week* index

3. PUBLICATIONS AS A PROXY FOR DEVELOPMENT ACTIVITY

In predicting the market pattern, it is useful to turn to the nearest and most apt experience for guidance. Texturing seems to fulfil this rôle, and it is interesting to consider publication rates as a proxy for commercial activity. It might be expected that patent activity would herald the inception stage, but it is very difficult to spot the key patents (which are hidden among many improvement and other patents). In fact, in sheer numbers, there is usually a surge in improvement patents well after the main inception stage.

When a new type of machinery is introduced, it is usually shrouded in secrecy until the grand opening. Following this there is usually a barrage of direct and indirect propaganda by the machine builder and his associates. This is necessary to overcome the inertia of the market, and several years may well be absorbed before there is a volume of sales of the new machine. Once the machine passes into use and a certain amount of time has elapsed, there are likely to be mill reports and discussions of the properties of the yarns, processing difficulties and procedures, etc.; this stage is later followed by reports about the nature of the fabrics. By plotting the publication rates and assigning the publications to each of several categories, the result shown in Fig. 3 is obtained. These data suggest that the acceptance lag is of the order of a decade and that the full information-flow path may extend over as much as two or more decades.

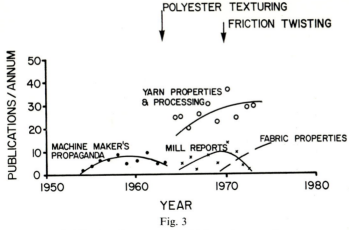

Fig. 3
Publications in conventional false-twist texturing

4.   OPEN-END-SPINNING ACTIVITY

Open-end spinning is not nearly so well established as texturing, but it is possible to make some comparisons. Fig. 4 shows the publication rates in open-end spinning, and the so-called 'propaganda hump' is evident. If the analogy were complete, one would expect great activity in respect of the yarns and the process in 1978–80; the fuller understanding of the fabrics would not be achieved until the 1980s. Unfortunately, the analogy is not complete because of varying economic conditions, and one cannot predict the development rate accurately. There has been a recession in 1974–75 as indicated in Fig. 2, and doubtless the downturn has damped down the commercial activity in open-end spinning. In the long run, this may not be as bad as might be expected. If the market system is likened to an oscillatory mechanical or electrical system, one might expect an overshoot on the first rise unless there is adequate damping. Consequently, the application of the damping effect of recession may have limited the initial overcapacity in open-end spinning that has been predicted by Brunet[1] and others. The increased sensitivity of the market to quality deficiencies during bad times

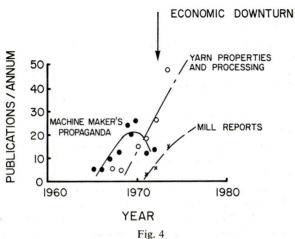

Fig. 4
Publications in open-end spinning

should lead to a more rapid textile-product development, which in turn should set the stage for a more ready acceptance of the product when the economy improves.

5. THE VARYING ECONOMIC CLIMATE FOR OPEN-END-SPINNING DEVELOPMENT

Figures 5 and 6 show how various economic parameters pertaining to the U.S.A. have varied over the period during which open-end spinning has attempted its penetration of the market. It is noticeable that the drop in fibre consumption anticipated the more general decline in the economy, and the herald for both seems to have been the upward surge in cotton prices. Doubtless the latter phenomenon had a considerable effect on the various decisions to buy cleaning or non-cleaning types of open-end-spinning machinery (for data, see Appendix II). It is also noticeable that staple-fibre usage has remained remarkably stable (Fig. 5), which implies that open-end spinning has a good future. The data on polyester fibres seem to suggest a slightly increasing preference for staple fibres.

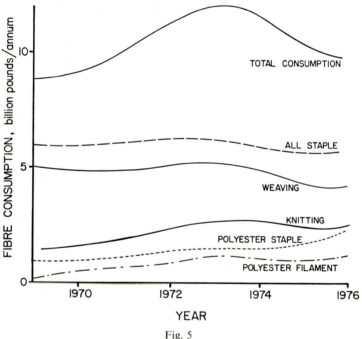

Fig. 5

U.S.A. fibre consumption

Fig. 6 shows that the cost of money rose sharply in 1973, and this implies difficulty for companies trying to raise capital to re-equip themselves, although there has been some improvement lately. Once again, this circumstance tended to act as a damper and lessen the tendency for an overshoot. In 1974, the cost of finished steel composites rose significantly, and similar pressures applied in other countries, as was evidenced by the cost of the cleaning type of open-end-spinning machine, which rose from about $500 per rotor to some $1200 per rotor. Not only does the rise in capital cost tend to reduce sales further, but, as has been shown, it also tends to require that the equipment be operated at higher speeds.

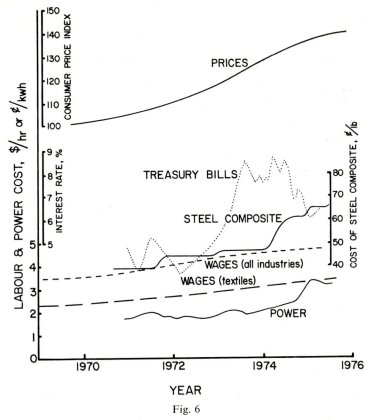

Fig. 6

Price and cost trends in U.S.A.

Also shown in Fig. 6 are the costs of power and labour. The incidence of the upsurge in energy costs in 1975 was significant, and, theoretically, the rise in energy costs should have caused the machine users to reduce operating speeds to conserve energy and associated costs. The opposing trends caused by increases in fixed and variable costs tend to cancel, but there is a limit to the upper speed for purely technical reasons, and there has been a downward revision in many of the higher operating speeds, a tendency that has been reinforced by considerations of machine efficiency and product-fault rates.

Fig. 7 shows that the quotient (cost of labour ÷ *per capita* productivity) for all industries has changed very rapidly in some countries. In particular, the cost of the labour content of German and Japanese goods has changed drastically as compared with those from the U.S.A. The differences are not so marked in the textile field because of the modest productivity gains in textile manufacturing. Open-end spinning should be able to make a contribution in this respect and help to hold a competitive position without sacrifices in wage rates. Indeed, the U.S.A. has seen the emergence of an export market; for example, textile exports from the U.S.A. increased by 40% in 1974. It will also be noted that German labour costs (which typify trends in many European countries) have also risen sharply, and, since a great deal of textile machinery comes from Europe, either the capital costs will escalate

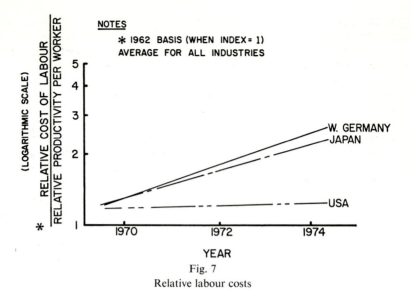

Fig. 7
Relative labour costs

(with the results discussed earlier) or machine production will be moved to lower-cost areas (perhaps even to the U.S.A.). In this respect, British companies seem to be in a good position.

6. TECHNICAL CONSIDERATIONS

During the course of development and use, some half-dozen major technical factors have emerged.

In spinning natural fibres (particularly cotton), it is important to remove most of the dust, trash, and other impurities before the fibre enters the rotor, since otherwise the machine efficiency is impaired because of the high rate of accumulation of these materials in the rotors and the necessity to clean frequently. A fouled rotor also produces a poorer-quality yarn. There are several schools of thought when it comes to a solution. One solution is to have a cleaning edge in the vicinity of the combing roller and another is to clean the material before it reaches the open-end-spinning machine. Yet another solution is to do both, because it is said that most yarn faults are associated with dust and trash particles even with a self-cleaning open-end-spinning machine; the cost of extra cleaning in the opening line might be recovered by dispensing with rewinding for the purpose of yarn-clearing. In any event, the fact that the cost of the non-cleaning open-end-spinning machines is a fraction of that of the others has motivated considerable development activity among makers of fibre-cleaning and carding equipment. In the latter respect, there is evidence of some advantage from double or tandem carding, but only part of that can be ascribed to improved cleaning, since part must be attributed to improved fibre orientation in the sliver, which tends to reduce fibre damage in the combing roller.

The use of man-made fibre does not eliminate the problems. For example, the use of surplus fibre finish can cause build-ups in the rotor, albeit at a slower rate than with cotton. Moreover, fibre breakage can, under adverse conditions, produce rapid build-ups of debris, and this is especially true of the relatively brittle fibres. The use of too great a fibre crimp or length can adversely affect yarn properties[2] and operating conditions. The use of improper materials (e.g., polyester fibre on soft steel) can cause remarkably rapid rates of metallic wear and erosion. Unfortunately, wear caused by fibres tends to be directed into the production of deep and most undesirable grooves in critical areas in the fibre-flow path; this causes local accumulations of fibre to build up, which at first adversely affect quality and ultimately lead to a high rate of ends-down. The critical metal parts must be sufficiently hard and abrasion-resistant to permit the use of the normal range of textile fibres. The fibre should be specially designed for open-end spinning, and, for most machines, the usual $1\frac{1}{2}$- or $1\frac{7}{16}$-in. (38- or 36·5-mm) staple length is probably too long. The length, crimp level, fibre finish, and fibre characteristics generally determine how well the comber roller will separate the fibres, it being remembered that good fibre separation is essential for efficient open-end spinning. In fact, it is fibre separation that imposes a low-count spinning limit on open-end spinning so that there are both high- and low-count spinning limits, and this has to be taken into account in estimating machine efficiencies because, as one approaches either limit, the machine efficiency falls. This also implies that many cost calculations are in error because most of them are made on the basis of fixed efficiency. Fig. 8 illustrates the effect, and it will be noticed that there is a limited range of linear densities over which there is an economic gain, and this will be fixed to some extent by the comber-roller design.

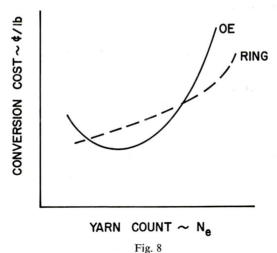

Fig. 8
The cost of making yarn: comparison of open-end-spun and ring-spun yarns

The ratio of fibre length to rotor circumference is important[3] since this, together with the crimp level, determines the percentage of wrapping and bridging fibres. In view of the needs to conserve power and to prevent unwanted eddy motion with the rotor, it is necessary to limit the rotor size, and thus staple length has to be correspondingly limited. It is estimated that, for the extant short-staple machines, the fibre length ought to be limited to a staple length of about $1\frac{1}{4}$ in. (32 mm) and the crimp levels ought to be kept below about 10 crimps/in. (3·9 crimps/cm). The reason for the latter is that an increase in crimp level tends to increase the size of the 'trailing anchor' formed at the point at which the yarn is peeled from the collecting surface inside the rotor[4]. Incidentally, the shape of that collecting surface not only affects the yarn quality but also affects the rate of build-up of debris[5].

One of the most critical areas is the design of the yarn-withdrawal funnel inside the rotor (i.e., the navel or nose-piece). Although it has been realized for a long time that the yarn rolls on the stationary funnel to produce a superimposed false-twist effect[3], the true significance has only just begun to emerge. The twist inside the rotor is different from that in the yarn placed on the package, but it is the twist inside the rotor that affects the machine efficiency and yarn structure[5-7]. The false twist produced is a function of the fibre–metal frictional properties, the funnel-flare radius and bore, the rotor size and speed, the yarn twist and linear density, the fibre properties, and possibly some other factors. This means that a spinner using any one machine design, with one type of funnel operating at a given speed to produce a particular yarn, will *not* manufacture the same product as another spinner who has varied any one of these parameters. No longer is it possible merely to describe yarn by twist and linear density alone. The slippage and disposition of the fibres as the yarn is made inside the rotor can give a remarkably wide range of yarn structures and properties. Changes in funnel design can produce dramatic effects, as shown in Fig. 9; changes in linear

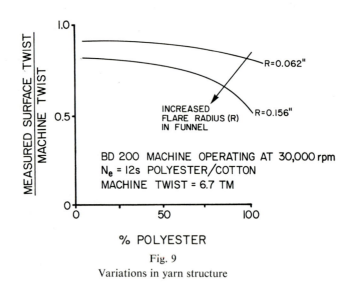

Fig. 9

Variations in yarn structure

density or twist or blend proportions also have large effects, and the resulting structures vary widely in performance from the norms established by ring-spinning. For example, the twist liveliness of the yarn is affected, as is shown by a simple yarn-self-twist test (Fig. 10). No wonder there is confusion in the market-place! Until it is realized that open-end-spun yarn cannot be used as a universal substitute for ring-spun yarn and that the fabrics and yarns have to be compatibly designed, open-end spinning cannot make the headway that it deserves. Strangely enough, the differences between open-end-spun and ring-spun yarns are small for cotton, but they can become remarkably significant with polyester fibre, and, since the popularity of the latter fibre continues unabated, it is likely that strenuous efforts will be made either to come to terms with the differences or to reduce them to the point of insignificance.

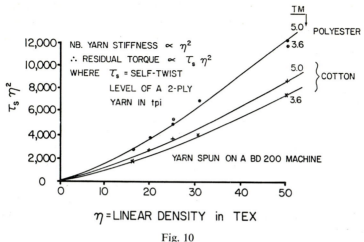

Fig. 10
Residual torque in open-end-spun yarns

7.   INTERACTIONS BETWEEN YARN AND FABRIC

Differences in yarn structure have varying importance according to the type of fabric, particularly according to whether it is a woven or knitted fabric. In a woven fabric, lateral-compression characteristics and chafing-resistance are important, whereas in a knitted fabric the torsional characteristics are more important. In both cases, the bending stiffness, hairiness, surface character, and evenness are important. Tenacity is much less important than many people imagine as has been shown by the various reports on work with twistless yarn.

In woven fabrics, the yarn crimp tends to be greater with open-end-spun yarns because the yarns do not compress as much as ring-spun yarns. The yarn crowns tend to protrude more, with the result that the fabric feels harsher and abrades or pills more rapidly than a fabric of the same construction made from ring-spun yarns. This lack of yarn compression due to the hard core[8] prevents the yarn from squashing and spreading as much as a ring-spun yarn, the result being that cover is sometimes disappointing despite the greater initial yarn diameter. The pilling, abrasion, and harsh handle can often be ameliorated to some extent by making the fabric tighter, but this reduces the tearing strength; this is a problem, because the low yarn tenacity is associated with a low tearing strength, and one can rarely afford to reduce it further. A compromise is necessary according to end-use, and it is the market that will ultimately determine what this compromise should be.

In knitted fabrics, the varying torsional characteristics affect the loop shape and out-of-plane distortion, which in turn affect shrinkage, permeability, spirality, etc. Open-end-spun yarn sometimes offers consider-able advantages in this respect, but on other occasions it does not[9]. It is beginning to appear that variations in staple type, machine type, operating conditions, and funnel design can have a profound effect. The use of a large flare radius in the funnel can make it possible to operate the open-end-spinning machine at a low twist factor, but, despite this, the yarn can be remarkably twist-lively, which gives adverse effects in the knitting operation and in the knitted fabric. Thus, there is a compromise needed between handle (low twist) and knitting productivity (low twist-liveliness), and this has to be worked out to the satisfaction of all parties.

8.   CONCLUSIONS

It has been shown that the development of a radically new type of machine to the point of full acceptance takes a remarkably long time, and this is likely to be true for open-end spinning. After a few years of propaganda, it is possible to launch a good idea despite the conservatism of the machine buyer. Unfortunately, competitive commercial pressures seem to cause a state of euphoria among the machine buyers that can lead to an overshoot in machine purchases. For open-end spinning in the United States market, some of this overshoot has been limited by exceptionally adverse economic swings; indeed, in some areas, a mood of pessimism has become evident. In all probability, both the earlier excessive optimism and the later pessimism are unjustified. Many signs point to continued and substantial progress as the economy expands once more. However, the progress could be hastened if the communications throughout the cascade of markets could be improved. It is perhaps significant that the Czechs set up their own pilot plant in the early days of the development rather than relying solely on customer reports. Before this time, it was unusual for Western yarn-machinery makers to concern themselves with more than the machine and its immediate product. Perhaps a leaf could be taken from the fibre maker's book: a significant and successful means of merchandising has been to control the quality of *fabrics* under certain fibre makers' brand names. Doubtless moves in these directions will occur as the industry tends to become more integrated. Thus one may expect some telescoping of the time scale that applied to previous developments (such as texturing). However, in view of the doubts about the progress of national and international economies, it is difficult to forecast the future exactly; nevertheless, it does seem probable that the fullness of the advance in open-end spinning will not become evident until the latter end of the current decade. A slack period may be expected in 1976.

It has been shown that there is a problem with a lack of understanding of open-end-spun yarn and that new standards of yarn specification are probably needed, which will have to be related to the performance of the yarn in fabric form.

REFERENCES

[1] I. Brunet. 'U.S. Market Outlook for Open-end Spinning' (presentation at Uster Corporation Open-end-spinning Symposium, Charlotte, N. C., April 16th, 1975).
[2] K. Motobayashi and R. H. Meadows in 'A Collection of Papers on Open-end Spinning', School of Textiles, North Carolina State University, Raleigh, N. C., 1974.
[3] P. R. Lord in 'Spinning in the 70's' (edited by P. R. Lord), Merrow, Watford, 1970.
[4] H. Landwehrkampf. *Textil-Praxis,* 1974, **29,** 272.
[5] J. W. Lünenschloss *et al.* 'The Influence of the False-twist effect and the Rotor Design on the Spinning Behaviour and the Properties of OE Rotor-spun Yarns' (private communication).
[6] P. R. Lord and P. L. Grady. *Text. Res. J.,* 1976, **46,** 123.
[7] P. R. Lord. *Trans. Amer. Soc. Mech. Engrs,* 1975, Paper No. 75 Tex-1
[8] M. H. Mohamed and P. R. Lord. *Text. Res. J.,* 1973, **43,** 154.
[9] P. R. Lord, M. H. Mohamed, and D. B. Ajgaonkar. *Text. Res. J.,* 1974, **44,** 405.

APPENDIX I

COST BALANCE

Let the labour cost/kg be divided into two portions, i.e., one that is unaffected by the productivity of the spinning machine but is affected by package size (e.g., creeling, doffing, etc.) and one that is directly affected by the productivity but is unaffected by the package size. Let the former be called a 'fixed' cost component and the latter a 'variable' cost component. A large part of the variable cost component is likely to arise from the repair of end-breaks. The cost/unit time of the variable cost component (C_1) is likely to be proportional to the quotient (yarn stress $\div$ yarn tenacity), that is:

$$C_1 > K_1 \frac{\omega^2 R^2}{\xi}, \qquad \dots (1)$$

where ω = rotor speed,
R = rotor radius,
ξ = yarn tenacity, and
K_1 = a constant.

In addition, part of the maintenance cost is likely to vary as at least the square of the rotor speed $\times$ rotor radius.

The power costs/unit time (C_p) also consist of fixed and variable components. The variable component, C_p, is given by:

$$C_p = K_2 \omega^a,$$

where K_2 = a constant dependent on machine design, and
a = an exponent such that $2 < a < 3$.

Over a restricted range, ($C_1 + C_p$) may be approximated to in the form:

$$(C_1 + C_p) = K_3 \omega^b,$$

where K_3 and b are appropriate parameters.

The total variable cost/unit mass is:

$$\frac{C_1 + C_p}{P},$$

where P = productivity in mass/unit time

$$= \frac{K_4 \omega \eta^{3/2}}{\tau},$$

where K_4 = a constant,
ω = rotor speed,
η = yarn linear density, and
τ = twist multiple.

Thus:

$$\text{total (labour + power) cost} = C_{pl} = C_f + \frac{(C_1 + C_p)\tau}{K_4 \omega \eta^{3/2}}$$

$$= C_f + \frac{K_3 \omega^{(b-1)} \tau}{K_4 \eta^{3/2}},$$

where C_f = summed 'fixed' costs.

The twist multiple (τ) can only be varied over a restricted range; thus, $K_3 \tau / K_4$ may be treated as a constant (K_5) and:

$$C_{pl} = C_f + K_5 \omega^{(b-1)} \eta^{-3/2}.$$

A further cost arises from depreciation, interest, rent, and other charges that exist irrespective of whether yarn is being produced or handled. Let this be called an 'investment' cost component (C_i').

The cost/unit yarn mass is given by:

$$C_i = C_i' P^{-1}$$

$$= \frac{C_i' \tau}{\omega \eta^{3/2}},$$

i.e.:

$$C_i = (C_i' \tau \eta^{-3/2}) \omega^{-1}.$$

The total cost is given by:

$$C_t = C_{pl} + C_i$$

$$= C_f + K_5 \omega^{(b-1)} \eta^{-3/2} + C_i' \tau \eta^{-3/2} \omega^{-1}.$$

Minimum cost is when:

$$\frac{dC_t}{d\omega} = 0.$$

Differentiation with respect to ω gives:

$$\frac{dC_t}{d\omega} = K_5 \eta^{-3/2}(b-1)\omega^{(b-2)} - C_i' \tau \eta^{-3/2} \omega^{-2}.$$

For a minimum:

$$K_5(b-1)\eta^{-3/2}\omega^{(b-2)} = C_i' \tau \eta^{-3/2} \omega^{-2}.$$

Multiplying both sides by ω gives:

$$K_5(b-1)\eta^{-3/2}\omega^{(b-1)} = C_i' \tau \eta^{-3/2} \omega^{-1},$$

i.e.:

$$(b-1)(C_{pl} - C_f) = C_i.$$

In other words, the ratio (investment cost/variable cost) must be maintained at a fixed value to give the minimum cost. Thus, for given machinery already in place (where investment cost is invariable), any increase in labour or power rates should be accompanied by a speed reduction that would just maintain the said ratio. In machinery development, however, the investment cost is a variable, and, the higher the machine cost (or land or money costs), the faster the machine has to be run to reach the minimum cost level, all other things being equal.

APPENDIX II

Table AI
Open-end-spinning-machine Positions in Production

Year	Cleaning Type	Non-cleaning Type	Percentage of Machines Producing Yarn for Direct Sale
1969	0	0	—
1970	0	1,400	0
1974	62,000	12,000	50
1976	100,000*	100,000*	40

*Estimated.

Department of Textile Technology,
School of Textiles,
North Carolina State University,
Raleigh,
N.C.,
U.S.A.

2—FIBRE CONFIGURATIONS DURING OPENING IN OPEN-END SPINNING

By E. Dyson and H. Behzadan

The development of a technique of ultra-high-speed fluorescent-flash photography and its application to a study of fibre configurations in the opening region of an open-end-spinning unit are described. The effects of variations in important machine parameters are discussed with reference to fibre configurations and yarn properties.

1. INTRODUCTION

As open-end spinning continues to become more and more widely used for the production of short-staple yarns of medium and coarse counts, the differences between open-end-spun yarns and their ring-spun counterparts have been extensively studied and reported upon. Briefly, the principal differences are that the open-end-spun yarns have improved regularity of linear density and strength, lower mean strength, greater extensibility, increased bulk and covering power, and improved abrasion-resistance. The first of these properties is due to the doubling action at the point of yarn formation and the last has recently been questioned[1]; moreover, all except the first one are generally taken to be reflections of the fact that the fibres in typical open-end-spun yarns are less well-aligned and more convoluted than those in ring-spun yarns and also undergo less intensive migration through the volume of the yarn[2]. The experimental technique described in the present paper was designed to permit the direct observation of fibre configurations in the opening region and transport channel of a typical open-end-spinning unit when it was operating as far as possible at speeds representative of commercial practice, and, after a description of these techniques, the results obtained to date will be summarized.

2. EXPERIMENTAL

2.1 The Open-end Spinner

The open-end spinner used in the work to be reported in this paper is a single-end unit of the circumferential-assembly type, with a combing-roller drafting system designed by the authors that is based on well-known commercial units such as the Czechoslovakian BD200 machine. The housing of the opening unit is constructed from acrylic plastics material, the rotor is of the self-pumping type, and the four drives, i.e., feed roller, combing roller, rotor, and yarn take-up, each have individual variable-speed fractional-horse-power motors. The unit will spin cotton yarns of good quality from drawframe sliver, for example, 20s-cotton-count (30-tex) yarn from 0·1-hank (6-ktex) sliver, and such a yarn will have an Uster regularity of 13% CV or better and an acceptable tenacity. All the results referred to in this paper are based upon observations made while the unit was actually producing yarn, usually at a rotor speed of 30,000 rev/min.

2.2 Photography

After investigating several possible photographic techniques, it was decided to adopt an ultra-high-speed fluorescent-flash technique developed by the former Central Unit for Scientific Photography (now renamed the Instrument and Ranges Department) of the Royal Aircraft Establishment. This utilizes a Q-switched ruby laser as its light source to obtain a very short (approximately 20-nsec), intense burst of red light, which is then passed through a frequency-doubling crystal to convert it to ultra-violet radiation of 347·1-nm wavelength.

If the fibres of interest have previously been rendered fluorescent by treating them with an optical brightener, they can be illuminated by this source and photographed by using normal emulsion to give pictures of good definition and excellent contrast even when the fibres are travelling at very high speeds. The laser system used in the present case was a Laser Associates model 211A ruby system, with Pockel cell-switching rated at 5 J. Frequency-doubling was by a potassium deuterium phosphate crystal, and the camera was an MPP 4 × 5 technical camera.

To permit illumination and viewing from appropriate angles, much of the housing of the opening roller was machined away so as to leave only a thin wall around the roller. The face of the transport channel opposite the opening roller was formed by a small glass plate (a 3-in. × 1-in. (7·6-cm × 2·5-cm) microscope slide), and windows were cut in the supporting frame of the machine where necessary. In many instances, it was possible to illuminate the fibres by directing the laser beam along the transport channel in the direction of fibre movement, although several other configurations were also used. Fig. 1 is a general view of the spinner and the laser equipment when they were on exhibition at a Royal Aircraft Establishment Open Day and Fig. 2 a close-up of the opening-roller housing and cover and a typical opening roller and rotor (in this case, machined from transparent plastics). Fig. 3 is a typical positive print from one series of experiments and shows fibres on the surface of the combing roller, rotating at 4800 rev/min, in the vicinity of the stripping point. The tips of the roller teeth are faintly visible, and several 'broken-hooked' fibres are evident. Similarly, Fig. 4 is representative of the records of the fibres in the transport channel.

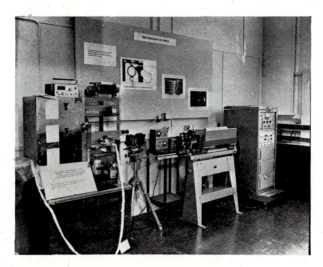

Fig. 1

View of the experimental arrangement, showing, from left to right: single-end open-end spinner, technical camera, laser head, etc., on optical bench, and laser-control unit

3. RESULTS AND DISCUSSION

3.1 Fibre Configurations in the Opening Region

Kášpárek[3] has used the tracer-fibre technique originally developed by Morton and his co-workers to study the fibre configurations in yarns, and he classified the fibres into ten types of configuration and related their relative

Fig. 2
Opening roller and feed roller in transparent housing, upper section of housing, transparent rotor, and opening roller

Fig. 3
Fibres on surface of combing roller, showing several broken-hooked fibres

Fig. 4
Typical fibres in the transport channel

frequencies to yarn tenacity. After preliminary observations of the fibre configurations in the opening region of the spinning unit, it was decided that in the present work the configurations could best be classified into the nine groups shown in Fig. 5. It will be noted that leading and trailing hooks are not distinguished from one another and that the 'open-hooked' class is intermediate between 'hooked' and 'crimped' or 'straight'. Folded fibres are those in which the two legs of the hook are approximately equal in length and the fibre is oriented in the direction of travel. The U-formation fibres are ones that are effectively hooked but with the legs of the U perpendicular to the direction of motion; these generally have the U shape in an open form. Class 9, 'grouped', is included to contain the closely entangled groups within which individual fibres cannot be distinguished. The most unusual class is class 7, 'broken hooks', which includes the very frequently observed fibres on the surface of the opening roller, which at first sight appear to have the apex of their leading hook hidden behind the tip of one of the wire teeth. Closer inspection of the photographs reveals, however, that this is not the case, and it is virtually certain that these fibres have been broken at their apex while still held by the feed roller and that the two halves have then been carried by the combing roller side-by-side. In the transport channel, such fibres become separated and lose their joint identity.

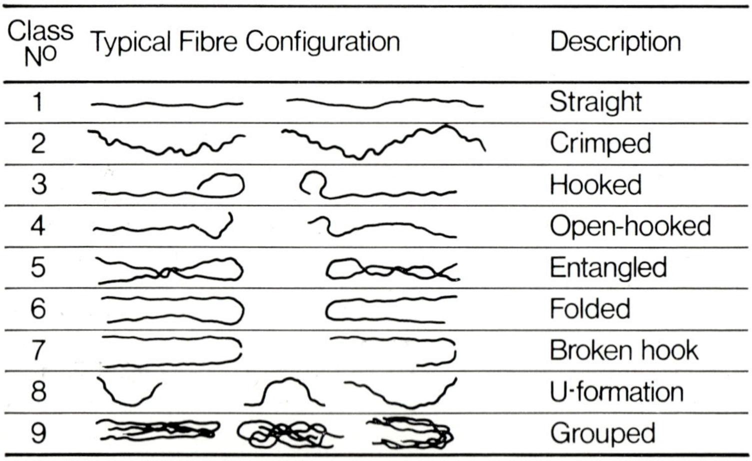

Class No	Typical Fibre Configuration	Description
1		Straight
2		Crimped
3		Hooked
4		Open-hooked
5		Entangled
6		Folded
7		Broken hook
8		U-formation
9		Grouped

Fig. 5
The nine classes of fibre configurations

3.2 The Effects of the Combing-roller Covering

Twelve combing rollers were available, each covered with a different commercially available type of wire and with principal characteristics as given in Table I. To investigate the effects of these rollers in the spinning of cotton yarns, series of photographs were taken, usually sixteen for each set of conditions, to permit analysis of the fibre configurations on the surface of the roller at the point at which the fibres are about to be stripped by the air-stream. In each case, the yarn being spun was collected for examination, and the standardized spinning conditions are given in Table II. Before each new trial was started, the roller was changed, and the whole of the fibre path and the rotor were thoroughly cleaned. Before collecting yarn for analysis or taking any photographs, the spinner was operated for about 15 min to stabilize the conditions.

Table I
Combing-roller Details and Yarn Parameters for First Series of Tests

Roller No.	Wire Front Angle (deg)	Points per cm^2	Yarn Tenacity (mN/tex)	Uster Irregularity (CV%)
8	63	22·7	93·7	13·8
11	73	26·3	90·6	13·7
10	75	23·8	97·9	14·0
9	76	26·3	89·5	14·5
6	80	47·6	97·1	14·5
7	80	35·7	100·0	15·0
12	80	29·4	99·1	14·8
1	80	19·2	107·3	15·5
3	85	15·6	98·1	14·5
2	90	20·0	98·3	14·6
4	95	11·1	96·5	14·6
5	105	10·0	98·0	15·3

Table II
Spinning Conditions

Combing-roller speed	5800 rev/min
Rotor speed	30,000 rev/min
Yarn-delivery speed	23·3 m/min
Yarn linear density	25 tex
Total draft	145·6
Sliver linear density	3656 ktex

The principal parameters of the yarns are also given in Table I and, in addition, the negatives were projected at a total magnification of 20× to permit the categorization of the fibre configurations according to Fig. 5.

To consider the extreme cases only, Table I shows that the strongest yarn was produced by using roller No. 1 and the weakest by using roller No. 9, roller No. 11 giving a similar result. The analysis of fibre configurations for rollers Nos. 1 and 9 gave the results of Table III, and a statistical examination by the technique of chi-squared with sequential deletions[4] demonstrates that the differences in proportions of fibres in classes 5 and 7 (entangled and broken-hooked) are statistically significant; an identical result was obtained in comparing the configurations for rollers Nos. 1 and 11. It thus appears that the use of a combing roller with too severe an action can cause a significant reduction in

Table III
Fibre Configurations for Rollers Nos. 1 and 9

Class	Percentage Number of Fibres	
	Roller No. 1	Roller No. 9
(1) Straight	27·2	12·0
(2) Crimped	21·0	6·0
(3) Hooked	11·1	6·0
(4) Open-hooked	17·3	8·7
(5) Entangled	7·4	12·0
(6) Folded	4·9	4·7
(7) Broken-hook	8·6	46·0
(8) U-formation	2·5	5·3

yarn tenacity as a result of fibre breakage. However, roller No. 11, with its greater point density, gave a yarn of relatively good regularity of linear density, and this is reflected in the regularity of fibre flow around the rollers. An analysis of the numbers of fibres in the fields of view of the several negatives for rollers Nos. 1 and 11 showed that, for roller No. 1, the CV of the number of fibres was 121%, compared with 61% for roller No. 11, again a statistically significant difference. Thus regularity of the opening action appears to be correlated with yarn regularity despite the large number of doublings within the rotor, and the intermediate values for the other rollers support this finding.

3.3 Wire-point Density

It has been demonstrated previously that the optimum wire front angle on the combing roller for the spinning of cotton by this technique is close to 80°, and four of the present rollers were clothed with such wire but had the range of point densities shown in Table I. Yarns from these rollers had tenacities that showed significant differences, and, again for the extreme pair, i.e., rollers Nos. 1 and 6, there are significant differences in the proportions of fibres in the several classes of Fig. 5. In decreasing order of importance these differences were in classes 7, 5, 4, 2, and 1, with the first one, broken hooks, having by far the most significant difference. As above, however, the roller with the densest distribution of wire points gave the most regular yarn and also the most even fibre flow around its periphery, with a coefficient of variation of 67% compared with 121% for roller No. 1.

3.4 End-breaks and Fibre Waste

During the operation of the open-end-spinning machine used throughout the present work, one of the principal problems was the frequency of end-breaks. Many of the breaks were a result of the fact that the unit was a hand-built prototype, with fibres trapped at various points of the fibre path, and these breaks could have been eliminated by a redesign of the equipment with the rounding of corners and polishing of surfaces. However, for the purposes of this study, it was considered impracticable to do this because it was necessary always to consider the problems of photography and the desirability of having flat or simply curved walls through which the fibres could be viewed with the minimum distortion. The other identifiable cause of end-breaks was the accumulation of trash, dust, and very short fibres in the rotor.

It was expected that the latter type of end-break would occur with similar frequencies, irrespective of the opening roller in use at the time. However, it was quickly found that this was not the case and that the rollers that gave the greatest frequency of end-breaks also made the restarting of spinning much more difficult, even after a considerable amount of practice by the operative. Because of this, an investigation was made of the conditions of spinning with rollers Nos. 1 and 9, which gave the best and worst results, respectively.

Roller No. 1 left in the rotor just a marginal amount of waste, which mainly consisted of very fine trash and dust, whereas roller No. 9 left a considerable web of short fibres mixed with trash and white powder. The short fibres, each not longer than a few millimetres, in the waste web clearly demonstrated the large amount of breakage of fibres when roller No. 9 was used. The build-up of this web on the collecting surface caused the frequent end-breakages when this roller was used, so that, after operation for only

5 min at 30,000 rev/min under the conditions specified above, the end would break down and any attempts to restart spinning were unsuccessful unless the waste web was removed and the rotor properly cleaned. In contrast, the operational performance of roller No. 1 was excellent and easily the best among all the roller types. It was possible to spin for long periods under the same conditions as for roller No. 9 without any end-breakage, and, if an end-breakage occurred after this time, it was possible to repiecen and continue to spin without the need to clean the rotor.

Priming and end-piecing were especially difficult when roller No. 9 was used. It was not possible to piecen the yarn at normal delivery speeds, and, even when the speed was reduced to 25,000 rev/min or less, several attempts had usually to be made before the end could be started. When roller No. 1 was used, the trash and fine particles accumulated in the rotor at a rate of 12 mg/hr, whereas for roller No. 9 the rate was 3·5 g/hr or 290 mg/5 min, which was the typical period before an end-break occurred in this case. This ring of trash represents about 8·5% by weight of the yarn spun during that time or approximately five times the weight of the web within the rotor that is incorporated in the yarn at any one time. This is the extreme example observed in the work done to date of the very harsh treatment that the combing roller can mete out to the fibres if the parameters are unsuitable. It should also be emphasized that much of the short fibre and many of the fine particles appeared to form a compact layer against the wall of the rotor and were not continuously stripped by the yarn tail, even when this layer contained a reasonable number of fibres having lengths of up to 1 cm.

3.5 Fibre Breakage during Initial Opening

The ultra-high-speed-photography technique was also used to record the fibre configurations at the opening stage immediately after the fibres were separated from the fringe and taken up by the opening roller. Sixteen photographs were taken during each run, and length measurements were made on at least 100 fibres from each of these runs.

Casual inspection of the negatives, even before any measurements were made, showed considerable differences in the number of short fibres, especially between rollers Nos. 1 and 9. The measurements were made on projected images such that there was a total magnification of $20\times$.

The enlarged images of the fibres were measured with a 'curvimeter' or map-tracer and confirmed the highly significant differences in mean fibre lengths in the two cases as summarized in Table IV. Combining these figures with the analysis of fibre configurations suggests that the large increase in the shorter fibres with roller No. 9 occurs because of the large number of broken hooks that this roller gives, whereas roller No. 1 has a more gentle action, which enables it to straighten the hooked fibres without breaking very many of them.

Table IV
Fibre-length Details for Yarns Produced with Rollers Nos. 1 and 9

Property	Yarn from Roller No. 1	Yarn from Roller No. 9
Maximum fibre length (mm)	28	26
Mean fibre length (mm)	10·9	5·9
Effective length (mm)	22·5	17·5
Percentage of short fibres	50	70

It must be noted that the figures for fibre length and fibre-shortening given here were not necessarily obtained by using the optimum machine settings determined by extensive previous experiments. It is virtually certain that appropriate investigations would lead to optimum machine settings that would give a considerable reduction in the amount of fibre breakage so that this parameter becomes more akin to the values experienced in commercial practice. However, the statistically significant and practically very real differences between the results given by the various rollers would no doubt remain.

3.6   Air-flow and Fibre Configurations

The air-flow in the transport channel has the dual functions of stripping the fibres from the combing roller and transporting them into the rotor. Preliminary observations demonstrated that the air-speed in the channel had a marked effect on the configurations of the fibres after they were removed from the combing roller. To enable a wider range of conditions to be utilized, the pumping action of the rotor was supplemented by an exhaust fan, and, as previously, the flow rate was measured by a float flowmeter.

The effects of air-speed can best be considered by taking the ratio of the air-speed at the stripping point to the surface speed of the combing roller and referring to this ratio as the *stripping draft*. Yarn samples produced by using a range of roller speeds and air-flows demonstrated that, within the range of values that could be obtained, i.e., stripping drafts from <1 to >3, the higher the stripping draft, the greater was the yarn tenacity. For example, with a combing-roller surface speed of $15 \cdot 6$ m/sec, a stripping draft of $2 \cdot 75$ gave a yarn tenacity of $89 \cdot 1$ mN/tex, whereas a stripping draft of $1 \cdot 17$ gave a tenacity of $82 \cdot 0$ mN/tex, and, when the stripping draft was reduced still further to $0 \cdot 88$, the yarn tenacity was $77 \cdot 3$ mN/tex. A more detailed study of the results obtained suggests that the effect of the stripping draft levels off at values around 3, which supports the claim[5] that this draft should preferably be in the range $1 \cdot 5$–4.

Use was made of the photographic technique described above to observe the fibre configurations in the transport channel under a range of conditions. Because of the tenuous nature of the fibre flow, it was possible to superimpose several records onto each negative, since the average number of fibres in the field of view at any one time was so small. The images of the fibres were classified into six of the nine groups used previously, for no fibres were recorded as broken-hooked or in groups. In addition, each fibre was recorded as having an over-all orientation within $45°$ of the direction of travel (parallel fibres) or in excess of $45°$ (perpendicular fibres). Hence the classification 'U-formation' was in effect superseded by that of 'hooked perpendicular'. The results of such a classification for a typical series of observations are given in Table V, from which it can be seen that an increase in the stripping draft does have the expected effect of increasing the proportion of parallel fibres and also increasing the proportion of open-hooked fibres, very probably by opening out what would otherwise have remained as hooked fibres. In addition, there is a significant reduction in the proportion of entangled fibres as the draft is decreased.

4.   CONCLUSIONS

The value of the photographic technique described has been amply demonstrated for the study of fibre configurations, and it is intended to extend this work to the interior of the rotor. It is also planned to use a multiple-flash technique in order that changes in the configurations of individual fibres can be observed.

Table V
Percentage of Fibres in Various Fibre-configuration Classes

Fibre Configuration \\ Stripping Draft	1·08		2·16		2·88	
	Para.*	Perp.*	Para.*	Perp.*	Para.*	Perp.*
Straight	5·50	0·92	8·13	0	2·42	0
Crimped	13·91	4·54	27·02	5·50	25·00	4·84
Hooked	15·60	11·92	9·76	4·87	11·29	3·23
Open-hooked	9·18	1·83	13·83	4·06	23·30	5·72
Entangled	15·59	13·77	10·58	4·87	11·29	3·23
Folded	3·67	3·67	6·51	4·87	5·61	4·07
Total	63·35	36·65	75·83	24·17	78·91	21·09
Yarn Tenacity (mN/tex)	77·25		87·28		89·09	

*Fibre orientation: 'Para.' = parallel; 'Perp.' = perpendicular.

ACKNOWLEDGEMENTS

The authors wish to thank the Director of the Royal Aircraft Establishment for permission to adopt photographic techniques first developed by that establishment and the staff of the Photo-Instrumentation Division, especially Mr. R. E. Perkins, for their invaluable advice; the Science Research Council for financial support; and the governing body of Teheran Polytechnic for allowing one of them (H.B.) to undertake the work described.

REFERENCES

[1] A. Barella and J. Vigo. *J. Text. Inst.*, 1973, **64**, 496.
[2] J. W. S. Hearle, P. R. Lord, and N. Senturk. *J. Text. Inst.*, 1972, **63**, 605.
[3] J. V. Kášpárek. *Proc. Symp. Int. Rech. Text. Cot., Paris*, 1969, 249.
[4] M. H. Quenouille. 'Introductory Statistics', Pergamon Press, Oxford, 1969.
[5] Výzkumny Ústav Bavlnářský. B.P. 1,113,003 (Czechoslovakia, 1 Oct., 1965).

Postgraduate School of Textiles,
University of Bradford,
Bradford 7,
West Yorkshire.

Present address of H. Behzadan:
Office of Budget and Planning,
Teheran Polytechnic,
Teheran,
Iran.

3—THE USE OF OPEN-END-SPUN COTTON YARNS IN TRICOT FABRICS

By J. M. BLACK and H. E. BROCKMANN

The purpose of this paper is to demonstrate and highlight the technology that is necessary to knit both fine and coarse singles cotton yarns properly and efficiently on tricot equipment. It begins with consideration of the minimum quality standard for the yarn to be knitted because no fabric can be any better than the yarn that was used to make it. It continues with a detailed view of the necessary modifications to existing warping equipment that will permit efficient high-speed quality warping. This study includes: (i) creel and yarn-tensioning systems that will minimize lint- or fuzz-ball formation and yarn-rolling—a major cause of fabric defects and lost ends; (ii) a discussion showing how a more symmetrical eye board at the front of the warper can help eliminate broken ends; (iii) means of scanning the warp sheet electronically and removing large slubs and long tails during warping; and (iv) a simple approach to the elimination of weak spots and lost ends. These changes will greatly improve the quality of the beams made. Beams of poor-quality yarn will knit very inefficiently and produce poor-quality cloth.

The paper continues with a discussion of the necessary modifications that should be made to the modern tricot machine for it to run efficiently at high speed. This includes a discussion of (i) the yarn linear density in relation to the machine gauge; (ii) a system to remove lint from the guide-bars, brackets, and presser-bar; and (iii) a method for minimizing lint fall-out and subsequent warp contamination. Also included in this section is a study of the effect of yarn position and stitch variation and the advantages of half-set threading.

The paper concludes with a discussion of the benefits of open-end-spun yarn compared with ring-spun yarn, fabric possibilities with ring- and open-end-spun yarns, and the expected defect levels of both types of yarn on tricot systems.

1. BRIEF HISTORY

Cotton yarns were among the first raw materials used in the production of fabrics by the tricot method of knitting. However, with the commercialization of continuous-filament man-made fibres early this century, an evolutionary change occurred in both the tricot machine and its utilization. During the last 50 years, substantial changes in the mechanics of the tricot-knitting machine have been developed to effect the efficient and high-quality knitting of 100% synthetic-fibre fabrics. A result of this evolutionary development was that cotton was virtually eliminated from consideration as a raw material in tricot fabrics. This was unfortunate because it effectively shut out the world's most important fibre raw material from the most efficient fabric-producing device. The research conducted at Cotton Incorporated in recent years has now accelerated the use of singles cotton yarns on tricot equipment. The authors will show in this paper that not only can traditional lingerie-type fabrics be knitted on this system with cotton yarns but shirtings, dress-weight fabrics, light-weight fabrics, and suedes can also be made. Illustrations of commercial fabrics, garments, and other products that have resulted from research and development executed by Cotton Incorporated will be given.

2. MINIMUM YARN STANDARD

How can the minimum specifications for a cotton yarn for use in warp-knitting be objectively discussed? Most of the problems associated with the warp-knitting of cotton yarns do not lend themselves to physical testing. Yarn strength and evenness are easily measurable, but they account for only a few defects. However, variables such as yarn hairiness, degree of lint-shedding, long tails, weak spots, and twist liveliness, which are responsible for most defects, are, in fact, very difficult to measure objectively. The yarn standards that have been set by circular knitters have little meaning for warp-knitters, although they do allow for general yarn classification. As an example, most singles yarns that have a Classimat rating between 6 and 9 major slubs/91,440 m (100,000 yd) are considered to be of good quality. If one accepted this standard and warped 4572 m (5000 yd) of yarn on a 21-in. (53·3-cm) beam with 504 ends, one would have 151 major defects/beam or one warp stop every 30·2 m (33 yd). Hardly acceptable for the warping operation, a 42-in. (106·7-cm) beam would have twice as many defects. All this is not a cause for despondency, however, because the great majority of these slubs will knit and not cause a defect, and the warping operative can let them pass through.

The specifications listed in Table I are to be used only as a guide. They do not specify a yarn that will always be suitable for warp-knitting, but they do indicate that the yarn spinner is producing a product of adequate quality.

Table I
Properties of Cotton Yarns for Warp-knitting

Property / Cotton Count of Yarn	Ring-spun Yarns		Open-end-spun Yarns	
	50/1	40/1	30/1	24/1
Linear density (tex)	11·8	14·7	19·7	24·6
Twist multiplier*	4·3–4·5	4·0–4·3	5·0–5·5	4·75–5·5
Twist multiplier†	41·2–43·1	38·3–41·2	47·9–52·6	45·5–52·6
Lea count–strength product‡	2200–2600	2400–2800	1500–1800	1500–1800
Uster evenness (CV %)	14–17	14–17	14–17	14–17
Classimat rating (top 4)	6–9	6–9	6–9	6–9

*On cotton-counts system.
†On Tex system (determined in units of (turns/cm)$\sqrt{\text{tex}}$).
‡Product of lea strength (lbf) and cotton count (also known as 'break factor').

3. MODIFICATIONS

It becomes obvious that what must be done to warp and knit cotton yarns efficiently is to engineer around the minor problems of the yarn and eliminate the major ones. It will be recalled that, when nylon yarn was first introduced to the tricot section of the textile industry in the 1940s, it was far from acceptable. The yarn ballooned in warping because of excessive static build-up, and this often resulted in broken filaments in knitting. The yarns were modified, new finishes were formulated, and warping and knitting machines were re-engineered to adapt to the yarn. Between fifteen and twenty years later, nylon yarn became a most suitable yarn to be knitted on a tricot machine and has now set an industry standard for good knitting efficiency. Most knitters have lost sight of the fact that the equipment has been designed to knit synthetic-fibre continuous-filament yarns.

At Cotton Incorporated, the last two years have been spent in active research, in formulating yarn data, and in modifying equipment so that cotton yarn will lend itself to the tricot machine and vice versa. With the technological changes that have taken place in yarn-spinning, coupled to the modifications to warping and knitting equipment that are recommended, cotton yarns can now be knitted at speeds of 400–600 m/min at acceptable defect levels. The work that has been done in this field is reported below.

Many knitting defects that were thought to be due to yarn faults have now been attributed to improper warping and creel-tensioning. It can be shown that most lint balls are formed on the creel and that most lost ends have occurred because of ineffective or improper stop motions. Yarn hairiness, a factor that causes yarn-rolling and yarn breakage, can be overcome by better yarn separation. Many long tails and large slubs can be removed by electronic warp-scanning methods. The first modification to be discussed is that to the creel and tensioning system.

4. CREEL MODIFICATIONS

The creel should be arranged so that a minimum amount of yarn-scuffing occurs and so that the lint that is generated on the creel during warping may be either removed by fans or kept from accumulating in the yarn path. On a sample Mayer warper, it was noticed that lint that was generated from the tension discs accumulated under the existing guide eye (see Fig. 1). As the warping progressed, the accumulated lint would build up until it eventually came into contact with the yarn and would be whisked off by it. It is this action that is responsible for lint-ball formation. In one modification, the tensioning device was changed to a vertical ball-tensioning unit (see Fig. 2). Although this unit also created some lint, there was very little lint accumulation, and, as a result, the number of defects caused by lint balls decreased drastically. An additional benefit was that less frequent creel-cleaning was needed. Carpet-yarn creels use a disc-tensioning system much like the Mayer unit, but they have a large hole next to the guide in order to let the lint fall away from the guide eye and prevent lint accumulation. Any number of devices can suffice, *but the key factor is to prevent lint accumulation in the yarn path.*

Within the confines of the creel is usually a form of stop motion, whose sole purpose is to trigger an electric impulse to the warper as soon as an end breaks so that it may be stopped and the end retied. Broken ends, although annoying, do not cause fabric defects, but lost ends do. In the authors' experience, most drop-wire stop motions are only about 50%

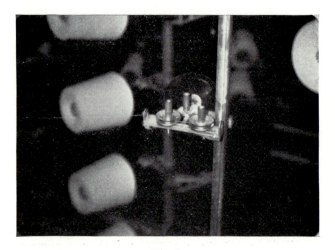

Fig. 1

The accumulation of lint generated from the tension discs under the existing guide eye of a Mayer warper

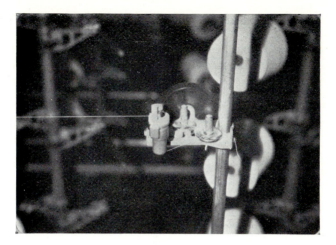

Fig. 2
Vertical ball-tensioning unit, fitted to Mayer warper to reduce the accumulation of lint

effective. Laboratory work has shown that, when an end breaks, the drop wire almost always drops but makes an electrical contact only 50% of the time. This is due to lint and dirt accumulation on the contact points of the drop wire or drop-wire unit. The Mayer drop-wire unit shown in Fig. 3 is typical of many units now being sold that create the same problem. There is, however, one unit on the market that does not have these inherent drawbacks and should be much more efficient than the units previously discussed. This unit bases its electrical contact on the mercury-switch principle. It has a drop-wire configuration similar to that of the Mayer unit, but each wire has a sealed mercury switch attached to it. When the wire drops, the mercury flows to the back of the switch, and electrical contact is made. Neither lint nor dirt can harm the electrical contacts in this unit because they are sealed. When this type of drop-wire system is used, hardly any lost ends occur. This type of stop motion also allows excessive weak spots in the yarn to be eliminated simply by increasing the warping-yarn tension to a value

Fig. 3
The Mayer drop-wire stop motion on a creel

above the known knitting-yarn tension and retying the broken ends as they occur in the warp yarns. Hence the warping tension should be related to the knitting tension if weak spots are not to cause defects and lost efficiency during knitting. As a general rule, the warping tension should probably be set to at least $0\cdot10$–$0\cdot15$ gf/den ($8\cdot8$–$13\cdot2$ mN/tex), with more tension added as necessary to prevent yarn-rolling and to maintain good control of the warp sheet.

5.   EYE-BOARD SELECTION

The purpose of an eye board is to keep all the yarns that enter it well separated to prevent yarn entanglement. Most cotton yarns should be kept at least 20 mm ($0\cdot8$ in.) away from each other. This is much greater than the space needed in warping continuous-filament yarns, and, because of this, most mills are not properly equipped to warp spun yarns. For a 504-end creel having nine positions/row and 28 rows on each side, the minimum dimensions for the eye board should be 112 cm (44 in.) in width by 18 cm (7 in.) in height. These dimensions could be modified, but any negative changes will increase the chances of yarn-rolling and entanglement. This width, however, is excellent for warp-scanning with a 42-in. ($106\cdot7$-cm) scanner, but more will be said about this later. From the eye board (Fig. 4), the yarn passes into the first reed. Here again, the spacing should be maximized, with at least 2 mm between successive yarns. A fan or blowing bar should be mounted in such a way that the reed is kept free of lint. This will eliminate the need for manual cleaning of the reed and prevent both broken ends and lint-ball formation. After passing through the reed, the yarns should be electronically scanned in order to eliminate whatever large slubs, lint balls, and long tails may be present. This can be done by using two 42-in. ($106\cdot7$-cm) optical yarn scanners (manufactured by Appalachian Electronics[1], the Lindly Company[2], or the Protechna Company[3]). The second scanning unit is used as a long-tail eliminator and as an additional stopping motion, which complements the drop-wire device. The set-up is described below.

Fig. 4
The eye board on a creel

6. OPTICAL SCANNING

Optically scanning the warp sheet permits high-speed warping without the need for manual inspection. This allows warping speeds to reach 300–500 m/min while effectively removing the yarn defects that may be present. The basis of the unit's operation is simply that a light beam is accurately aimed across the warp sheet and its resultant intensity is measured by a photoelectric detector. If the intensity of the light beam is not equal to or greater than a predetermined setting, a relay is activated, and the warper is shut off. By changing the setting of a potentiometer, the predetermined intensity needed to stop the warper can be either increased or decreased. For spun yarns from which only large slubs are to be removed, the sensitivity of the unit is turned down until the warper stops only at slubs of such a size that they are considered likely to cause a knitting defect. In general, this is about half the diameter of the guide eye, although finer settings can be used. In this manner, not only are defects removed, but one can also accurately assess the quality of yarn in the entire beam. This can be equal to as many as 4·5 million linear yards (4·1 million linear metres). About 2 ft (60 cm) in front of the first unit (Fig. 5) is placed a second unit, whose function is to remove long tails and detect lost ends. In this case, the warp sheet should be below the light beam. A blowing device is placed below the yarn sheet, and the air-stream is aimed at about 45° towards the warper. The air-pressure used should be sufficient for any long tails or broken ends to lift off the warp sheet and be blown into the light path to effect a stop. It is necessary to keep the yarns well separated so that they are allowed to be blown free of the warp sheet. This method works best when the yarns have at least 2 mm of separation between them, and this is the reason for using a wider scanner unit than normal. This extra space is not

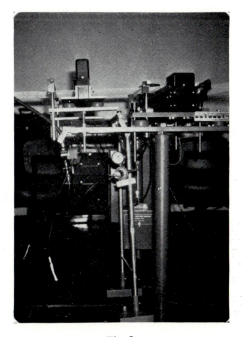

Fig. 5
An optical-scanning unit

needed in the warping of continuous-filament yarns because they do not affix themselves to the warp sheet as do hairy spun yarns. From this point, the warp sheet begins to be narrowed down to its proper width. Because of the large distance between the scanning unit and the last reed, it is advisable to go back into another eye board, which can be of standard dimensions, since the yarn sheet must narrow down. The yarns are leased over a chrome rod (1 up, 1 down) in order to maintain yarn separation and then drawn through the final reed, which should also be continuously cleaned by means of a fan or compressed air. The yarns are not oiled or lubricated during warping because the authors have not seen enough evidence to show that it is necessary in warping and knitting 100% cotton yarns. Although the above warping scheme is only a modification of an existing system, it does possess some of the changes that are felt to be necessary to warp spun yarns efficiently. The research is still not complete and more data must be obtained. The authors believe, however, that the resultant improvements in both warping and knitting are predictable on the basis of substantial trials.

7. TRICOT-MACHINE MODIFICATIONS

For many years, the research that was done on the warp-knitting of cotton yarns on tricot equipment was confined to 28-gauge machines. This was and still is the most popular gauge of tricot machine; however, in the late 1960s and early 1970s, many warp-knitters ordered three- and four-bar machines in coarse gauges, i.e., 20 and 24, in order to compete in some outerwear markets against double-knitted fabrics. The coarse-gauge machines have allowed singles cotton yarns to be knitted on tricot equipment at acceptable defect levels.

Knitters have for years related yarn count or linear density to machine cut. Many formulae are available, such as:

$$\text{ideal yarn cotton count} = (\text{machine cut})^2/20. \qquad \ldots \ldots (1)$$

Although no formula is perfect, this one does hold within certain limits for circular knitting. If it is applied to tricot equipment, it does not take into account the complexities that arise in trying to keep 4000 separate ends from entangling and creating lint. Although the authors are not aware of a more precise mathematical relation between yarn count and machine cut, Equation (1) certainly holds between 12 and 24 gauge but falls drastically short for 28 gauge. The difficulties involved in trying to keep 28 ends/in. (11 ends/cm) separated are almost insurmountable with a 50/1-cotton-count (12-tex) spun yarn, let alone one of 40/1 cotton count (15 tex) as the formula gives. The finest work now being done by Cotton Incorporated is on 24-gauge tricot and requires a 40/1–50/1 (15–12-tex) cotton yarn. For 20 gauge, a spun yarn as coarse as one of 18/1 cotton count (33 tex) can be knitted, but this requires changing the guide eye to an oversized unit that will allow large slubs and knots to pass through.

One of the first things that Cotton Incorporated tried to evaluate was the knitting efficiency of ring-spun yarns compared with open-end-spun yarns. The yarns selected were 18/1 (33-tex) 100% cotton yarns, and they were knitted on a 20-gauge, 84-in. (213·2-cm), Mayer KC4 tricot machine. In yarns of this count, weakness was not expected to be a major problem, nor was yarn-rolling because of the gauge. Lint accumulation was the greatest problem on the machine for both yarns. The machine was stopped and cleaned after every 200–300 racks of knitting because of severe lint accumulation on the guide-bars, brackets, and presser-bar. This performance was not considered acceptable. If coarse cotton yarns were to be commercially knitted on tricot equipment, some form of lint removal would clearly be necessary. Experiments with vacuum systems failed. Because of this, some time was spent in experimenting with air-cleaning systems. After several systems had been examined, an invention marketed by Edco Textile Air Systems[4] that is the most effective device the authors have seen for keeping lint from accumulating on the tricot machine was fitted. It is a blowing unit that uses compressed air to clean off one of eight sections of the machine for a 3-sec interval before switching to another section through an intermittent-gear arrangement. This allows the unit to reach pressures as high as $2 \cdot 8 – 4 \cdot 22$ kgf/cm^2 (40–60 lbf/in^2 or 276–414 kPa) while using a relatively small amount of air because there are only ten small holes per section. The air-stream is aimed at the tops of the guide-bars in order to keep them clean (Figures 6 and 7). Some improvement in this device is warranted, but the principle is well thought out. This same type of unit could be used to keep the combs clean during warping.

Fig. 6
The Edco Textile Air Systems blowing unit

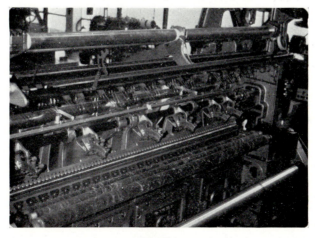

Fig. 7
Another view of the Edco Textile Air Systems blowing unit

The simplest method for eliminating much of the lint fall-out on the knitting machine and subsequent contamination during knitting can be accomplished by hanging a plastics sheet between the cotton and the synthetic-fibre warps and then fastening it to the flutter bar (Fig. 8). This will act as a shield and help keep lint off the continuous-filament yarn as well as the guide-bars, brackets, and presser-bar. The sheet can later be cleaned manually. For this to be most effective, however, it is strongly recommended that the cotton yarns be kept on the front two bars. Not only will this make shielding easy, but it will also allow for fast replacement of broken cotton ends should they occur. It further allows the blower bar to be mounted behind the warps out of the fixer's way. In this position, the lint is blown forward, which prevents contamination of the synthetic-fibre yarns.

Fig. 8

The elimination of lint fall-out on a warp-knitting machine by hanging a plastics sheet between the cotton and synthetic-fibre warps

The choice of stitch also affects the amount of lint generated. Laboratory work has shown that the quantity of lint produced on the machine is proportional to the number of needles shogged. This undoubtedly occurs because of the greater angle of abrasion in the guide eyes and the rapid back-and-forth movement of the yarn sheet. A 1–0/3–4 stitch for yarns coarser than 20/1 cotton count (29·5 tex) is not recommended on 20-gauge equipment.

One final point to be considered is the advantage of part-set threading the cotton yarns into the front two bars and then shogging them both to knit as one. In order to do this properly, one must now use a three-bar machine for producing standard two-bar cloth. This entails warping twice the usual number of cotton beams, a lengthy process. However, the resultant trade-off might be worth the extra warping time. Firstly, if the warping operation were not modified as recommended in the initial presentation, the proper spacing between yarns would now be obtained. This spacing would allow for the use of faster warping speeds. Secondly, twice the normal yardage would now fit on a beam, which would allow greater running time between beam run-outs. Finally, the yarns would be better separated and yarn-rolling minimized during knitting. Work currently in progress at Cotton Incorporated should determine just which method is the most economical way of producing a cloth.

Open-end-spun yarns have been referred to, and the authors feel that they are a major improvement in allowing coarse cotton yarns to be knitted efficiently on tricot equipment. A brief discussion of the work that has been done at Cotton Incorporated will conclude this paper.

8. OPEN-END-SPUN COTTON YARNS IN TRICOT-KNITTING

Earlier yarn and knitting studies indicated that an open-end-spun yarn should warp and knit more efficiently than a conventional ring-spun yarn. This is due primarily to the presence of fewer knots and slubs, a larger package size, and a marked decrease in lint accumulation of the open-end-spun yarn (Table II). These four items can be responsible for as large a proportion as 90% of all warping and knitting defects. In order to confirm the validity of this theory, a series of fabrics was knitted on tricot equipment from 18/1-cotton-count (33-tex) 100% cotton yarn of both ring- and open-end-spun types. All pertinent warping and knitting defects were recorded. (The ring-spun and open-end-spun yarns were purchased from the same manufacturer.)

Table II
Comparison of Ring-spun and Open-end-spun Yarns of 18/1 Cotton Count (33 tex)

Property*	Ring-spun Yarn	Open-end-spun Yarn
Cotton count	18·03	17·77
V_0 (%)	4·13	1·70
Twist multiplier†	3·68	4·24
Linear density (tex)	32·75	33·23
Twist multiplier‡	35·22	40·58
Single-thread strength (gf)	402·5	327·3
(N)	3·95	3·21
V_0 (%)	8·39	3·50
Single-thread elongation %	7·30	8·88
V_0 (%)	4·58	2·41
Uster evenness, CV %	14·6	14·4
V_0 (%)	2·84	1·62
Classimat rating (top 6)	8·0	4·0
Yarn friction (μ)	0·281	0·244
Lint test (g/lb)	0·237	0·117

* V_0 is coefficient of variation of results.
†On cotton-counts system.
‡On Tex system (determined in units of (turns/cm)$\sqrt{\text{tex}}$).

The machine chosen was an 84-in. (213·2-cm), 20-gauge Mayer KC4 tricot machine (duplication on a 90-in. (228·6-cm), 40-gauge Mayer R4N raschel machine also confirmed these results). The tricot machine was run at 400 courses/min, but the speed could easily have been increased to 500 courses/min.

The fabrics knitted on the tricot machine were made with the 18/1 (33-tex) cotton yarn on one bar and a 40-den (4·4-tex) polyester-fibre yarn on the other in a jersey, a reverse-jersey, a lay-in, and a queen's-cord construction.

The results of the knitting on the tricot machine are given in Table III: in all cases, the open-end-spun yarn performed from two-and-a-half to three-and-a-half times as efficiently as the ring-spun yarn in knitting. This was due primarily to a large decrease in lint accumulation on the guide-bars, brackets, and presser-bar. This accumulated lint causes lint balls and yarn entanglements to form, which in turn cause yarn breaks. This decrease in lint accumulation was also seen during warping, where the reeds were cleaned only half as often as in the warping of the ring-spun yarn.

9. LATER WORK

After these initial trials with the 18/1 (33-tex) cotton yarn, the creel was modified in order to eliminate several places at which lint had previously accumulated. A blowing device was installed on the tricot machine to blow the lint off the guide-bars, brackets, and presser-bar before it could accumulate.

These changes greatly improved the warping efficiency and reduced the lint accumulation on the tricot machine to an extent at which it was no longer a problem. A series of fabrics from yarn-dyed 18/1 (33-tex) open-end-spun cotton yarn on the front bar and a 40-den (4·4-tex) nylon yarn on the back bar was now knitted in order to produce fabrics for display and wear-testing. For the sake of brevity, the results are summarized; however, all the relevant details can be found in Table IV.

Simply stated, a reverse-jersey stripe, a 2 × 2 check, and a three-bar argyle (two cotton bars threaded 1 in, 1 out) were knitted. The average defect rate was 31·5 m/defect (34·5 yd/defect), and 346 m (379 yd) of fabric were knitted. There were eleven cotton defects, four defects due to lint balls, three due to lost ends, two due to weak spots, and two to knots and slubs. This average fairly represents what can be expected in knitting an 18/1 (33-tex) 100% cotton open-end-spun yarn on 20-gauge tricot equipment.

10. SUMMARY

It is quite apparent from these trials that it can safely be said that coarse open-end-spun cotton yarns will perform better than their ring-spun counterparts. It has also been determined that two- and three-bar outerwear fabrics can be knitted at 27–32 m/defect (30–35 yd/defect) on tricot equipment at speeds of 500–600 courses/min. It is important to note, however, that the tricot system does need an auxiliary blowing attachment in order to prevent the accumulation of lint. Furthermore, by utilizing electronic scanning equipment, which will help eliminate slubs and lost ends, the defect rate may be further improved by another 50%. It is therefore quite likely that a knitting efficiency of 100–150 racks/defect can be achieved on the tricot system in the very near future. At present, six commercial tricot knitters are at various stages of fabric development and sales and are using predominantly cotton. The products are elastic fabrics for underwear, foundation garments, and swimwear; terry cloth for sportswear; shirtings; athletic wear; and other outerwear.

Table III

Comparison of Use of 18/1 (33-tex) Open-end-spun and Ring-spun 100% Cotton Yarns in Warp-knitting

Fabric Type	Cotton Bar	Number of Racks	Racks/Defect	Yd/Defect	Loops and Slubs	Knots	Tails	Lint Balls	Weak Spots	Lost Ends	Lint Accum.
Open-end-spun Yarn											
Jersey	Top	200	50·0	20·8	0	0	0	3	1	0	4
Reverse jersey	Back	257	28·5	11·9	0	0	0	4	1	4	3
Queen's cord	Back	407	15·65	7·0	1	2	3	7	4	8	2
Three-bar lay-in	Back	460	24·2	7·4	0	6	0	5	3	2	3
Jersey	Top	530	48·1	23·4	0	0	2	2	2	4	5
Ring-spun Yarn											
Jersey	Top	200	8·33	3·5	1	1	2	11	1	8	2
Reverse jersey	Back	152	8·0	3·5	—	—	—	16	1	2	2
Queen's cord	Back	157	5·6	2·4	—	—	—	22	2	3	1
Two-bar lay-in	Back	228	57·0	17·4	—	1	—	3	—	0	3
Regular guides: three-bar lay-in	Back	735	10·4	3·2	2	4	—	51	10	2	3
Large guides: three-bar lay-in	Back	477	14·5	5·1	—	1	—	20	8	4	3

Table IV

Analysis of Defects in Knitting of 18/1 (33-tex) Open-end-spun 100% Cotton Yarn

Fabric Type	Number of Racks	Length Knitted (yd)	Yd/ Defect	Total Cotton Defects	Cotton Defects				
					Lost Ends	Weak Spots	Lint Balls	Knots and Slubs	Tails
Stripe	295	115	23·0	5	2	1 (Selvedge)	2	—	—
2 × 2 Check	225	88	29·0	3	—	1 (Selvedge)	1	1	—
Three-bar argyle (2 bars, 1 in, 1 out)	453	176	58·7	3	1	—	1	1	—
Totals	973	379	34·5	11	3	2	4	2	—

REFERENCES

[1] Appalachian Electronic Instruments, Ronceverte, W. Va., U.S.A.
[2] Lindly & Co. Inc., Mineola, N. Y., U.S.A.
[3] Protechna Herbst & Co. KG, Munich, West Germany.
[4] Edco Textile Air Systems, Sarasota, Fla., U.S.A.

Cotton Incorporated,
Raleigh,
N.C.,
U.S.A.

4—THE ECONOMICS OF OPEN-END SPINNING

By H. Catling

This paper presents an assessment of the relative advantages of both open-end-spun and ring-spun yarns and leads to a techno-economic profile of both spinning systems in which the primary economic aspects and product values for both types of yarn are evaluated and compared.

The greater difference in investment requirements occurs in the spinning room, with the unit price of open-end-spinning machines from six to eight times that of ringframes. However, in terms of productivity, the difference factor is small for coarse open-end-spun yarns and becomes progressively greater for finer yarns. Operating costs are also important. power and labour costs varying significantly between the two systems and, in the case of power, with operating speeds. Package form and size and performance in later stages of processing are sectors in which open-end-spun yarns have a useful advantage.

Fabrics produced from open-end-spun and ring-spun yarns differ in several respects, not all the advantages lying with one particular system. Open-end-spun yarns are consistently lower in strength than corresponding ring-spun yarns, but there is considerable doubt as to the real importance of this weakness; in weaving, weft and warp breaks may be halved, and in knitting subsequent processing performance can be markedly superior.

1. THE CHANGED SITUATION IN SPUN-YARN MANUFACTURE

Until relatively recently, the ringframe had long been the universal machine used for the production of spun yarn of all types. It has two great limitations, speed and package size, both of which are associated with the need to rotate the yarn package in order to introduce twist. With the coming of open-end spinning, it is now technically and economically possible to produce yarn three or four times as rapidly as was possible on the ringframe and in addition to have the advantage that the yarn is delivered directly in the form of cheeses weighing 2 kg or more each. As a result, it is now necessary for every spun-yarn manufacturer to examine the situation and appraise the merit of the new system of spinning in relation to the established system for his own particular circumstances.

2. WHAT OPEN-END SPINNING HAS TO OFFER

For more than fifty years, a machine that would spin staple-fibre yarns without the need of package rotation for the purpose of twisting was the philosopher's stone of the textile-machinery industry. Everyone wanted it for its greater speed potential and for the freedom it gave to produce yarn directly on any size or type of package. When, with the introduction of the Czech KS200 machine in 1965, the dream became a commercial reality, the mood changed. Doubts began to be expressed. By some, the new method of spinning was damned because the yarn it produced was not so strong as ring-spun yarn. Others complained that the new machines were too expensive to buy or doubted that their life expectation would be equal to that of the traditional ring-spinning machine.

At that time, precise economic appraisal was impossible because of the lack of experience in relation to several aspects of the new process. Nevertheless, spinning companies throughout the world set out to gain experience with the new machine. Some did little more than wet their toes, but others plunged boldly into the new element and began to appreciate both the difficulties and the merits of open-end spinning on a commercial scale. In the event, the new process has not by any means been rejected. After a cautious beginning, interest is increasing rapidly as early fears are being allayed, and it is clear that ring-spinning now has a serious rival. It is still too early to predict the extent to which ring-spinning will ultimately be displaced, but now is an opportune time to reappraise the economic situation.

From time to time, an innovation appears that is incontestably beneficial over the whole field of potential application. It gives a significant reduction in direct processing costs, produces an undeniably better product, and requires a lower capital investment than does the machine or process that it displaces. Open-end spinning is not that sort of innovation. Over part of the range of potential application, it gives marginally lower direct-processing costs, the product is in some respects superior yet in other respects inferior to the established product, and, finally, although for coarse yarns there is little difference, for medium-to-fine yarns an appreciably higher capital investment is required for the new process. In other words, it is not possible to make a simple and unqualified economic balance.

In this situation, it would be misleading to offer a single-figure appreciation of the situation based on quantification of costs and benefits in purely monetary terms, however reasonable the assumptions one might make. Instead, the four primary economic aspects of:

  investment requirement;
  fixed charges;
  operating costs; and
  product value

will be considered separately, and the position will be summarized by means of a techno-economic profile.

3. INVESTMENT REQUIREMENT

Broadly speaking, the difference in investment requirements is not great except in the spinning room itself, and then only for yarns of linear density (or count) finer than average. Up to the first passage of drawing, there need be no difference at all between a ring-spinning mill and an open-end-spinning mill. At the second drawing, it may be necessary to have a small-can drawframe, but this is a trivial difference. Open-end spinners will accept second-passage drawframe sliver, and this means that no roving frames are needed. On the operational side, this is a very substantial advantage, since roving frames are notorious for the introduction of medium–long-term count or linear-density variation, but, in the matter of capital investment, although important, it is by no means a crucial factor.

A modern roving frame, with accessories, costs about £200 per spindle, and, for an average cotton count of 20s (30 tex), one spindle will feed 25 ring spindles. Thus the need for a roving frame can be seen as adding £8 to the cost of each ring spindle. The most important factor influencing the investment requirement is the relationship between the cost of ringframes and the cost of open-end-spinning machines.

There is, in fact, no unique relationship, because the investment to be made in ringframes can be varied widely depending on local conditions and the preference of the investor. Not only do small-package ringframes have a lower unit price than that of large-package frames, but, in addition, they can be run at much higher speeds. Thus the investment requirement may be reduced at the expense of package size. Similarly, where power is cheap, the number of spindles purchased may be minimized by the use of spindle speeds that in other circumstances would be uneconomic. At the present stage of development, this second consideration is not really applicable to open-end spinners in which the speed is still limited by mechanical rather than power-economic considerations. The required package size has only a marginal direct effect on the cost of open-end spinners.

In round figures, the unit price of a present-day open-end spinner is from six to eight times that of the ringframe to which it is the alternative, but, if account is taken of the cost of the roving frames necessarily associated with the ringframe, the ratio is reduced to between five and seven. The productivity relation is very much dependent on the linear density of the yarn to be spun—or, more strictly, on the package size and spindle speed used on the ringframe. With the choice of these variables usual in Europe to-day, the ratio of open-end-spinning productivity to ring-spinning productivity ranges progressively from 5 : 1 for an average cotton count of 8s (74 tex) to 2·5 : 1 for an average cotton count of 36s (16 tex). Thus, at the coarsest end of the range, there is virtually no difference between the investment requirements, but, as the average yarn spun becomes finer, the investment required for open-end spinning becomes progressively and significantly greater than that required for ring-spinning.

Table I shows specific machinery-investment requirements for new mills to produce 1000 lb/hr (454 kg/hr) of yarn on *(a)* ringframes, and *(b)* open-end spinners. The calculations have been made for four average yarn counts covering the greater part of the conventional short-staple-yarn range. The machinery chosen is in line with current good practice. The prices do not include installation costs.

Table I

Cost of Machinery for a Mill to Produce 1000 lb/hr (454 kg/hr) of Yarn on Ringframes and on Rotor-type Open-end Spinners

Machinery / English Cotton Count	10s (59 tex)	16s (37 tex)	24s (25 tex)	36s (16 tex)
(a) Ring-spinning	Machinery Costs (£'000)			
Opening, carding, and drawing machines	272	292	325	373
Roving frames	87	112	145	176
Ringframes	268	499	655	928
Total	627	903	1125	1477
(b) Open-end Spinning	Machinery Costs (£'000)			
Opening, carding, and drawing machines	272	298	339	391
Open-end spinners	386	757	1325	2130
Total	658	1055	1664	2521
Additional Cost of Open-end Spinning				
(i) In £'000	31	152	539	1044
(ii) As a percentage of the cost of a ring-spinning mill $\left\{100\dfrac{(b-a)}{a}\right\}$	4·9%	16·8%	47·9%	70·7%

It will be seen that, although for a mill with an average cotton count of 10s (59 tex) the extra cost for open-end spinning is only about 5% of the cost of the machinery needed for ring-spinning, the picture changes rapidly as the count becomes finer, and the additional cost for 36s is 70%. There are, however, two factors that to some extent ameliorate the situation.

Firstly, there is the question of space. Open-end spinners fed from small cans (*c.* 12 lb or 5·4 kg), such as would be installed for the finer yarns, take up appreciably less space than the corresponding ringframes and associated roving frames. Where existing buildings are available, this may be unimportant in terms of investment requirement, but, where a new building is concerned, it is a significant advantage. For the mill spinning 36s (16-tex) yarn, there would be a saving of about 6000 ft² (557 m²), which, at current building costs in Britain, represents a reduction in investment requirement of at least £50,000.

Secondly, and of the greatest importance, is the question of shift-working and machine utilization. For several operational reasons, rotor-type open-end spinners are far better suited to the most intensive operation. It is true that, with good organization, ringframes can be operated for 168 hours a week, but the differences are such that, whereas with ringframes it is merely possible, with open-end spinners 168-hr working is both natural and, particularly in terms of operational economics, very much more attractive. In the present context (i.e., in relation to investment requirement), this is of the greatest importance where the choice is between ring-spinning on three shifts (112½ hr) and 168-hr working of open-end spinners. In this situation, there is actually a reduction in investment requirement for the 10s- and 16s-count (59- and 37-tex) open-end-spinning mill of 30% and 22%, respectively, of the investment requirement for comparable ring-spinning mills. For the 24s-count (25-tex) mills, there is virtually no difference, and, for the 36s-count (16-tex) mills, the additional investment required for open-end spinning is reduced to 14% of that required for ring-spinning.

4. FIXED CHARGES

Under this heading are included the depreciation of machinery and buildings, the upkeep of buildings, insurance, and an interest charge on the value of material in process. It might be argued that an interest charge on the residual value of machinery and buildings should also be included, but there are very serious difficulties here that make it more appropriate to take account of this cost as a concomitant of investment requirements.

There is now a fair amount of evidence to suggest that the normal operating life of rotor-type open-end spinners will be the same as that of ringframes, and on this basis one might reasonably assess depreciation differences simply on the differences in the original cost of the machinery that have already been discussed. The rapidly changing situation, however, raises some doubt as to the soundness of this approach. Two future situations that can be envisaged are:

(i) significant improvements in the performance of open-end spinners without a rapidly expanding demand for open-end-spun yarn could make open-end-spinning machinery of current design prematurely obsolete; and

(ii) the development of a strong preference for open-end-spun yarns could render much of the world's ring-spinning capacity redundant and result in premature scrapping of ringframes.

Acceptance of the first situation as the more likely would counsel accelerated depreciation of open-end-spinning machines, but, conversely, the second situation would demand accelerated depreciation of ringframes.

A third possibility, that of significant improvement in the performance of open-end spinners together with the development of a strong preference for open-end-spun yarns by almost all users, is a strong one, with important implications in relation to investment policy and depreciation assumptions.

Not surprisingly in the present situation of uncertainty as to the technical (not to mention the commercial) future of spinning, no completely rational basis for machinery depreciation exists. Here we must fall back on directional flair and gamble.

With the depreciation and upkeep of buildings, we are on firmer ground. Open-end spinning requires less space, and, for a mill producing 1000 lb/hr (454 kg/hr) of average count 20s (30 tex), the saving will be of the order of 4000 ft² (372 m²). If one assumes depreciation over twenty years on a building cost of £8·50 per ft² (£91·80 per m²) and annual-upkeep costs of £0·60 per ft² (£6·48 per m²), this gives a monetary saving of £4100.

Insurance of both machinery and building will be on the same cost basis for both mills and may be assumed to be directly proportional to the initial investment. The value of materials in process is, in fact, very much the same for both ring-spinning and open-end spinning. Although larger creel and delivery packages are used for open-end spinning, this is more or less balanced by the higher unit productivity and a corresponding reduction in the number of packages in process. Thus insurance and interest charges on material in process are not appreciably different.

All in all, there is little under the heading of fixed operating costs that is significant in relation to the investment decision of ring-spinning or open-end spinning except, of course, the vital matter of the depreciation period of the asset. A subjective element is inevitably involved here, and the two remaining aspects discussed below will aid judgement on this point.

5.   OPERATING COSTS

The major operating costs incurred in actual manufacture are those of materials, power, and labour, and these costs only are dealt with below. A mill has, of course, many other operating costs, such as sales, warehousing, and despatch, but, since these are not germane to the present issue, they are not considered here.

The cost of materials per unit of production is dependent on the quality of material needed to produce a satisfactory product and on the amount of waste made during processing. In the early days of open-end spinning, it was necessary to use cleaner (and hence more expensive) cottons because of difficulties caused by trash accumulation in the spinning rotors. More recent machines incorporate a trash-rejecting device, and it is now claimed that dirtier (and hence cheaper) cottons can be used. There is as yet insufficient information available as to the value of this feature, and it has therefore been assumed that there will be no difference in the unit cost of materials. This is certainly true for man-made fibres, although it may be appreciable for cotton. The effect of reduced waste losses is, however, real and significant. Waste is made in two ways: in creeling and by the release of fibres during processing. Open-end spinning has clear advantages here in that the roving-frame process is eliminated and the increased creel-package size reduces creeling waste. In addition, it is claimed that less fibre is released during the spinning process itself.

A typical over-all waste-loss figure for the two processes of the production of roving and ring-spinning is 4%, and the corresponding figure for open-end spinning is $1\frac{1}{2}$%. The value of this saving of $2\frac{1}{2}$% depends very much on the extent to which the waste may be reprocessed or the price for which it can be sold. On the assumption that the net loss on each pound of waste made is 14p, the annual value of the $2\frac{1}{2}$% saving in waste loss to a mill producing 1000 lb/hr (454 kg/hr) of yarn is £19,800—a very useful sum.

For both open-end spinning and ring-spinning, power costs are critically dependent on the operating speed, and in the latter case the package size is also important. As has already been mentioned, this involves a compromise in which the effect of the operating speed on power costs and the value of package size are balanced against the effect of both these factors on investment requirement. The power-cost figures given in Table II have been calculated in relation to the speeds and package sizes assumed to give the best compromise for U.K. conditions in the compilation of Table I. An over-all unit power cost of 1·0p per kWhr has been assumed.

Table II

Annual Cost of Power for a Mill Producing 1000 lb/hr (454 kg/hr) of Yarn on Ringframes and on Rotor-type Open-end Spinners*

Process / English Cotton Count	10s (59 tex)	16s (37 tex)	24s (25 tex)	36s (16 tex)
(a) Ring-spinning	Power Costs (£'000)			
Opening, carding, and drawing	15·7	14·4	13·5	12·5
Roving production and spinning	32·6	42·8	58·0	79·9
Totals	48·3	57·2	71·5	92·4
(b) Open-end Spinning	Power Costs (£'000)			
Opening, carding, and drawing	15·7	14·4	13·5	12·5
Spinning	11·3	24·4	44·5	83·9
Totals	27·0	38·8	58·0	96·4

*Unit charge 1·0p/kWhr; three-shift operation.

The table shows that, although open-end spinning gives a very useful saving in power costs for the mill producing the coarsest yarns, this saving is progressively eroded as the yarn becomes finer until, for the finest yarn, ring-spinning has a marginal advantage. The physical explanation of this arises from the fact that it is economically necessary to use both greater lifts and larger-diameter rings for the spinning of coarser yarns on ringframes, and this greatly increases unit power consumption. For rotor-type open-end spinners, however, unit power consumption is not materially affected by linear density or package size.

Reduced labour requirement is, to the spinner, the most attractive feature of open-end spinning. In the first place, all roving-frame labour is eliminated, and, secondly, the use of very large creel and delivery packages greatly reduces the labour requirement for materials-handling, creeling, and doffing. In addition, the end-breakage rate per unit of production is lower, and the amount of short fibre liberated during spinning is reduced. Both these factors help to reduce further the need for attention during spinning.

Table III shows the annual cost of salaries and wages for a mill producing 1000 lb/hr (454 kg/hr) of yarn *(a)* on ringframes and *(b)* on rotor-type open-end spinners. Four average counts are considered, and the machinery concerned is that on which the investment requirements of Table I were based. The costs are for three-shift operation at wage rates prevailing in Britain to-day.

Table III

Salaries and Wages of a Mill Producing 1000 lb/hr (454 kg/hr) of Yarn on Ringframes and on Rotor-type Open-end Spinners*

Process English Cotton Count	10s (59 tex)	16s (37 tex)	24s (25 tex)	36s (16 tex)
(a) Ring-spinning	Salaries and Wages (£'000 per annum)			
Management and other indirect items	44·6	49·4	56·1	66·2
Opening, carding, and drawing	30·0	33·0	37·0	42·7
Roving production and spinning	70·5	92·5	122·9	176·6
Totals	145·1	174·9	216·0	285·5
(b) Open-end Spinning	Salaries and Wages (£'000 per annum)			
Management and other indirect items	44·6	49·4	56·1	66·2
Opening, carding, and drawing	30·0	34·2	38·6	45·5
Spinning	28·6	33·0	39·7	51·8
Totals	103·2	116·6	134·4	163·5
Annual saving by use of open-end spinning	41·9	58·4	81·6	122·0

*The figures given are for three-shift operation.

To summarize the situation, it is clear that open-end spinning offers savings in annual operating costs throughout the counts (or linear-density) range for which it is used. The crucial consideration is the relationship between this saving and the greater investment required to be made in machinery. As has already been discussed, the problematic future with regard to the acceptance of (or even preference for) open-end-spun types of yarns and the likelihood of significant improvements in machine performance becoming available makes it difficult to assess the depreciation position for either method of spinning to-day. In addition, there is the further complicating factor of differences in company situations with regard to the availability of funds, the effect of regional investment incentives, and the present inflationary situation. Nevertheless, an over-all balance has been made in Table IV on the basis of a uniform capital charge equal to 20% of the required investment in machinery.

On this basis, the attractiveness of open-end spinning as a cost-saving innovation depends on the average count (or linear density) being spun. The saving is greatest at the coarsest count and a little less at 16s (37 tex). At 24s count (25 tex), it has been reduced almost to vanishing point, and it

Table IV

Cost-savings for Open-end Spinning*

English Cotton Count Source of Saving	10s (59 tex)	16s (37 tex)	24s (25 tex)	36s (16 tex)
	Savings (£'000 per annum)			
(a) Operating Cost-savings				
Fixed Costs				
Space, insurance, etc.	1·2	1·5	−0·2	−2·3
Processing Costs				
Waste	19·8	19·8	19·8	19·8
Power	21·3	18·4	13·5	—4·0
Labour	41·9	58·3	81·6	122·0
Totals	84·2	98·0	114·7	135·5
(b) Additional capital charge†	6·2	30·0	107·9	208·6
Net annual saving	78·0	68·0	6·8	−73·1

*For three-shift working at production rate of 1000 lb/hr (454 kg/hr) of yarn.
†Charge rate = 20% of machinery cost.

becomes an additional cost of £73,000 per annum at the finest count. It is tempting to pursue this aspect of open-end-spinning economics further and to explore the sensitivity to the capital-charge rate, but, before yielding to this temptation, let us step back a pace and get a perspective view of the situation. For each count, we are concerned with a mill producing more than 5 million lb (2270 tonnes) of yarn per annum. Expressed in terms of unit costs the savings come out at:

> 1·47p/lb (3·24p/kg) of 10s (59-tex) yarn;
>
> 1·29p/lb (2·84p/kg) of 16s (37-tex) yarn;
>
> 0·12p/lb (0·26p/kg) of 24s (25-tex) yarn;
>
> −1·10p/lb (−2·43p/kg) of 36s (16-tex) yarn.

If the products were identical, there would be some justification for regarding these differences as significant. But, since the products are not by any means identical, it is clear that we have already gone quite as far as is worth while in our studies of cost, and it is high time that we gave some attention to the matter of differences in product value.

6. PRODUCT VALUE

6.1 Introduction

In comparing product value, there are several points of difference between ring-spun and open-end-spun yarns, and the following are discussed below:

> package form and size;
>
> appearance, cover, and handle;
>
> strength and durability; and
>
> performance in later processes.

6.2   Package Form and Size

The most obvious difference between the products is the form and size of the yarn package. There is no doubt whatever that the large cheeses produced by the open-end spinner are more attractive than the small bobbins produced by the ringframe. Even when rewinding is necessary, the open-end-spun package will command a premium:

>   *(a)*   because rewinding from a cheese is cheaper than rewinding from a ring bobbin;
>   *(b)*   because of the considerable reduction in the number of knots per unit mass that the rewound yarn will contain;
>   *(c)*   because of the reduced incidence of barriness caused by linear-density variation between successive packages; and
>   *(d)*   because of the convenience in package-handling and the reduced risk of mixed yarn.

It is difficult to quantify this premium, but it could well exceed the greatest differences in production cost estimated above. Where the open-end-spun package can be used directly but the ring-spun package requires rewinding, there is no doubt at all. In addition to the value of factors *(b)*, *(c)*, and *(d)*, the direct saving in rewinding cost will be of the order of 2p/lb of yarn (4·4p/kg of yarn) for an average count of 20s (30 tex) and very much more for finer yarns.

6.3   Appearance, Cover, and Handle

Appearance, cover, and handle are all different. The same visual cover in woven and knitted fabrics is obtained with from 2 to 5 % less open-end-spun yarn. This can be a very useful economy. Fabric appearance is improved because of the higher uniformity, but it is difficult to express the value of this in monetary terms except where the conditions are such that on this account a singles open-end-spun yarn can replace a two-fold ring-spun yarn. The handle of the yarn is even more difficult to quantify economically. In woven constructions, there is certainly no loss in value, but for knitting the situation is complex. Knitted fabrics so far produced from open-end-spun yarns have not as soft a handle as those made from ring-spun yarns. In some circumstances, this may render them unacceptable; in others, it may be an attractive feature.

6.4   Strength and Durability

There is no doubt whatever that the strength of open-end-spun yarns is consistently and significantly lower than that of corresponding ring-spun yarns. There is, however, considerable doubt as to the real importance of this weakness. Even in such obviously strength-demanding end-uses as conveyor and driving belts, the ultimate tensile strength (UTS) is not in itself an absolute criterion of suitability. The UTS, as such, is never used in service where modulus and fatigue life (i.e., life under repeated loading cycles) are the parameters that determine performance. In practice, it has been found that the lower strength of open-end-spun yarns is not reflected in inferior yarn or fabric performance, but that, on the contrary, open-end-spun yarns generally give improved durability and abrasion-resistance.

6.5   Performance in Later Processes

As experience has been gained in the warping, weaving, and knitting of open-end-spun yarn, it has become clear that, once processing conditions have been optimized in relation to the new yarns, subsequent process performance can be markedly superior to that achieved by conventional yarns. This is now well documented in relation to both weaving and knitting.

The number of both warp- and weft-yarn breaks during weaving is typically halved, and the number of minor fabric faults caused by yarn irregularities, such as slubs, is even more strikingly reduced. This has an immediate effect in reducing loom stoppages and hence weaving costs but is even more important in relation to the value of the fabric produced. A recent Shirley Institute study of the cost of cloth faults at the garment-making stage has shown that the cost of such yarn faults varies typically from *c.* 2 to 8p/lb (i.e., from *c.* 4·4 to 17·6p/kg) weight of fabric. Thus the use of open-end-spun yarn, by halving the yarn-fault rate, can be expected to enhance cloth values by from 1 to 4p/lb (i.e., from 2·2 to 8·8p/kg), in addition to the bonus of a reduction in weaving costs. As this situation becomes more widely appreciated, users will begin to insist on, and be prepared to pay a premium for, open-end-spun yarn for many cloths.

7. THE TECHNO-ECONOMIC PROFILE

Although these features of product value are to some extent subjective and not readily quantifiable, they are nevertheless real and important. They are generally large in relation to the differences in production cost discussed in the earlier part of this paper and will undoubtedly provide the major incentive to innovation. An attempt has been made to relate these factors in Fig. 1. In this techno-economic profile, the over-all economic situation for each of four counts and the costs and values involved are shown on the basis of a uniform-area scale. Although precise quantification is not possible in this form of presentation, it is felt that weighting of the various factors has been done with at least the degree of precision that the situation justifies.

TECHNO-ECONOMIC PROFILE OF
RELATIVE ADVANTAGES OF RING AND OPEN-END SPINNING

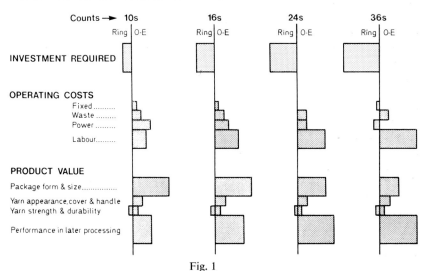

Fig. 1
Techno-economic profile of the relative advantages of ring-spinning and open-end spinning

Cotton Silk and Man-made
  Fibres Research Association,
Shirley Institute,
Didsbury,
Manchester 20.

5—THE IRREGULARITY OF OPEN-END-SPUN WOOL YARNS

By P. GROSBERG and I. M. ABOU-ZEID

The work described in this paper is an investigation of the irregularity of yarns spun from long-staple fibres produced on a rotor type of open-end spinner. The cutting-and-weighing method was used to investigate the irregularity of the fibre band before and after 'doubling' on the rotor wall. As a result of these determinations, modified spinning equipment was designed and constructed to improve the flow irregularity; better results were obtained with this equipment. Both photographic and high-speed-cinematic methods were used to investigate the fibre-flow irregularity in the feed tube and to measure the velocity of fibres travelling through the feed tube. It was found that fibre speeds equal to 80% of the rotor-wall surface speed produced more even yarns.

1. INTRODUCTION

Long-staple open-end-spun yarns are considerably weaker than the corresponding ring-spun yarns, despite the greater amount of twist that has to be used. This effect is even more pronounced than in short-staple yarns. In contrast to the short-staple yarns, long-staple open-end-spun yarns are slightly less extensible than the equivalent conventional yarns. In general, the regularity of the yarn produced in short-staple open-end spinning is very good; it is usually assumed that this is due to the number of doublings given to the fibre stream that issues down the feed tube when it is formed into the ribbon lying in the groove of the rotor. The number of doublings is given approximately by v_2/v_4, where v_2 is the velocity of the fibres as they reach the end of the feed tube and v_4 the speed of the take-up mechanism. (There is a very small error due to yarn-length contraction during twisting.) The maximum value of v_2 is given by the speed of the rotor wall (to prevent fibre-buckling), and, since this speed is given by $2\pi RN$, where R is the rotor diameter and N the speed of rotation of the rotor in rev/min, the maximum number of doublings is $2\pi RN/v_4 = 2\pi RT$, where T is the twist in turns/unit length. The larger the drum and the higher the twist, the better will the yarn regularity therefore apparently be. In general, this is not found to be the case, partly because the number of doublings is not as great as the value given by the above expression (in practice, v_2 is usually smaller than the rotor speed), but more fundamentally because the irregularity of the final yarn is only indirectly affected by the number of doublings. For a random or quasi-random fibre flow, the index of irregularity of the fibre flow down the feed tube is the principal determining factor[3]. The index of irregularity has been found to be closely related to the number of fibres in the cross-section of the flow down the inlet tube.

The work described in this paper is concerned with the cause of irregularity in the open-end spinning of long-staple fibres. It is known that less fibre breakage and on the whole more even yarns are produced with drafting-unit feeds than with beater feeds. Drafting-unit feeds were therefore used to ascertain whether there is any fundamental reason why long-staple open-end-spun yarns are relatively more irregular than short-staple yarns.

2. EXPERIMENTAL STUDIES

2.1 Effect of Feed-roller Speed

Experiments were made on an SKF drafting system at different front-roller speeds, and their effect on the irregularity of the fibre band deposited in the groove of the collecting surface for a fixed time of feed was determined. This procedure was repeated with a different front-roller covering, and 20 samples were taken at each front-roller speed. The results obtained are shown in Table I.

Table I

Expt No.	Front-roller Speed (rev/min)	CV_a*	CV_i†	Index of Irregularity ($= CV_a/CV_i$)	Roller Draft	Average Number of Fibres in Feed Tube
1	4000	16·97	7·94	2·14	686	4·15
2	3500	16·00	7·70	2·08	600	4·75
3	3000	14·05	7·21	1·95	514	5·5
4	2500	15·83	7·19	2·20	428	6·6
5	2000	17·94	7·56	2·37	343	8·3
6	1500	19·38	7·91	2·45	257	11·0

*Actual coefficient of variation.   †Martindale coefficient of variation.

2.2 Irregularity of the Wedge

The rotor was adjusted to rotate at 10,000 rev/min and to produce a yarn of 100 tex at a front-roller speed of 3000 rev/min. The machine was left to run under normal running conditions. By using a pair of scissors, the outgoing yarn was cut at the nearest point to the yarn-withdrawal tube while the feed tube was simultaneously blocked by a piece of Perspex to stop the feed to the rotor. The parts of the machine were then stopped. The rotor continued to rotate under the effect of the inertia force holding the wedge sample in direct contact with the groove surface until it finally came to rest and released the sample, which would be distorted only by the effect of the internal twist left in the portion of the yarn being formed. To facilitate the extraction of the wedge, a plastics drum, 10 cm in diameter, was placed concentrically with the rotor before it came to rest. When the rotor came to a complete standstill, the wedge contracted and encircled the plastics drum so that it could be lifted easily out of the rotor without disturbing the relative position of the fibres. From the results obtained, the circumferential index-distribution curve was plotted as shown in Fig. 1.

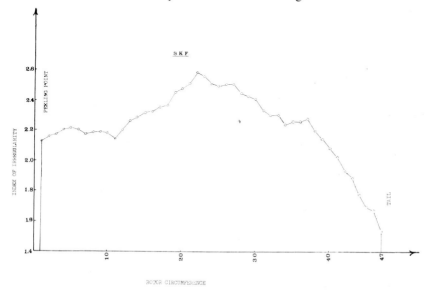

Fig. 1

Distribution curve of index of irregularity in relation to rotor circumference for SKF drafting system

The same procedure was carried out with an Ambler Superdraft (ASD) drafting system, and the results obtained are given in Table II and illustrated in Fig. 2.

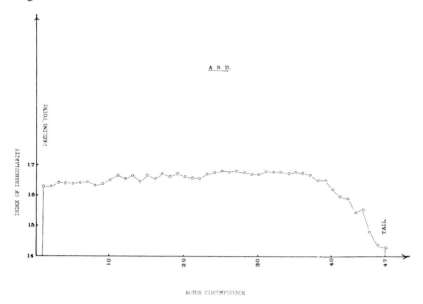

Fig. 2

Distribution curve of index of irregularity in relation to rotor circumference for ASD drafting system

Table II

Expt No.	Front-roller Speed (rev/min)	CV_a*	Index of Irregularity	Roller Draft	Average Number of Fibres in Feed Tube
1	3000	19·25	1·81	665	4·3
2	2625	18·62	1·74	581	4·95
3	2250	17·25	1·62	498	5·75
4	1875	18·34	1·72	415	6·85
5	1500	19·30	1·81	332	8·5
6	1125	20·72	1·94	249	11·0

*Actual coefficient of variation.

It can be shown that the index of irregularity does not rise during doubling unless the fibre-flow variation contains a periodic component. It can be seen by comparing Figures 1 and 2 that the ASD system produces a more uniform flow as well as one having much smaller periodic components, so that after doubling the irregularity of the doubled sliver is much lower. The level of irregularity of even the ASD yarn is still high, however. To investigate the possibility of reducing this irregularity still further, it was decided to study the actual irregularity of the fibre flow down the feed tube by means of several photographic techniques.

2.3 The Irregularity of Fibres in the Feed Tube

All the mechanical parts were adjusted and set while the speed of the front roller was kept at a constant speed of 2250 rev/min, the optimum value obtained from the experiments described in Section 2.2. A constant feed of twistless sliver of 60 dr/40 yd (2·9 ktex) was maintained. The venturi feed tube was placed with its input set close to the nip of the front roller and its delivery end directed to the rotor wall through the rotor cover. To investigate the fibre straightness and flow irregularity when the fibres were travelling through the feed tube under normal conditions, it was considered best to photograph the lower part of the tube nearest to the rotor, since by this time the fibres should have achieved their maximum straightness orientation and separation. The part of the tube to be investigated was defined by two pairs of screws shown in the photographs. For each of the four different processing conditions already mentioned, 36 exposures were taken. A summary of the results obtained is given in Table III. For each condition, frequency-distribution curves such as those shown in Fig. 3 were derived and the values given in Table III calculated. The expected and observed frequency-distribution curves for the four processing conditions are plotted in Figures 4 and 5, respectively.

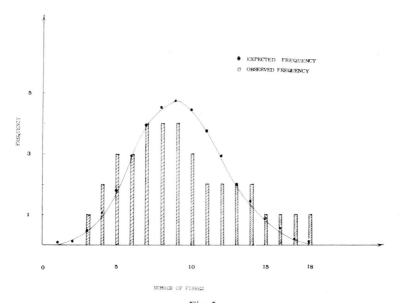

Fig. 3

Expected frequency curve and observed frequency histogram of numbers of fibres in feed tube

Table III

Rotor Speed (rev/min)	10,000		12,000	
Twist Factor	8	5	8	5
Mean number of fibres	4·91	7·06	6·03	9·33
CV_a*	49·05	44·68	44·61	41·23
CV_i†	45·13	37·65	40·73	32·74
Index of irregularity	1·09	1·19	1·10	1·26

*Actual coefficient of variation.
†Martindale coefficient of variation.

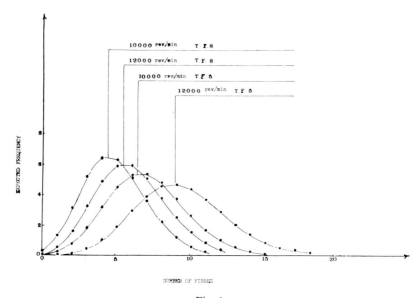

Fig. 4

Expected frequency curves of number of fibres in feed tube for rotor-surface speeds of
10,000 and 12,000 rev/min and twist factors (T.F.) of 5 and 8

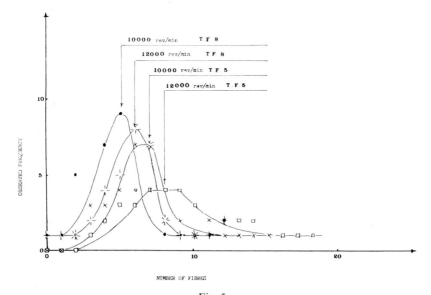

Fig. 5

Observed frequency curves of number of fibres in feed tube for rotor-surface speeds of
10,000 and 12,000 rev/min and twist factors (T.F.) of 5 and 8

It is clear from Table III that the minimum index of irregularity is
obtained when the number of fibres is at its minimum at approximately 5
fibres in the cross-section of the tube. The irregularity rises as the number
of fibres increases, which is in agreement with the results obtained by
Cormack[1].

With more fibres in the feed tube, the index of irregularity does not rise
very much when the number of fibres is doubled. This is shown in Fig. 6.

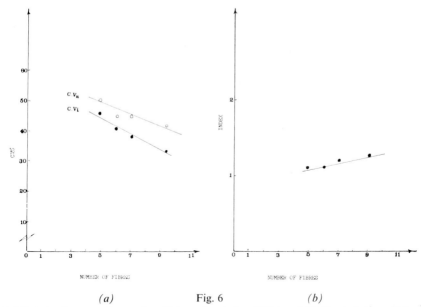

(a)   Fig. 6   *(b)*

(a) Relation between (i) actual coefficient of variation (CV_a) and (ii) Martindale coefficient of variation (CV_i) and number of fibres in feed tube

(b) Relation between index of irregularity and number of fibres in feed tube

The lowest index of irregularity is very nearly random, i.e., an index of irregularity of 1·09, and this is considerably lower than the irregularity of the band laid down in the groove of the rotor. As shown in Fig. 2, the index of irregularity of the weight of the band never falls below 1·48. Even with allowance made for the weight variation of the fibres themselves, there is clearly still a noticeable difference, which necessitates further investigation. The most probable reason for the increase in irregularity as the fibre moves down the feed tube and is laid in the groove is the difference between the speed of the fibres as they approach the rotor wall and the speed of the rotor wall itself. If the rotor is going at a much higher speed, the fibres could be plucked in tufts from the feed as the fibres are accelerated to the speed of the rotor wall. If the fibre feed is faster than the rotor speed, the fibres will be decelerated and therefore buckled as they reach the wall, which once more increases the possibility of an increase in the fibre-band irregularity. To investigate this possibility, it is clearly necessary to determine the velocity of air-flow through the venturi feed tube and the speed of the fibres as they travel down the feed tube to the rotor.

Table IV gives the experimentally determined velocity ratios at different rotor speeds.

Table IV
Ratio of Velocity of Air-flow to Rotor-surface Speed

Expt No.	Rotor Speed (rev/min)	V_{air} (m/sec)	V_{fibres} (m/sec)	Rotor-surface Speed (m/sec) $= V_{rotor}$	$\dfrac{V_{air}}{V_{rotor}}$
1	10,000	49·18	46·65	78·50	0·63
2	11,000	52·75	52·30	86·35	0·61
3	12,000	56·16	57·20	94·20	0·59
4	13,000	59·48	61·32	102·05	0·58
5	14,000	62·98	65·43	109·90	0·57

2.4 High-speed Cinematic Studies

A high-speed cinematic film was taken of the movement of the fibres down the feed tube to enable the fibre speed to be measured, and the film obtained clearly showed the positions of the fibres as they are released from the front-roller nip and move down the feed tube. As the fibres leave the front-roller nip before entering the opening of the feed tube, they take up a wavy configuration. As soon as they enter the feed tube, they start to straighten as they are gradually accelerated until they finally attain a completely straight shape on their journey down the feed tube. The fibre velocity was found to be $10 \cdot 22$ and $51 \cdot 37$ m/sec at the inlet and outlet of the tube, respectively. It was evident that the fibres were accelerated throughout their journey down the tube until they finally acquired the air-velocity at the outlet point. From Table IV, it is clear that the ratio of both the air and the fibre velocities inside the tube to the rotor-surface speed is less than unity at all spinning speeds. These results suggest that it would be possible to improve the band irregularity and hence also the yarn irregularity by increasing the flow rate down the feed tube. An induced suction through an external-vacuum device was the simplest way of increasing the fibre speeds down the feed tube.

Yarns were spun to a twist factor of 5 at speeds of 10,000 and 12,000 rev/min, and the index of irregularity was reduced to $1 \cdot 37$ and $1 \cdot 40$, respectively, when the velocity ratio was increased to $0 \cdot 732$ and $0 \cdot 702$. These were the maximum ratios that could be achieved with the suction pumps available.

3. GENERAL DISCUSSION AND CONCLUSIONS

It is clear from Table I that the highest efficiency of fibre separation occurs with a front-roller speed of 3000 rev/min. At higher front-roller speeds, turbulent air-movements around the rollers have the effect of changing the configuration of the fibres during their passage from the front-roller nip to the feed tube. This results in a poorer yarn structure and lower yarn strength. At lower front-roller speeds, both the coefficient of variation and the index of irregularity increase with decreasing front-roller speeds. This is mainly due to a deterioration in the efficiency of fibre separation and constitutes a major disadvantage in the use of the drafting system as a feed device.

The irregularity-index variation along the collecting-surface circumference is shown in Fig. 1. The increasing trend of the index of irregularity starts at the peeling point with a value of $2 \cdot 13$, and the index reaches its peak at twice the mean fibre length. Its value then starts to decrease until it reaches a lower value at the final tail end, which has, however, a considerably higher index than the first layer. This indicates that a periodic irregularity must be present in the feed to the rotor. By direct analysis of the shape of the curve, it has been shown[2] that there is a periodicity with a wavelength of $1 \cdot 5$ m or some sub-multiple of this length. There is no obvious reason for a periodicity of this particular wavelength, and it should be noted that no wavelength of less than $0 \cdot 5$ m can be detected from the variation in the index of irregularity along the collecting surface. Values of the index of irregularity of the yarn from tests on the Uster Evenness Tester and from cutting and weighing are in agreement with those of the index of irregularity of the fibre web in the rotor at the peeling point, which indicates that the insertion of twist does not affect the irregularity, i.e., there is no fibre slippage in groups as the fibres are twisted into different radii while held only by friction.

The circumferential-index-distribution relation obtained when the ASD drafting system is used is plotted in Fig. 2, which shows the irregularity values for each unit length along the whole length of the measured wedge, and, from this graph and other results already reported earlier in the paper, the different components of irregularity were calculated, the results being given in Table V.

Table V

Analysis of Components of Irregularity

Type of Irregularity	I	I^2
(1) Irregularity of the yarn	1·62	2·61
(2) Irregularity of the fibre band in the groove before twisting	1·61	2·58
(3) Irregularity of the first layer deposited	1·43	2·04
(4) Irregularity due to fibre-diameter variation		0·24
(5) Irregularity due to random fibre placement		1·00
(6) Irregularity added during doubling (due to periodic components still not removed)		0·54
(7) Irregularity still unaccounted for		0·80

It is clear that, even though the irregularity variation around the rotor shows no marked peaks, the increase in the index that occurs during doubling is relatively large compared with the remaining irregularity, for which the cause is unknown. It must therefore be assumed that there is still some periodic component of irregularity in the feed despite the improvements that have occurred as a result of the use of the ASD drafting unit. Krause[3] found that the minimum index occurred when the number of fibres in the inlet tube was about two, and similar work done at the University of Leeds with long-staple fibres indicated a minimum when the number of fibres was four. In Krause's experiments, the minimum index was relatively high, i.e., 1·5. In his findings, however, it can be noted that there is a bimodal distribution of the number of fibres. This could be due to the fact that, in this work, a long horizontal tube of 50-cm length and 3-mm internal diameter was used to contain the fibre flow. Such a tube would be relatively crowded with fibres owing to the small internal diameter, so that there would be a clumping together of the fibres in the tube itself. In the present authors' experiments, it is probable that clumping of this type was prevented by the shape of the fibre-feed tube, so that the bimodal frequency distribution is not observed in Fig. 3.

Increased fibre-flow rates caused an increase in the index of irregularity, but the frequency distribution was unchanged. From the measurement of the fibre-flow irregularity down the feed tube, the analysis of the build-up in irregularity in the spinning process can be summarized as shown in Table VI.

Table VI

Analysis of Build-up of Irregularity

Type of Irregularity	I	I^2
(1) Fibre-flow irregularity in the feed tube	1·19	1·41
(2) Irregularity due to random fibre placement	1·00	1·00
(3) Irregularity due to drafting and fibre transport in the feed tube		0·41
(4) Irregularity of first layer deposited in the rotor	1·43	2·04
(5) Irregularity due to fibre-diameter variation		0·24
(6) Irregularity added in laying down fibres		0·39
(7) Yarn irregularity	1·62	2·61
(8) Irregularity added during doubling		0·57

The fact that the index of irregularity of the fibre band laid on the wall is greater than that of the fibre flow (with account taken of the fibre-diameter variation as indicated in Table I) shows that the process of laying down the fibres on the wall has resulted in an increase in irregularity. Since it has been shown that the air-speed in the feed tube is less than the rotor-surface speed, this is most probably due to the fact that the rotor wall plucks the feed in tufts as the fibres are accelerated suddenly to the rotor speed. This may also account for the existence of a periodic component in the irregularity of the fibre band deposited on the wall, which has had to be postulated to explain the results obtained during the doubling of the fibre band in the rotor.

With this hypothesis in mind, two yarns were spun with an increased air-flow down the feed tube. The results of these trials are summarized in Table VII, in which it is shown that, when higher air-velocities are used, the yarn irregularity becomes smaller and is almost completely determined by the random fibre-positioning, the variation in the fibre diameter, and the irregularity of the fibre feed. This last component of irregularity is governed only by the number of fibres in the feed when the ASD system is used and can be made almost zero when only four fibres occupy the feed-tube cross-section.

Table VII
Analysis of Build-up of Irregularity at Two Rotor Speeds

	10,000 rev/min, TF5*		12,000 rev/min, TF5*	
Type of Irregularity	I	I^2	I	I^2
(1) Fibre-flow irregularity in the feed tube	1·19	1·41	1·26	1·59
(2) Irregularity due to random fibre placement	1·00	1·00	1·00	1·00
(3) Irregularity due to drafting and fibre transport in the feed tube		0·41		0·59
(4) Irregularity due to fibre-diameter variation		0·24		0·24
(5) Irregularity of yarn with increased external suction	1·37	1·88	1·40	1·96
(6) Irregularity unaccounted for		0·23		0·14

*Twist factor.

It appears from this discussion that a 'random' or 'Martindale' yarn can be produced on an open-end spinner when long-staple fibres are used. The deviation from this minimum irregularity previously found both in work by one of the present authors[2] and in published work seems to be due to imperfections in the fibre-feed device and to fibre slippage, which can occur when the fibres are being deposited on the rotor wall.

ACKNOWLEDGEMENTS

The authors would like to express their gratitude to the International Wool Secretariat for its support for the work reported in this paper.

REFERENCES

[1] D. Cormack. Ph.D. Thesis, University of Leeds, 1972.
[2] I. M. Abou-Zeid. Ph.D. Thesis, University of Leeds, 1975.
[3] H. W. Krause in 'Studies in Modern Yarn Production' (edited by P. W. Harrison), the Textile Institute, Manchester, 1968, p. 109.

Department of Textile Industries,
University of Leeds,
Leeds 2.

Present address of I. M. Abou-Zeid:
Misr Beida Dyers,
Egypt.

6—NEW DEVELOPMENTS IN THE OPEN-END SPINNING OF WOOL AND LONG-STAPLE MAN-MADE FIBRES

By J. E. Burlet

Difficulties encountered in the open-end spinning of wool and blends containing wool are discussed and suggestions made for overcoming them. These relate to the effects of fibre length and diameter, yarn twist, and damage that occurs to the wool on machines fitted with beaters. The appearance and properties of open-end-spun wool yarns are briefly considered. The advantages of blending wool with man-made fibres to obtain a comparatively fine open-end-spun yarn are pointed out, and there is a brief discussion of open-end spinning on the woollen system.

1. INTRODUCTION

The International Textile Machinery and Accessories Exhibition in Milan in 1975 proved to sceptics that the spinning of short-staple fibres, often called cotton-type spinning, was experiencing a very profound technological evolution because of the extension of the open-end-spinning system. The consequences in the economic field are such that it is feasible to foresee the application of this technique in the wool textile industry and more generally in the long-staple-fibre industry, particularly for yarns intended for knitted or woven garments.

Experience has shown that it is not impossible to process combed wool on the rotor system. Nevertheless, there are some difficulties that must be resolved before one can achieve a satisfactory industrial result.

Some of the essential points will be reviewed in this paper to give an indication of their importance and suggest existing or possible future solutions.

2. FIBRE LENGTH

It is well known that the maximum length of fibres that may be processed on a given machine is approximately equal to the diameter of the rotor. It is also known that the energy consumed by the machine increases very rapidly with the rotor diameter, and the same applies to the cost of the spinning head.

In practice, experience has shown that the first rule, namely, that the maximum fibre length should be approximately equal to the rotor diameter, depends on the fibre-length diagram; when this is of the type found in combed wool, it is essential that the prescribed limit is not exceeded by 5% of the fibres. This is, of course, an order of size that can vary somewhat from one model of machine to another.

In order to avoid the necessity of using an excessively large rotor, it is more convenient to use short wool, and this may be achieved in several ways: wools shorn at 6–8 months, as is common practice in South Africa, may be used, or skinwools of suitable length may be selected. Finally, it is easy to stretch–break the wool on existing machines basically designed for converting man-made fibres.

This procedure has its limitations, however: all spinners know that, all other things being equal, a yarn produced from short fibres has inferior characteristics to a yarn spun from longer fibres. There is an additional factor in open-end spinning: the fibre used must possess suitable flexural rigidity and torsional rigidity for the twist of the yarn to rise up to the throat of the rotor; thus it may be noted that it is difficult to spin on an industrial scale a 3·3-dtex polyester fibre cut to 40 mm.

It may be mentioned that, with 60-mm rotors, it is possible to spin merino wools without encountering this difficulty. This point must not be overlooked if it is recalled that a wool of 24-μm diameter corresponds approximately to a fibre of 6·3 dtex, with a large proportion of distinctly coarser fibres. The flexibility of the wool is thus a very favourable factor.

3. WOOL FINENESS

The above remark on the relative coarseness of merino wools assumes full importance when it is considered that in open-end spinning the apparent minimum number of fibres in the cross-section is of a high order. The apparent number of fibres in the cross-section signifies the value obtained by dividing the linear density of the yarn by the linear density of the fibres, the linear density being expressed in the same units in both cases. It must be said that this apparent number is actually overestimated because of some lack of parallelism of the fibres. However, in numerous cases, there are approximately 100 fibres.

There are machines that are less discriminating: for instance, Société Alsacienne de Constructions Mécaniques has built the ITG 300, which permits a yarn to be spun with as few as 70 or 75 fibres in the cross-section. This is outstanding for an open-end-spinning machine, but it is a very high figure for a worsted spinner, who commonly thinks in terms of 40–45 fibres! This therefore means that, even with merino wools, it is only possible to spin fairly coarse yarns.

This factor places great interest on the spinning of wool blended with man-made fibres of 2·5–3 dtex to obtain relatively fine yarns, and Table I contains some very significant figures.

Table I

Limiting Yarn Linear Densities for Wool and Blended-fibre Yarns

Number of Fibres in Cross-section	Minimum Yarn Linear Density (tex)	
Fibre Content of Yarn	75	100
100% Wool (diameter 22 μm)	40	53
100% Wool (diameter 26 μm)	55	74
45% Wool (diameter 26 μm)–55% polyester fibre (3 dtex)	31	41

This raises an important problem in relation to crossbred wools.

4. YARN TWIST

It is well known that open-end-spun yarns are generally of high twist, higher than that in conventional yarns. It must be noted, however, that it can be close to the values obtained on the ringframe. Consequently, wool has been spun on the Krupp Perfect 300 machine with a twist factor, α, of the order of 90. The value of α is calculated by the formula:

$$\alpha = \frac{\tau\sqrt{T}}{\sqrt{1000}}$$

where τ is the twist in the yarn in turns/m; and

T is the linear density of the yarn in tex.

On the ITG 300 machine, it is possible to have lower twist factors, of the order of 70–75.

In Continental worsted spinning, a value of α of 70–75 corresponds to weft yarn and a value of 90 to warp yarn.

These results, which are rather favourable to wool, are probably partly explained by the fibre-length diagram. It has been found, in fact, that it has been possible to reduce the twist of man-made-fibre yarns by changing from cut-converted fibres to stretch–break-converted fibres, both on the 40-mm machine and on the 60-mm machine; the reduction in twist was obtained, of course, without any increase in end-breaks.

5. WOOL DAMAGE

The tests so far made at l'Institut Textile de France on machines with beaters have shown a rapid build-up of dust in the rotors. This fault is apparent with both card-wire beaters and pin beaters. It is very harmful, since it results in a progressive lowering of yarn quality, and an increase in the coefficient of variation of mass (Uster) of $1 \cdot 5$ points has been observed in a period of three hours. Moreover, this phenomenon is the cause of a high rate of end-breaks.

Chemical analysis of samples shows that this powder that is produced in the rotors is composed of 95% wool. This result is a little surprising when compared with observations in tests made on similar deposits resulting with man-made fibres, which contained 20–25% of lubricating agents.

For wool, the 5% of lubricant does not appear to be influenced by the initial content in the wool up to a value of $1 \cdot 1$% as measured by the IWTO standard.

Estimations were made of the amino acids in both the wool and the residue found in the rotor. The latter has a high cysteic acid content and a lower cystine content compared with the wool used, and this has been observed in all the cases studied. This leads one to suppose that the action of the beater detaches from the fibre portions that were already degraded, particularly the extreme tips of the fibres, and that these portions are 'trapped' in the rotor.

In view of the disadvantages caused from the industrial aspect, it appears difficult to process wool in the pure state or in wool-rich blends on machines with beaters without taking special precautions: selection of wools, very careful backwashing of the top, and the use of special card wire or pins.

These observations apply to dry-combed tops, since l'Institut Textile de France has not yet carried out any trials on oil-combed tops of the Noble type. It should be noted that the practice of backwashing has been largely discontinued in Continental combing and that the amount of damaged tips is higher when the top is not backwashed than when it is.

The situation is different when drafting is used for fibre separation: the less severe action exerted on the wool treats the fibres much more gently. It should be added that the form of the rotor plays an important rôle. The yarn does, in fact, pick up the residue to some extent, and in some cases it is possible to arrive at a state of equilibrium between the accumulation and removal of the dust. It appears that the results obtained with the ITG 300 machine are due on the one hand to the reduction in severity of treatment of the wool and on the other to the form of the rotor.

6.   YARN APPEARANCE AND PROPERTIES

The wool yarn produced by open-end spinning does not have the same appearance as a conventional worsted yarn. It resembles woollen yarn somewhat, but the appearance differs fairly appreciably according to the type of machine used. 'Bunching' is never absent from rotor-spun yarn, but here again this fault varies in severity according to the machine and fibre characteristics.

As a rule, the specific strength of open-end-spun wool yarn is lower than that of conventional yarns. For instance, on the Perfect 300 machine, a specific strength of 3 cN/tex was obtained with a yarn of twist factor 90, which corresponds to a reduction of approximately 30% compared with a conventional yarn. On the other hand, an increase of the order of 20% in the extension at break was observed. These results agree with results obtained in short-staple-fibre spinning.

It may also be noted that the yarn has very good covering power at the same linear density, which imparts a pleasing appearance to fabrics produced from open-end yarns, and it is often possible to reduce the fabric weight somewhat.

7.   BLENDS

It has already been shown that blends of wool and man-made fibres are necessary if one wishes to produce fairly fine yarns. The open-end system of spinning has the power of imparting a very high degree of cross-sectional homogeneity. This is an advantage at the preparation stage, since it is sufficient for the proportion of each constituent at any point in the sliver to be of suitable size; the cross-sectional homogeneity of sliver is not necessary. However, the appearance of the yarn with an equal proportion of wool is less wool-like than that of yarn produced on the conventional system; on the latter system, the wool tends, in fact, to be orientated on the outside of the yarn.

Provided that the man-made fibre is selected from those fibres suitable for spinning by the open-end process, the results will be satisfactory at the spinning stage. In woven or knitted fabrics dyed in the piece, the high degree of homogeneity produces a very pleasing appearance.

The fabrics made from open-end-spun yarns do not appear to have a greater tendency to pilling; this is of the same order as with conventional yarns.

Finally, there is a reduction of the order of 25–30% in yarn strength. This cannot fail to raise some problems in weaving, since one may be tempted to produce from singles yarn fabrics usually made from folded yarn: the evenness of open-end-spun yarn would permit this, but it would then be necessary to size the warps.

8.   WOOLLEN YARN

It is tempting to try to spin on the open-end-spinning machine the slubbings produced on woollen cards from the raw materials used in the woollen section of the industry.

With tops containing up to 1·1% of lubricant, no difficulty has been found, nor was there any deposit of fatty matter in the rotors. The same does not apply to woollen blends, which for carding require higher levels of lubricant, and it has not been possible to achieve a satisfactory result.

Another open-end-spinning system, without a rotor, has also been studied at l'Institut Textile de France for woollen spinning. The functions of yarn formation and imparting yarn twist are separated. Yarn formation occurs from a fringe of fibres obtained on a comb circle from a beater.

The results obtained up to now show that this is a possible solution, but development work is still required.

9. CONCLUSION

The technological changes taking place in spinning are of the utmost interest to the wool textile industry. Experience obtained to-day in this field shows that the principal technical obstacles can be overcome, and it is now possible to envisage development continuing on favourable lines.

The results obtained by research workers remain to be confirmed on an industrial scale. Here, however, it is not only the technological factors that are involved; economic factors are an essential feature, and one may say that the future is largely dependent on the advantages that can be gained from the use of the open-end-spinning system in the spinning of long-staple fibres.

Institut Textile de France,
Section Nord,
Villeneuve d'Ascq,
France.

7—OPEN-END-SPUN YARNS: THEIR PROCESSING PERFORMANCE AND FABRIC CHARACTERISTICS

By H. V. Shaw

The properties of open-end-spun yarns are briefly compared with those of ring-spun yarns, and the differences are attributed to differences in yarn structure, supported by evidence of the properties of model yarns produced at different levels of twisting tension.

The processing performance of open-end-spun yarns is considered in respect of winding, beaming, weaving, warp-knitting, and circular weft-knitting. Evidence is presented of yarn-fault content and warp-breakage in weaving.

Fabric properties are discussed in relation to factors other than yarn properties, and fabric characteristics are related to appropriate yarn characteristics in the open-end-spun product. Examples of end-uses are quoted in several different categories.

1. OPEN-END-SPUN YARNS

1.1 Yarn Properties

1.1.1 Introduction

A considerable amount of evidence is already available in the published literature with regard to the more common properties of open-end-spun yarns, and it is not necessary in this paper to produce corroborative evidence of properties such as regularity, tenacity, or extension of cotton yarns produced by this method. Since some of the properties of open-end-spun yarns bear different relationships to those of their ring-spun equivalents in the case of man-made-fibre yarns, the properties are summarized below so that some of these differences can be recorded.

1.1.2 Tenacity

The tenacity of open-end-spun yarns is some 15–25% lower than that of equivalent ring-spun carded cotton yarns and up to 40% lower than that of ring-spun combed cotton or man-made-fibre yarns. Factors affecting the degree of difference include linear density, material, preparatory processes, and type of machine.

1.1.3 Extension

In all cases, the extension at break of open-end-spun yarns is higher than that of similar ring-spun yarns.

1.1.4 Regularity

Open-end-spun cotton yarns are superior in short-term regularity to carded ring-spun cotton yarns, and there is a complete absence of the pronounced drafting-wave type of irregularity that is characteristic of the latter. The measured regularity of man-made-fibre yarns is similar for both systems of spinning.

1.1.5 Imperfections

As for regularity, the open-end-spun product is superior to its ring-spun equivalent for carded cotton yarns and is similar for combed cotton yarns or yarns spun from man-made fibres.

The Uster Imperfection Indicator records the presence of neps in similar quantities to those in combed yarns for cotton, but blackboard examination of yarns indicates that nep is less apparent in the open-end-spun product.

1.1.6   Yarn Bulk

Open-end-spun yarns have greater specific volume than their ring-spun equivalents.

1.1.7   Hairiness

Evidence has been produced by Barella[1] that open-end-spun yarns are less hairy (as assessed by both frequency and length of hairs) than ring-spun yarns, and the variation in hairiness that exists within a ring-spun package is not present in an open-end-spun package.

1.1.8   Abrasion-resistance

This is considerably higher in yarn form for the open-end-spun product, but the degree to which this advantage is obtained in fabric is always reduced and depends mainly on the fabric construction.

1.1.9   Twist

Although the same methods of measurement and expression of yarn twist are used for open-end-spun and ring-spun yarns, the results are not really directly comparable because of the differences in yarn structure. The levels of twist used in the production of open-end-spun yarns are usually those that are necessary to give satisfactory spinning performance and are usually higher than those used for ring-spun yarns. All comments in this paper refer to yarns spun with normal 'commercial' twist.

1.1.10   Stress–Strain Relation

Fig. 1 illustrates the stress–strain diagrams of equivalent open-end- and ring-spun cotton yarns in which some of the differences mentioned are evident, i.e., the lower breaking stress, higher breaking strain, and lower modulus of the open-end-spun product.

1.2   Yarn Structure

All the differences in properties listed above are the results of structural differences between open-end- and ring-spun yarns. It has been shown[2] that the structure of open-end-spun yarns is bipartite in nature and that some of the differences in properties are due to one or other or even both parts of the yarn structure. The differences due to the basic structure have been reproduced in model yarns made by twisting different materials at different levels of twisting tension; the models produced at high tension had properties similar to those of ring-spun yarns and those produced at relatively low tensions had properties similar to those of open-end-spun yarns. For example, the stress–strain diagrams in Fig. 2 are for model yarns produced by twisting under different conditions a bundle of five flat polyester-fibre continuous-filament yarns, each of 28 tex. It is apparent that these exhibit a remarkable similarity to the stress–strain curves shown in Fig. 1.

Examination of the structure of the model yarns and of that of ring-spun and open-end-spun yarns indicated that the spinning tensions affect the way in which the assembly of fibres twists to form the yarn, the low-tension models and the open-end-spun yarns forming a cylindrical spiralling ribbon, whereas the models produced under high tension and the ring-spun yarns form a collapsed twisted-ribbon structure. These different structures are illustrated in Fig. 3, which shows strips of woven fabric twisted in different ways. The strip shown in Fig. 3(a) had been twisted under tension and had formed the typical ring-spun structure, in which both sides of the fabric

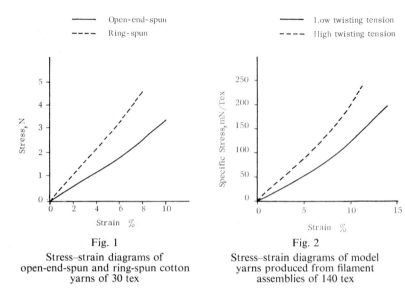

Fig. 1

Stress–strain diagrams of
open-end-spun and ring-spun cotton
yarns of 30 tex

Fig. 2

Stress–strain diagrams of model
yarns produced from filament
assemblies of 140 tex

appear on the surface of the model: Fig. 3(b) illustrates the appearance
of the ring-spun structure during untwisting just before the point at which
all the twist had been removed.

The model shown in Fig. 3(c) had been produced without tension
by laying the fabric strip on a table and rolling the twist into it by twisting
one end; only one surface of the fabric is visible in the twisted structure.
Fig. 3(d) illustrates the typical 'corkscrew' effect apparent when an open-
end-spun yarn is untwisted. This structure not only accounts for differences
in tenacity between open-end- and ring-spun yarns, but also explains the
difference in extension, the greater bulk, and the reduced fibre migration
of open-end-spun yarns.

1.3   Comment

Initially, comparisons have been made between open-end-spun and
ring-spun yarns because no other standard was available. In the light of
experience, it can be seen that such comparisons can be unfortunate, e.g.,
in the prediction of weaving performance from yarn strength, and it is
therefore important to recognize open-end-spun yarn as a distinct yarn
type and to assess it accordingly.

2.   PROCESSING PERFORMANCE

2.1   Introduction

The factors that determine the performance of open-end-spun yarns
in subsequent processing are many and their interrelationships complex:
their low modulus, low fault content, and strength regularity all contribute
to performance at one or more stages, and each processing stage can be
considered separately.

2.2   Winding

It has been claimed that the large package produced on open-end-
spinning machines means that the yarn need not be rewound but can be
used directly in the creel of the next process, e.g., in beaming or knitting
or as the weft-supply package in high-speed weaving, and it has been established that it is possible to use the spinning package in all these areas.

Fig. 3 Models of yarn structure

(a) Ring-spun yarn, fully twisted
(b) Ring-spun yarn, untwisted
(c) Open-end-spun yarn, fully twisted
(d) Open-end-spun yarn, untwisted

The decision to rewind therefore depends upon two main factors: the degree of freedom from fault required in the end-product and the suitability of the spinning package for the next process.

Some evidence has been published to support the claim that the fault content of open-end-spun yarns is significantly lower than that of ring-spun yarns. Leeming[3] quoted Uster Classimat test results for individual samples to illustrate the difference, and an analysis of records over a period of approximately two years confirms this evidence. Table I contains averages for different yarns, the open-end-spun results representing yarn from the spinning package, whereas, for 100% cotton, the results for ring-spun yarns represent yarn that has been rewound to cone and cleared. The Classimat categories have been simplified into three larger categories: minor, containing the Classimat categories A1, A2, and B1; small, containing A3, B2, and C1; and larger, containing the remainder, i.e., A4, B3 and 4, C2, 3, and 4, and all D faults. It is evident that, in 100% cotton, open-end-spun yarns are superior to ring-spun yarns in the minor- and small-fault categories and equivalent to cleared ring-spun yarns in their content of larger faults. For yarns spun from man-made fibres, the differences are not as great, but the open-end-spun yarns are superior to the ring-spun in both the small- and larger-fault categories.

Table I
Fault Content of Open-end-spun and Ring-spun Yarns

Fibre and Linear Density (tex)	Spinning System*	Package	Faults per 100,000 m (Non-cumulative)		
			Minor†	Small†	Larger†
100% Cotton					
42	OE *(a)*	Spool	54	5	7
30	OE *(b)*	Spool	61	4	9
66–25	OE *(c)*	Spool	146	10	6
37	Ring	Cone	303	30	9
59–37	Ring	Cone	1488	60	56
Man-made Fibres 100% Viscose					
37–30	OE	Spool	260	22	21
66–37	Ring	Spinning bobbin	378	57	56
Polyester-fibre– Vincel Blend					
59–23	OE	Spool	273	23	16
49–23	Ring	Spinning bobbin	226	36	49

Notes
*OE = Open-end.
(a) BD 200 machine.
(b) Platt type 885 machine.
(c) BD 200 machine—different cottons from those indicated by *(a)*.
†See text for definition of categories.

If open-end-spun yarn is rewound, it is obvious that the efficiency of the process will be much higher than that for ring-spun yarn because of the much larger spinning package and the fewer interruptions to winding due to clearer cuts if a similar standard of residual fault content is assumed, and the cleared yarn will have far fewer knots than a ring-spun yarn of the same linear density and raw material.

2.3 Beaming

A comparison of the performance of ring- and open-end-spun yarns in beaming indicates a superior performance of the latter, machine stops per million end–metres for an open-end-spun yarn being 33% fewer than the figure for the same linear density of ring-spun yarn, both yarns in this case having been rewound to cone before being beamed.

2.4 Sizing

The control of conditions in the sizing of open-end-spun yarns is critical in order to obtain the best performance possible in weaving. For cotton or other cellulosic fibres, similar size formulations to those used for ring-spun yarns have proved to be satisfactory, but, because of the more open structure of open-end-spun yarns, lower concentrations are necessary in order to prevent the addition of an excessive quantity of solids. Early recommendations were for a 25% reduction in solids in the size liquor, but more recent work by Vincent and Gandhi[4] suggests that very small quantities of size are adequate for the open-end-spun product.

At this processing stage, stretch control in the wet state is critical, since the initial modulus of the yarn can be permanently changed by over-extension in this state.

2.5 Weaving

All the published results indicate that the weaving performance of open-end-spun yarns is superior to that of ring-spun yarns, but a search of the records of Courtaulds Ltd for additional evidence yielded very little owing to the absence of direct comparisons with ring-spun equivalents. Table II illustrates the available evidence: in the comparable constructions for which data are available, the frequency of end-breaks when open-end-spun yarns are used is only 63% of that for ring-spun yarns; this proportion varied from 57 to 71% over the whole range of comparisons.

Table II
Weaving Performance: Warp Breaks

Loom Type	Warp Linear Density (tex)	Breaks per 1000 Ends per 100,000 Picks	
		Open-end-spun Yarn	Ring-spun Yarn
Air-jet	25	0·83	1·34
Sulzer	30	1·38	2·19
Conventional shuttle	25	1·75	2·45
	37	0·91	1·53
	R 100/2*	2·32	3·65

*Unsized warp.

The abrasion-resistance of open-end-spun yarns can be discounted as a factor of any significance in this superior performance, since, although this abrasion-resistance is impaired by the addition of size, the two-fold yarn quoted in the table was unsized, and it had the highest end-breakage rate of any of the open-end-spun yarns. The improved weaving performance of open-end-spun yarns is probably due to a combination of factors, of which the main ones are the strength regularity of these yarns, their lower knot content, and their lower modulus.

With regard to strength regularity, the advantage of open-end-spun over ring-spun yarns depends upon the particular ring-spun yarn with which the comparison is made: in some cases, the coefficient of variation of single-thread strength is very similar, whereas in others that of the ring-spun yarn is significantly higher. Dyson and El-Messiry[5] have demonstrated that the claim of improved performance due to strength regularity is only valid under certain conditions.

Because of the much larger spinning package and the lower incidence of larger-type faults, there are fewer knots in any given quantity of open-end-spun yarn than in the same quantity of ring-spun yarn, and consequently the probability of the occurrence of a yarn break that is attributable to the presence of a knot is lower.

It is evident from Fig. 1 that, at any given strain, the stress in an open-end-spun yarn is lower than that in a ring-spun yarn. In weaving (and in warp-knitting), the stresses in the warp are determined mainly by the strains imposed on the yarns owing to the mechanisms involved, and in these processes the stresses to which the yarns are subjected are therefore lower for open-end-spun than for ring-spun yarns.

Combined with the strength regularity of the yarn, this factor will probably result in a reduction of the frequency with which the strength of the weakest points is exceeded. It should be noted in this connexion that the weak points in a yarn that fail during processing lie well below the lower extent of the normal distribution expressed as $x - 3\sigma$ and occur only rarely. Since the figures quoted in Table II represent total warp breakages, then, according to van Harten's analysis[6], this type of failure could be classified as yarn fatigue through failure at weak spots, which represents a total of 20% of all warp breaks.

2.6 Knitting

The two factors that affect the performance of open-end-spun yarns in knitting are their reduced hairiness and fewer knots. In the case of the former, the result is a significant reduction in the release of fly during knitting and consequently fewer machine stops due to end-breakages resulting from fly and fewer fabric faults due to fly. The advantages of fewer knots are the reduced frequencies of machine stops due firstly to the weak points that occur at knots, secondly to tension breaks caused by knots snagging, and thirdly to knots slipping. In addition, knitting-machine efficiency is often affected by faults that are introduced at the winding process, the frequency of which is related to the number of knots tied: the fewer the knots, the less frequent is the occurrence of this type of fault. In one particular example, the faults were long-tailed or multi-tailed knots, which accounted for 12·8% of the knitting-machine stops; this number represented one faulty knot in every 2100 tied. Since the open-end-spinning package is relatively large and contains only a similar number of faults to that of a cleared ring-spun yarn and no knots, it would seem reasonable to assume that it should be used in the creels of circular-knitting machines.

This practice has been common in Czechoslovakia for some years, and knitting trials in the U.K. have been satisfactory. In some cases, it is possible to knit unwaxed yarn, but, for the exceptions, a waxing device could be incorporated into the yarn path at the knitting or spinning machine.

In warp-knitting, the reduced hairiness of open-end-spun yarns, combined with the other properties of strength regularity, freedom from knots, and lower modulus, results in significant improvements in performance in comparison with ring-spun yarns and therefore makes open-end-spun yarns more attractive than ring-spun in this field, where standards of performance have for many years been related to either flat or textured continuous-filament yarns.

3. FABRIC PROPERTIES

The major factors that determine the properties of fabrics are the properties of the yarns from which they are produced. It is therefore to be expected that fabrics produced from open-end-spun yarns will have lower tensile, tearing, and bursting strengths and higher extensions at break than their ring-spun equivalents. The actual differences, however, are influenced by other factors, such as the construction of the particular fabric under consideration.

The significance of levels of strength as measured by the tensile, tearing, or bursting method in relation to performance in use is doubtful, particularly for two such different products as ring-spun and open-end-spun yarns. The evidence presented above in comparing the warp-weaving performance of the two types of yarn illustrates this point, since, from yarn-strength tests alone, superior weaving performance would be predicted for the ring-spun product.

In the early days of open-end spinning, it was extremely difficult to convince weavers that open-end-spun yarns would give improved performance in weaving because the main criterion for weavability was yarn strength. At the present time, fabric specifications are based on experience of the performance in use of fabrics produced from ring-spun yarns, and it is likely that criteria will be adjusted to allow for the different character and behaviour of open-end-spun yarns.

In the circumstances in which a minimum fabric strength is essential, it is possible to adjust constructions to control properties, and in some cases relatively minor adjustments will alter the fabric properties sufficiently to meet the specified levels of strength.

Examples of the effect of changes in construction on fabric properties are provided by Mohamed and Lord[7], who have recently published work on fabrics produced from open-end-spun yarns that illustrates increases in weft-direction strengths with increases in picks/cm for the same linear density of weft yarn.

Another approach to the same situation would be to retain the fabric construction while using a coarser yarn. Figures 4 and 5 illustrate the effect of using different linear densities of open-end-spun yarn in the weft direction of a plain-weave fabric. To make this comparison, the warp was a 24·6-tex open-end-spun yarn and the construction, which remained constant throughout the experiment, was 24 ends/cm and 24 picks/cm.

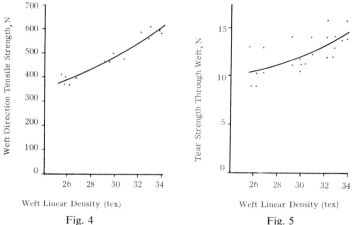

Fig. 4

The effect of change in weft linear density on fabric tensile strength

Fig. 5

The effect of change in weft linear density on fabric tearing strength

In this particular example, the changes in weft linear density resulted in weft-weight increases of 20 and 33%, respectively, and in strength increases of 21 and 49% for the tensile test and 13 and 31% for the tearing test. The relation between weft linear density and fabric properties, however, is not simple: a coarser weft yarn will affect the amount of crimp in the warp, and greater crimp will result in lower tensile and tearing strengths in the warp direction. Under certain conditions, a coarser yarn with unaltered pick-spacing will restrict thread slippage during the tearing test and result in a lower tearing strength even in the weft direction, and care must be taken in designing a fabric to ensure that all relevant factors are taken into account. In cases in which tearing strength is important and the weaver is free to adjust the structure, it is probable that satin, sateen, twill, or matt constructions will be used more widely, since fabrics containing longer floats have higher tearing strengths than those in plain weave.

Recent work with open-end-spun yarns in denim constructions at the Textile Research Centre of Texas Tech University[8] has shown that existing tensile- and tearing-strength specifications can be met by using coarser yarns and a less dense thread-spacing.

4. FABRIC CHARACTERISTICS

4.1 Introduction

The structure of open-end-spun yarns determines their properties and characteristics, and these in turn determine the characteristics of the fabrics produced from them. Table III illustrates the effect of various yarn characteristics on the processing performance of yarns and on the characteristics of the resultant fabrics.

Some of the items listed in the table have been considered under the heading of properties in the preceding section, and processing performance has also been discussed above: the remainder can be discussed generally under this heading.

4.2 Appearance

Yarn regularity, fault content, absence of nep, hairiness, and lustre all affect the appearance of the resultant fabric. The degree or magnitude of the effect is relative and depends upon the ring-spun criterion

Table III Effect of Differences in Method of Spinning on Yarn and Fabric Characteristics and Processing Performance

Effect on:	Yarn Property or Characteristic		Processing Performance	Fabric Property or Characteristic	
	Primary	Secondary		Primary	Secondary
Basic Difference between Ring- and Open-end-spun Yarn					
Strength				Tensile strength, tearing strength, bursting strength	
		Modulus	Sizing, weaving, knitting		
Regularity				Appearance, surface smoothness	Print clarity
		Strength variation	Weaving, knitting		Tearing strength
Yarn Structure					
Fault content		Fewer knots	Winding, weaving, knitting	Appearance	Print clarity
Nep				Appearance, surface smoothness	Print clarity
Bulk				Handle, drape, crimp	Tearing strength
		Absorption	Sizing		Print clarity, dyeability
Hairiness			Sizing, knitting	Appearance, permeability	Tearing strength, bursting strength
Lustre				Appearance	
Elastic recovery			Winding, sizing, weaving, knitting		

used, e.g., in the extreme case, a substantial improvement is evident in appearance when a fabric produced from open-end-spun cotton yarns is compared with a similar product made from ring-spun carded cotton yarns; much less obvious differences are apparent if comparison is made with combed cotton yarns in fabric or if man-made-fibre yarns produced by the two methods are compared.

In fabrics produced from man-made fibres, the greatest difference in appearance is the reduced lustre of the yarn and fabric, which is due to the difference in orientation of the fibres in the open-end-spun yarn structure. Where fibres of bright lustre are used, this difference results in an improvement in the fabric appearance, the glossy surface associated with bright fibres in ring-spun yarns being eliminated.

4.3 Surface

The regularity, absence of nep, and hairiness of open-end-spun yarns result in smoother surfaces for equivalent fabrics, which, in addition to the effect that they have on appearance and handle characteristics, also enable greater clarity to be obtained in printed designs by either roller or screen methods.

This characteristic is particularly apparent in certain end-uses, such as some apparel uses and drapes, in which satin constructions are often used.

4.4 Handle

In addition to being influenced by those factors listed in Section 4.3, the handle of fabrics produced from open-end-spun yarns is also affected by the increased bulk of this type of yarn. This aspect of fabric characteristics is particularly apparent in man-made-fibre fabrics. Those produced from cellulosic and polyester fibres and from blends containing these types are fuller and warmer in handle than their ring-spun equivalents, and this characteristic is particularly appropriate in apparel end-uses. A further factor that affects the handle of a fabric is the twist in the yarns: in this respect, it is appropriate to note that open-end-spun man-made-fibre yarns are produced with lower twist levels than open-end-spun cotton yarns, and the handle of fabrics produced from them is quite different from that of fabrics produced from either open-end-spun cotton or ring-spun man-made-fibre yarns.

4.5 Drape

The factors that influence the drape of a finished fabric are many and their interrelationships complex. Fibre type and fineness, yarn linear density and twist, various aspects of fabric construction, and, by no means least, the type of finish applied are all examples of the major factors that influence drape, and, among these, the differences in yarn structure between ring- and open-end-spun yarns constitute an additional variable rather than a fundamental factor. The individual characteristic of open-end-spun yarn that has the greatest effect on drape is bulk.

If all other factors remain unaltered, the fabric produced from open-end-spun yarns will be stiffer than one produced from ring-spun yarns because of the greater space occupied by the yarns. This characteristic was evident in certain tightly constructed cotton drill fabrics produced some seven years ago, and changes in finished construction were necessary to compensate for it.

4.6 Summary

In all aspects of fabric characteristics, differences are evident between the open-end-spun and ring-spun products. The magnitude of the difference is greatest with carded ring-spun cotton yarns, less with blends of carded cotton with man-made fibres, and least with combed cotton or 100% man-made fibres, although different characteristics, such as lustre and handle, are more noticeable when comparison is made between man-made-fibre fabrics than between those produced from cotton. The effect of these differences will be seen in the development of different end-uses for particular fabrics.

5. END-USES

5.1 Classification

End-uses for yarns can be conveniently arranged in one specific and three general categories: pile yarn for carpets and rugs, apparel, household textiles, and industrial uses. In a recent publication[9], the total fibre consumption for the U.S.A. was given by end-use and broad fibre type (wool, cotton, rayon and acetate, and non-cellulosic man-made fibres). Since the pattern of use of fibres varies from country to country, in, for example, the proportion of wool or of regenerated-cellulose fibres, it would be unwise to conclude that the exact pattern would apply elsewhere, but it is interesting to classify the total fibre consumption into end-use categories and to comment on the uses of open-end-spun yarns in each area of use.

5.2 Carpet Pile

This specific category accounted for 19% of U.S. fibre consumption, and several machinery manufacturers are offering open-end-spinning equipment designed to produce yarns of appropriate linear density from wool or long-staple man-made fibres to supply this market.

5.3 Apparel

The largest single category, 47% of all fibre, was used for apparel, which includes hosiery and apparel linings. It is in this category and that of household textiles that open-end-spun yarns have been mainly used up to the present time.

In 1969, the author[10] drew attention to the advantages of open-end-spun cotton yarns in several fabrics and selected six as examples of particular interest from a general list of fabric types. Of these six, four have been in continual production since that time: satins, combinations of continuous-filament warp and spun weft, lightly raised winceyette types of fabrics, and denims. Since that time, the use of open-end-spun yarns in denims has increased rapidly, and several vertical organizations in various parts of the world have established plants exclusively producing denim fabrics from yarns spun on open-end-spinning machines. The prime reasons for this type of development are firstly economic and secondly particular suitability for the market. The various constructions of denim all use relatively coarse yarns, and this type of market is therefore appropriate for open-end spinning, which is most economical at the coarse end of the cotton-count range; the appearance of denim produced from open-end-spun yarns is attractive and suitable for a wide range of end-uses and in particular for the fashion wear into which it has been introduced.

In addition, fabric properties suitable for workwear and fabrics intended for other heavy-duty uses can be obtained by appropriate adjustment to the fabric construction. The appearance advantages of this type of fabric when produced from open-end-spun yarns have been extended into lighter-weight constructions for use in dresswear and shirtings, the coloured warp and undyed weft being retained, but with the construction changed to something more suitable for lighter-weight end-uses. In order that the denim market might be developed successfully, howevei, modifications to fabric structure and finishing techniques were necessary and were made according to established principles, which illustrates the need for the skills of the textile technologist in the field of marketing and sales development.

Other areas in which open-end-spun yarns are being used in apparel are woven fabrics for rainwear, dresswear, and shirtings in cotton and man-made fibres and in blends. With the introduction of man-made-fibre yarns, the quantity of open-end-spun yarn used in circular knitting is increasing, particularly in leisure shirts and some areas of knitted dresswear, and this type of use should continue to increase as the production of open-end-spun man-made-fibre yarns increases.

5.4 Household Textiles

Some 21 % of U.S. fibre consumption was used in the household-textile field, in addition to carpet- and rug-pile yarns. Of the fabrics discussed in 1969[10], the smooth surface and drape of the satin construction has proved particularly suitable in either plain-dyed form or as a print base for drapes and in lighter-weight versions for drape linings.

Other examples of end-uses in this field are colour-woven or printed bedspreads, brocades, plain or printed pillowcases and sheets, tapestries, towels, and window blinds. In addition to the less critical requirements of some of these products, the tearing-strength specifications of upholstery and loose-cover fabrics can be achieved by modification of the fabric structure. Most of the fabrics falling within the category of household textiles are constructed from yarns that are within the economic linear-density range for open-end spinning, and this field of end-uses is therefore particularly appropriate for open-end-spun yarns.

Some penetration of this area and that of apparel is being achieved by the use of open-end-spun yarns in warp-knitting, a subject dealt with in an earlier paper in this conference[11].

5.5 Industrial Uses

Although some fabrics in this category, such as filter cloths and cleaning cloths, are being produced from open-end-spun yarns, the majority are heavy-duty fabrics for which strength specifications have to be met, so that the use of open-end-spun yarns is precluded. As the number of open-end-spinning machines installed increases and the labour element of the production cost also increases, the need to produce all coarse yarns by this method will become pressing, and the question of the performance of open-end-spun yarns in industrial fabrics, such as tarpaulins, canvases, hoses, conveyor belting, etc., will inevitably arise. It is therefore suggested that the research organizations and universities look closely at this area and endeavour to produce fabric specifications that will enable open-end-spun yarns to be employed in these end-uses.

6. FUTURE PROGRESS

At the International Textile Machinery and Accessories Exhibition in Milan in October, 1975, over twenty machinery manufacturers showed open-end-spinning machines, most of which were capable of processing cotton and short-staple man-made fibres at rotor speeds in the region of 35,000–45,000 rev/min. It can be concluded that the short-term prospect is an increasing share of the coarse-yarn market within the present economic linear-density range. Factors that may affect the commercial linear-density limit are the availability and cost of labour and a significant increase in rotor speed for equivalent yarn properties, which at the present time appears to be a medium-term target, but this factor could be affected by increasing power costs. There is considerable scope for research into fabric properties where open-end-spun yarns are used and, more importantly, into the relationship of fabric properties to performance in use. In the long term, open-end-spun yarns will penetrate areas of the market that are at present exclusively the province of ring-spun yarns and will probably cover a wider linear-density range than they do at present.

ACKNOWLEDGEMENTS

The author wishes to state that this paper reflects his own views and opinions, which are not necessarily those of Courtaulds Ltd. He also wishes to express his thanks to those colleagues and customers who have assisted with information and the provision of fabric samples and to the Directors of Courtaulds Ltd for permission to publish this paper.

REFERENCES

1 A. Barella. *J. Text. Inst.,* 1971, **62,** 702.

2 J. V. Kášpárek in 'Spinning in the '70s' (edited by P. R. Lord), Merrow, Watford, 1970, p. 215.

3 R. Leeming. *Text. Inst. Industr.,* 1975, **13,** 139.

4 J. J. Vincent and K. L. Gandhi. *Text. Month,* 1974, July, 48.

5 E. Dyson and M. A. El-Messiry. *J. Text. Inst.,* 1975, **66,** 301.

6 K. van Harten. *Symp. Int. Rech. Text. Cot. Paris,* 1969, 331.

7 M. H. Mohamed and P. R. Lord. *Text. Res. J.,* 1973, **43,** 154.

8 J. D. Towery. Private communication, 18 Nov., 1975.

9 *Amer. Text. Rep./Bull.,* 1975, **AT–4,** No. 2, 24.

10 H. V. Shaw in 'Spinning in the '70s' (edited by P. R. Lord), Merrow, Watford, 1970, p. 242.

11 J. M. Black and H. E. Brockmann in 'The Yarn Revolution' (edited by P. W. Harrison), the Textile Institute, Manchester, 1976, p. 24.

Courtaulds Ltd,
Northern Spinning Division,
Heron Mill,
Hollinwood,
Oldham,
Lancs.

8—FROM YARN INNOVATION TO COMMERCIAL EXPLOITATION *

By I. GLASMAN

Yarns, and the raw material from which they are made, have played, over the ages, an important rôle in the quality, performance properties, and aesthetics of fabrics and garments.

From as long ago as Biblical times—as the author has discovered from an examination of textile fabrics found in caves of the Judean Hills—there is impressive evidence of the human ability to utilize, even in those days, the fibres then available, which were spun into yarns by hand to produce attractive fabrics coloured with natural dyes, some of which, for instance, Indigo, still inspire fashion to-day.

During the last few hundred years, remarkable developments have taken place in the textile industry, and, especially in the last fifty years, scientists and technologists, as well as those possessing practical craftsmanship and commercial ability, have established a man-made-fibre—and particularly a synthetic-fibre—industry that ranks in its concept and its execution with some of the major discoveries from which mankind has profited.

As far as this country is concerned, the abolition of the Utility scheme in the early 1950s allowed the floodgates of innovation to open wide and put before the British public fabrics and garments incorporating finishes and dyes to make them attractive, comfortable, fashionable, and endowed with performance properties that remain adequate during the life of the garment.

With the internationalization of life generally, brought about by improved travel and communications, speeded up through technology and science by means of the 'instant news' made available even in colour in almost every home in an industrialized society, the pace of development and of customer requirements in particular has quickened significantly.

The variety of new ideas in fibre types and spinning machinery has resulted in yarn effects that the knitter, the weaver, and the garment maker have turned into merchandise that is sold throughout the world.

No time is better suited to innovation and a rapid realization of new developments than a period of economic difficulties, when the challenge facing everyone requires a speedy and practical response to capture the market.

Marks & Spencer Ltd,
Baker St,
London W.1.

*This paper is presented in summary form. The complete paper will be published in *The Textile Institute and Industry*.

9—USES OF PRODUCER-TEXTURED YARNS

By K. West and N. M. MacInnes

The technological development of texturing has been accompanied by remarkable increases in speeds from 10 to 200 m/min, which have allowed texturing and drawing to be combined into one process. Future speed increases may even allow texturing to be combined with extrusion processes. There are quite remarkable similarities in the development of producer-textured yarns in hosiery, carpets, and apparel; there is some tendency in each area for the novel products to succeed at first in terms of novelty and low cost, but the next phase is then a massive diversification of the product range in which the new yarns seek to simulate the factors of consumer appeal that have been traditional for centuries.

1. INTRODUCTION

The textile industry is one of the oldest principal industries meeting mankind's basic needs for food, clothing, and shelter. With agriculture and housing, it is established on a complex interaction of crafts that have arisen to satisfy not only the simple demand for cover (whether for warmth or for modesty) but also more intangible expectations of fashion and attractiveness.

Although textile clothing dates from at least 4000 B.C. (the oldest known textile garment of this period being made from woven flax), major advances in the textile industry began only about 200 years ago with the application of power to textile processes. Really dramatic developments have taken place only over the past 30–40 years with the advent of synthetic fibres. Synthetic fibres, particularly in continuous-filament form, quickly found application where they satisfied the conversion requirements of the industry and the expectations of the consumer and, in particular, where individual processes or crafts could be combined together into simpler processes or eliminated completely. Table I compares traditional natural-fibre conversion routes with the simplicity of those for producer-textured polyester-fibre yarns in typical apparel outlets.

Table I
Processes in Conversion of Fibre to End-use

100% Wool Suiting		100% Cotton Shirting	100% Crimplene Dresswear
Lambing		Planting	Oil-refining
Rearing		Weeding	TA/glycol manufacture
Shearing		Feeding	Polymerization
Grading		Picking	Spinning
Washing		Shipping	Draw-texturing
Blending		Opening	Knitting
Carding		Blending	Scouring/dyeing/finishing/printing
Gilling		Carding	Making-up
Combing		Combing	
Gilling	—Top-dyeing	Drawing	
	Gilling	Spinning	
Drawing		Sizing	
	Combing	Warping	
Spinning ⌐	Gilling	Weaving	
	⟩Yarn-dyeing	Desizing	
Doubling ⌐		Scouring	
Warping		Bleaching/dyeing/printing	
Weaving		Finishing (resin, etc.)	
Pre-setting		Making-up	
Scouring/milling			
Piece-dyeing			
Brushing			
Cropping			
Decatizing			
Pressing			
Making-up			

It is in those textile areas in which continuous-filament synthetic-fibre yarns have achieved domination that producer-textured yarns have allowed technology to progress even further. In this paper, three diverse areas are examined—hosiery, carpets, and weft-knitting—and a common theme for the trend in producer-texturing is postulated, an attempt thereby being made to predict the future.

Even as recently as fifteen years ago, it would have taken considerable foresight to detect any real thread of continuity between the three sectors selected for examination and the processes by which the required yarns were made. Although hosiery had by then moved into the false-twist era, the speed characteristic of the conventional twisting and rewinding process was about 10 m/min; textured polyester-fibre yarn was of 167 dtex, on the point of explosion, and processed at around 20 m/min; and 3650-dtex yarn was offered for nylon carpets and processed at up to 500 m/min. But now the general development and evolution of these processes have increased both the running speed and linear-density range to such a degree that one can see much more a continuum of products rather than three isolated and distinct areas of technology. Hosiery yarns are now available in linear densities from 15 to 44 dtex, and running speeds are 300–500 m/min; the textured polyester-fibre product range has widened from 167 dtex down to around 50 dtex and up to 333 dtex and, with the development of fine-gauge knitting machines, could well go down to 30 dtex while characteristic process speeds are now from 250 to 600 m/min; the carpet linear-density range has come down from the heights of 3650 to around 1000 dtex, and speeds of around 1000 m/min are achievable.

We no longer think in terms of bulking as a series of specific process tricks for particular products but regard it more as a family of techniques of general application to making yarns of different characters, the most appropriate of which can be selected as needed. Those techniques of main importance are:

(a)   twist-texturing, based either on pin-twisting (where the yarn is 'driven') or on friction-twisting (where it is 'rubbed');

(b)   compression bulking, based mainly on a variant of the stuffer-box theme; and

(c)   impact bulking, based mainly on jet-texturing, by steam or air.

A major omission from this list, which ten years ago would have been regarded as an almost inevitable route to textured yarns, is self-bulking, based on heterofil spinning. This, in practice, has made an impact only in hosiery with Du Pont's Cantrece, and it does not now seem to have a major part to play in the technology of texturing.

2. HOSIERY

Before 1920, hosiery for women was very much an undergarment, and the lifting of the hemline to just above the ankle, while greeted by the acclaim of half the population, set the other half and the textile industry the problem of satisfying new expectations, particularly in emphasizing leg shape. Whereas the technology for producing the garments existed, the only yarns available were either continuous-filament silk and rayon or mercerized-cotton yarns (lisle). The first were expensive, and all had severe performance limitations. The only way to obtain leg shape and fit was by full-fashioning and by producing a wide range of leg lengths and foot sizes.

On its introduction, multifilament nylon was seen as a direct substitute for silk, and the initial yarns were highly twisted and gummed as in the traditional silk process. The lack of availability created a huge demand, which did much to foster Anglo-American relationships.

Monofilament nylon yarn, albeit still twisted and gummed, gave the industry a completely novel concept in the mid-1940s and afforded it the opportunity to produce sheerer (and dearer) stockings without the difficulties that would have been associated with finer multifilament yarns.

Textured multifilament yarns, sequentially uptwisted, set, and detwisted, although expensive, offered further opportunities to the industry and improved conversion efficiency, and the consumer benefited through the greater wear life of the garments produced.

Development co-operation between the fibre producers and machine builders provided the industry with a major breakthrough in the mid-1950s. This was the false-twist process, which combined three separate processes into one, dramatically increased production, and significantly reduced labour costs and overheads. This had the effect of bringing well-fitting nylon stockings into the realms of mass-production techniques and made silk-like stockings available to all women. No less important, the stretch characteristics allowed the industry to replace the wide range of sizes with two or three basic sizes, which still gave a better fit than the previous complex combinations of leg lengths and foot sizes.

In the mid-1960s, the introduction of producer-textured fine multifilament yarns, the development of multifeed knitting machinery, and further raising of the hemline in the fashion change to the miniskirt coincided to produce a transformation in the industry, which now was knitting seamless tights in one piece. It is this combination of simplicity of textile sequences, aptness of product, and satisfaction of consumer requirements that is the key to the success of producer-textured yarns, which now account for almost the entire hosiery consumption of textured yarns. Table II illustrates the simplification of conversion that has occurred between 1945 and 1975.

Table II
Conversion of Nylon into Ladies' Hose

1945	1975
Spinning	Spinning
Drawing	Draw-texturing
Twisting	Knitting of multifeed one-piece tights
Steam-setting	Scouring/dyeing
Gumming	Packing
Coning	
Single-feed knitting	
Seaming/linking	
Pre-boarding	
Scouring	
Dyeing	
Post-boarding	
Examining	
Pairing	
Packing	

To digress for a moment, it is interesting to postulate that hosiery, as we know it to-day, is such a recent ladies' outerwear garment that it may still be being considered by the trade, and by the consumer, as underwear, which may explain the preoccupation with fit rather than fashion. Uncertainty as to the future height of the hemline may prolong this indecision, but it may well be that, as the hemline is lowered again, decoration in terms of heel designs or clocking effects may represent the next innovation.

Producer-texturing of hosiery yarn has thus participated in the combination of two highly significant trends occurring simultaneously: a reduced number of processes, providing efficient methods of conversion for the fibre producer and the industry, and consumer satisfaction through meeting fashion requirements at very modest prices. We shall probably never know which was the cause and which the effect.

3. CARPETS

Before 1950, carpets were exclusively woven, and the carpet-manufacturing sector of the industry was based on wool as the preferred fibre, rayon being a cheap substitute. The introduction of tufting provided the opportunity for rapid expansion of the sector to meet the needs of the rising consumer market, and the economics of this new process made the concept of wall-to-wall carpeting an expectation of all social classes. Table III illustrates the explosive growth of tufting, which, like circular weft-knitting, allows yarn-to-fabric conversion without the expense and inconvenience of warping and thus significantly shortens the conversion route.

Table III

Carpet Production

Year	Production in million m^2			
	U.S.A.		U.K.	
	Tufted	Woven	Tufted	Woven
1954	59	55	—	44
1964	319	39	28	50
1974	866	23	103	49

Producer-bulked continuous-filament nylon was introduced in the early 1960s and provided the tufting section of the industry with a yarn of the required linear density, strength, uniformity, and absence of loose fibres, which gave greater conversion efficiency. Unlike the hosiery development, there never was a prior phase of a separate throwster industry, introducing bulk by twisting. The earlier use of rayon yarns had given tufted carpets a reputation for being inferior owing to the poor wear and appearance characteristics of rayon. Producer-textured nylon yarns provided the means of greatly improving tufted carpets by vast improvements in abrasion-resistance and pile-resilience and allowed the manufacturers to upgrade their market image. Table IV illustrates the growth of the use of producer-textured nylon yarns in the tufted-carpet section of the industry.

Table IV

Consumption of Producer-textured Nylon in Tufted Carpets

Year	U.S.A.		U.K.	
	%	million kg	%	million kg
1954	—	—	—	—
1964	30	288	8	4·4
1974	46	1250	42	62

The simpler conversion and piece-dyeing facility were at first enough to drive this trend, but then, with the vast reductions in weight (from 40 to 10 oz/yd^2, i.e., from 1360 to 340 g/m^2) made possible by the high bulk and strength of textured nylon, the cost element dominated, and was enough to overcome, for a time, the lack of design and customer appeal. But gradually interaction among tufted-carpet manufacturers, fibre producers, and machinery manufacturers led to a series of developments significantly improving the range of variety in the colour and pattern characteristics achievable.

Multilevel tufting, cut–uncut pile, differential-dyeing yarns, marls, greater ranges of linear density, novel cross-sections, and lustre characteristics have all been introduced to meet this demand. An example of the extent of this expansion is shown in Table V. Similar successful innovations have been achieved by all manufacturers of producer-textured yarns in the U.S.A. and Europe.

The U.K., with a long history of patterned carpets and a woven-carpet section of the textile industry left intact by the Second World War, demanded still greater similarity to traditional woven appearance in colour, design, and surface texture. Printing-equipment manufacturers were quick to recognize this demand, and full-width machines giving excellent print penetration of the pile, with superb design scope and definition, were available by the end of the 1960s. This led to further explosive growth, and this printed-carpet sector alone has grown fifteenfold over the past five years.

Initially, this innovation led to serious price-cutting, and there was a tendency to use printing as a means of disguising low pile weights. However, the excellent printing characteristics of producer-textured nylon yarns and the clarity and complexity of print achievable by the new processes have encouraged tufters to produce higher-quality carpets, closely imitating and directly competing with woven Axminster carpets. Fibre producers in Europe have responded by supplying products for both loop- and cut-pile types that retain their tuft identity sufficiently to simulate woven carpets. In the U.S.A., where there is less history of woven carpets, the producer-textured yarns are designed to burst more in finishing and lose their distinct tuft identity to give a velour-type appearance.

This growing emphasis on quality and surface texture in tufted carpets, whether plain or printed, provides the fibre producer with the challenge of progressing from the initial objective of a strong, hard-wearing, uniform yarn to the areas of yarn character, where irregularity on a controlled basis satisfies the expectations of both the industry and the consumer.

Table V

ICI Product Range in BCF Nylon for Tufted Carpets

1965				1975*			
Linear Density (dtex)	Number of Filaments	No.	Type	Type	No.	Number of Filaments	Linear Density (dtex)
3650	204	K805	Trilobal, standard dye	Bright, standard dye	K101 O	68	1360
3650	204	T215	Circular, internal dye	Bright, standard dye	K101 O	100	1780
3650	204	K815	Trilobal, deep dye	Bright, extra-deep dye	K101 E	100	1780
3650	204	K835	Trilobal, ultra-deep dye	Bright, random marl	K108 OE	100	1780
3650	204	G2	Marl (2K805; 1K815)	Bright, random marl	K108 LE	100	1780
3650	204	G3	Marl (1K805; 2K815)	Bright, random marl	K108 OB	100	1780
2450	136	K805	Trilobal, standard dye	Bright, random marl	K108 OBE	150	2670
2450	136	T215	Circular, internal dye	Quarter-dull, extra-deep dye	K201 E	136	2720
2450	136	K815	Trilobal, deep dye	Bright, random marl	K108 OE	136	2720
2450	136	G4	Marl (1K805; 1K815)	Quarter-dull, twisted marl	K201 OE	136	2720
				Bright, random marl	K108 LE	136	2720
				Quarter-dull, basic dye	K201 B	136	2720
				Quarter-dull, twisted marl	K201 OB	136	2720
				Bright, standard dye	K201 O	136	2720
				Bright, random marl	K108 OB	272	5500
				Bright, standard	K101 O	272	1100
				Bright, random marl	K108 OBEL	100	1600
				Bright, high-bulk standard	K106 E	100	1600
				Bright, high-bulk, extra-deep dye	K106 B	100	1600
				Bright, high-bulk, basic	K106 O	136	2650
				Bright, high-bulk, standard	K106 E	136	2650
				Bright, high-bulk, extra-deep dye	K106 B	136	2650
				Bright, textured bulk	K128	136	2650

*All yarns are also available with anti-static protection.

We may therefore say that carpets have followed the same development trend as hosiery in that the first innovation was to produce a simpler route from raw material to fabric (throwster-twisting in hosiery, tufting in carpets), and this was then followed by further condensation and the elimination of separate processes, largely involving producer-texturing, which is now having to become more diverse to cater for the growing demand for a wide product range and continuing customer satisfaction.

4. APPAREL

4.1 Weft-knitting

In comparison with the virtually single-end-use textile sectors of carpets and hosiery, textiles for outerwear apparel form a very complicated amalgam of production and consumption criteria.

To appreciate the impact of producer-textured yarns, it is important to remember that they have only a five-year history in apparel, whereas synthetic fibres have been available for 30 years and natural fibres have been used for about 6000 years. Up to the mid-1940s, wool and cotton were the predominant fibres, and even in 1970 wool and cellulosic fibres still accounted for 80% of the world's apparel-fibre consumption. The situation is changing rapidly, however, with synthetic fibres increasing at a growth rate of approximately 15% per annum, and it is expected that by 1980 they will represent 40% of the world's fibre consumption.

The situation in the developed countries is significantly different from the world's average, and synthetic fibres achieved 50% market penetration in the early 1970s. This discrepancy is highlighted by the *per capita* textile consumption of fibres in 1973, i.e.:

world average	6·6 kg;
West European average	12·7 kg;
U.K. average	16·0 kg;
U.S.A. average	24·8 kg.

Although the usage of textiles in the developed areas is abnormally high, textile production grows more slowly in the advanced countries than in the poorer ones because imports of textiles into advanced from developing countries grow faster than trade in the reverse direction.

It is in response to some of the less obvious discrepancies that the importance of producer-textured yarns for apparel outlets must be related. Broadly speaking, in the more developed countries, knitting has had a larger impact on the business and made a higher penetration into apparel that it has done in underdeveloped countries. Where knitting has grown, the use of polyester fibre has followed it, and, after the development of regular polyester fibre, the introduction and increasing usage of producer-textured polyester-fibre yarns have followed in its train.

The expanding penetration of knitting in the developed countries is shown in Table VI, and the associated usage of polyester fibre in the U.K., where the consumption has leapt in ten years from 0·1 million kg to 60 million kg per annum, is shown in Table VII. One reason for the preferential

Table VI
Knitted Fabrics and Garments as Percentage of Total Production of Apparel Fabrics

Country	1961	1970	1973
U.K.	25	50	55
Germany	31	44	45
Italy	20	38	45
France	17	32	34
Holland	20	26	27
Belgium	19	23	20
Japan	3	10	10
U.S.A.	23	30	40

Table VII

Fibre Consumption in Apparel Fabrics in the United Kingdom, 1963 and 1973

Consumption in million kg

| Fibre | Weaving | | Warp-Knitting | | Weft-Knitting | | | | | | | |
| | | | | | Hosiery | | Underwear | | Outerwear | | Jersey Fabrics | |
	1963	1973	1963	1973	1963	1973	1963	1973	1963	1973	1963	1973
Wool	88	57	—	—	4·5	1·8	1·4	1·4	14	9	7	9
Cotton and cellulosic fibre	124	72	5	5	1·8	0·4	18·1	11·1	4	7·5	2·3	5·5
Acrylic fibre	—	3	—	—	0·5	0·5	—	0·1	6	27·5	3·5	21
Polyamide fibre	6	12	11	43	10·6	21·3	1·8	6·5	4	4·5	2·0	4·5
Polyester fibre	5	24	1	4	0·1	0·5	—	—	—	1·5	0·1	60·0
Total	223	168	17	52	17·5	24·5	21·3	19·1	28	50	14·9	100

development of knitting in the developed countries is concerned with its fairly recent technological development. Whereas hand-weaving and knitting have existed from antiquity and power looms revolutionized weaving in the mid-nineteenth century, weft-knitting was mechanized only early in the twentieth century, and warp-knitting did not achieve industrial status until the middle of the century.

This expansion of jersey fabrics has not occurred across all apparel outlets, and consideration of the market share of textured polyester-fibre weft-knitted fabrics in Table VIII provides an interesting picture of their penetration.

Table VIII
Percentage Market Share of Textured Polyester-fibre Knitted Fabrics in the United Kingdom, 1974

Women's Wear	%	Men's Wear	%
Dresses	51	Trousers	13
Suits	45	Suits	9
Trousers	41	Jackets	7
Skirts	41	Shirts	2
Blouses	25		
Coats	3		

The enormous differences shown in Table VIII between the high penetration in women's wear and the modest penetration in men's wear, and even within women's wear the high penetration into dresses, suits, trousers, and skirts compared with the relatively modest penetration into blouses and coats, require some further explanation. To the technologist, it would seem obvious at a glance that the penetration is greatest where the technical factors most favour the usage of knitted fabrics made from producer-textured yarns, and, to check this point, an image profile was obtained in women's dresses, which represented the area of greatest acceptance and obviously an important market of 50 million units per annum in the U.K. alone. This is shown in Fig. 1.

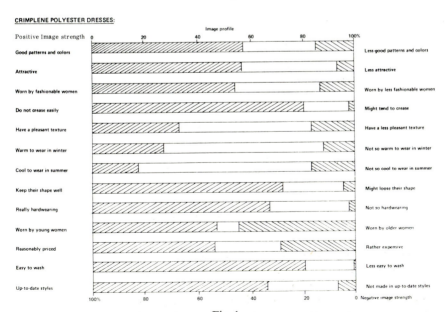

Fig. 1
Image profile for Crimplene polyester-fibre dresses

It should be noted that the response indicated in Fig. 1 was achieved in the U.K. at a time when the novelty value of dresses made from textured polyester-fibre yarns was long past. As a technologist might have expected, the most positive image strengths relate to performance attributes—crease-resistance, shape retention, and easy care—but these are very significantly augmented by the images of fashion and design. This is a clear illustration of the extent to which the textile industry thrives on change (real or imaginary), and the feedstocks for the industry must allow knitters and weavers the opportunity of achieving variety in their merchandise.

In the early 1960s, the introduction of throwster-bulked continuous-filament polyester-fibre yarns of low shrinkage and relatively low extensibility set new standards in mechanical conversion on double-jersey equipment, typical figures being over 90%. This ease of knitting encouraged knitters to introduce and develop structures that were impracticable in staple-fibre yarns. The move to textured surface structures also circumvented a deficiency in the early bulked polyester-fibre yarns, namely, dye irregularity and the consequent high risk of barré in plain fabrics. The introduction of producer-textured polyester-fibre yarns in the mid-1970s finally removed this constraint and improved knittability even further. It is interesting to speculate that, had these uniformly dyeable yarns been available from the start, the development of the knitting industry may well have shown a close parallel to that of producer-textured nylon yarns for tufted carpets. What has happened instead is that the blister-fabric variety of structures with plain dye and jacquard patterning, although it originally provided some break-up of a fairly plain structure, has now mainly moved to a few simple plain structures, predominantly piece-dyed, with fabric quality and aesthetics now verging on those of lustrous sheets of plastics gauze.

This phase of using the improved regularity and uniformity of producer-textured yarns to effect a fabric-quality and price decrease, together with overproduction, unattractive merchandise, and the poor economic climate, is placing knitters in a vulnerable position as opposed to weavers, and it mirrors an early stage in the development of tufted carpets. All the evidence is that, throughout the developed countries, weavers are making a significant recovery by concentrating on aesthetically pleasing fabrics of traditional appearance. There are signs that the more responsible and progressive knitters are responding to this challenge. There is now a growing demand for fine yarns for fine-gauge knitting, which enables high-quality lightweight fabrics to be produced to meet the market demand. This again mirrors tufting developments with fine-gauge machines, printing, and a move back towards the traditional aesthetics (established over centuries by woven goods). Underweight fabrics knitted from 167-dtex yarns on 18-gauge machines are a poor substitute, and the knitters must move on to producing fabrics that are attractive in their own right and regain the performance characteristics that the consumer associates with textured polyester-fibre yarns, even if this means re-equipping with fine-gauge equipment.

It is in the area of traditional fabric appearance that, like the tufter, the jersey knitter must concentrate. The fibre producers are contributing with the introduction of modified continuous-filament yarns, such as Crimplene Hi Spun, Diolen GV, etc., which give a measure of the aesthetic qualities of spun yarns. Variations in linear-density ranges, number of filaments, cross-section, lustre, and bulk have been and are being introduced in producer-textured yarns to match the range of machinery available and the fashion dictates of the apparel market.

A major breakthrough will come when manufacturers desist from equating prints with a cheap fabric made from second-grade yarn. Producer-texturing must be seen not only as a quality improvement but also as a means of introducing effects and textures by a cost-effective route to enable the developed countries to compete on a world-wide basis.

Printed woven fabrics have a high-quality and desirable image in Italy and France, and, as in the tufted-carpet section of the industry, knitters will probably utilize the print potential of producer-textured yarns to achieve traditional fabric appearance. Either jersey knitters must exploit screen-printing with the same ease as weavers or the printing trade and machinery manufacturers must develop a printing process that will combine the flexibility and pattern definition of transfer-printing with the retention of aesthetics of screen-printing.

Weft-knitting is the shortest conversion route from raw material to fabric and therefore requires a minimum of working capital. It also has the enormous advantage of quick response to fashion changes. Weft-knitted fabrics, however, can no longer expect to enjoy success on novelty value alone but will need to establish themselves on their intrinsic merits in the various apparel outlets. The industry needs to re-equip and master the techniques for improving aesthetics, such as printing and the use of the new ranges of producer-textured yarns. The recent success of fine-gauge printed fabrics knitted from yarns of low linear density that has occurred in every West European country demonstrates the potential for rational fabric developments. Even in a world depression, the growth of these particular fabrics has outpaced production.

4.2 Weaving and Warp-knitting

Whereas the major areas for producer-textured yarns have largely been confined to the three sectors examined in this paper, there are optimistic expectations of commercial success for polyester-fibre producer-textured yarns in weaving and warp-knitting fabrics from continuous-filament yarns. Weaving has the appeal of traditional appearance and is capable of producing a wide range of aesthetics because any character built into the yarn translates very easily into the fabric, especially from weft yarn. Producer-textured yarns modified to give some staple-fibre-like aesthetics, such as Hi Spun and Wondel, offer the weaver of continuous-filament yarns the opportunity of direct competition with weavers of staple-fibre yarns as well as producing distinctive fabrics in their own right. In France, Italy, and Japan, the section of the industry that is concerned with weaving continuous-filament yarns is located in areas where good design is a way of life, and producer-textured yarns are beginning to be used to great effect; in Japan, the weaving of producer-textured yarns continues the traditions established by centuries of weaving silk; and, in the U.S.A., the large and efficient weaving sector has already begun to exploit the potential for new cloths from producer-textured products.

Warp-knitting, being heavily dependent on conversion efficiency and yarn quality, could utilize the fundamental merits of producer-textured yarn. This is the major fabric-production route that does not have traditional staple-fibre feedstock, and the major advance in this area may come from the availability of a producer-textured yarn that allows the attainment of some degree of staple-fibre aesthetics. This may well be a novel yarn allowing bulk generation after knitting, since warp-knitters depend heavily on high-quality yarns to achieve good conversion efficiency in knitting. In contrast with weaving, where any yarn characteristic is easily translated into the desired fabric aesthetic property (especially for the weft), warp-knitting is a cruel process to textured and fancy yarns, and most of the bulk and surface interest in current producer-textured yarns is destroyed in the knitting process. This is an additional reason why the development of producer-texturing for warp-knitting will probably be via a latent bulk developed after knitting.

5. THE FUTURE

A consideration of past developments in producer-texturing gives some indication of likely future trends. Texturing equipment, such as Scragg, Barmag, and ARCT machines, was made to run at 200 m/min just a few years ago. At this speed, it can be fed with undrawn yarn to combine the two processes of drawing and texturing (the combined process is patented by ICI) or it can be fed with high-speed spun yarn that is partly oriented (POY) and therefore requires less drawing. Texturing speeds have recently increased to 600 m/min, and there are indications that 4000 m/min may be possible in the future. If this speed is, in fact, achieved, then it may be possible to combine the three processes—spinning, drawing, and texturing—into one combined producer-texturing process. Bearing in mind the past history with hosiery, carpets, and weft-knitted fabrics, however, one might expect that this first development of simple spin–draw–texture yarns would be followed some years later by a wave of diversification aimed at increasing the benefits required by consumers and preserving a more traditional aesthetic quality.

ICI Fibres,
Harrogate,
North Yorkshire.

10—THE PROPERTIES AND PRODUCTION OF PURPOSE-BUILT FALSE-TWIST YARNS

By K. Greenwood and O. T. Stutz

Since the inception of the Helenca trade mark, many new fibres have appeared on the market and the demands made on fabrics with regard to their appearance, properties, and variety have increased. In order to maintain and expand the market appeal of Helenca yarns, it has therefore been necessary to carry out continuous development work, designed to adapt them more closely to the requirements of different end-uses and tastes.

This paper describes some recent yarn developments, including combinations of man-made and natural fibres, that have produced new possibilities with regard to bulk, stretch, and lustre. Proceeding from the assumption that, in the foreseeable future, there will be a buyers' market, the paper emphasizes the need for machines and equipment that allow a rigorous control of yarn quality and maximum versatility. The conflicting requirements of speed and quality are discussed, and it is shown how they are reconciled in modern false-twist machines. Particular attention is given to the design and operation of high-speed pin and friction twisters and to energy-savings in high-speed texturing.

1. INTRODUCTION

It is an old saying that 'nature abhors a vacuum', and, perhaps with even greater truth, it could be said that nature abhors smoothness. Whether we regard inanimate manifestations of nature, such as water, soil, rock, or sand, plant life, or the skins of living creatures, roughness and texture are the rule and smoothness is the exception. The surfaces of all the large expanses of water are broken by waves and ripples, and even the apparently smoothest of all substances, ice, assumes a rugged texture when it persists for long periods.

When considered in this context, the continuous-filament yarn as it emerges from the spinneret is a distinctly 'unnatural' product, and it is therefore not surprising that great efforts have been made to 'naturalize' it, i.e., to give it texture. The most obvious way to do this is to chop the yarn into short staple fibres and then to spin these into a yarn that has texture because of its hairiness. In spite of the rapid growth of other methods of texturing, staple-fibre spinning of man-made fibres is still widely used, particularly because it offers the possibility of blending man-made with natural fibres and thus combining the advantages of both.

The disadvantage of 'texturing' man-made fibres by staple-fibre spinning is that the very smoothness of a continuous-filament yarn that makes it unattractive from the final user's point of view is of considerable advantage in the processing stages, where the yarn is converted into fabric, particularly in warp- and weft-knitting. A smooth yarn can easily pass round guides and through needle eyes without entanglements and breaks, and it is free from the problem of fly, which besets all staple-fibre processing. Furthermore, in staple-fibre spinning, the utilization of the inherent strength of the man-made fibres is rather poor, and a staple-fibre yarn has only 30–40% of the strength of a comparable continuous-filament yarn.

For many types of end-use, it is therefore the ideal state of affairs to have a yarn that retains most of the fibre strength and remains smooth during processing but acquires texture in the finished fabric. The essence of the false-twist process and the secret of its success are that this is precisely what it achieves. The yarn, as it emerges from the false-twist machine, has approximately 80% of its original strength, and, because it is under tension, it has no apparent texture. It remains smooth throughout its subsequent storage on various types of package and during various stages of processing until, in fabric form, it is released from tension and only then really becomes a textured yarn.

The function of the false-twist process is to give the yarn a 'message' to deform itself long after it has left the false-twist machine. In order to be effective as a textured yarn, it must retain this message over long periods and in the face of considerable stresses, which tend to delete the message and restore the yarn to its original smooth state. The message must therefore be very clear and intensive, and the great advantage of the false-twist process is that it applies great force in imparting the message to the yarn and tells every filament quite clearly where and how to deform when the chance arises.

The false-twist process twists and untwists the yarn in one operation, the twisted state being conveyed to the yarn as the message by heat treatment. When the yarn is freed from tension, the individual filaments attempt to return to the original twisted state but cannot do so because this would necessitate a rotation of the yarn. The filaments are therefore forced to take up a shape corresponding to the lowest potential energy that is geometrically possible. This shape is the 'reversing helix', which has been described by Denton[1] and by other workers. The reversing helices of the individual filaments cannot fit into each other in the same compact way as the original (non-reversing) helices of the twisted yarn, and this accounts for the high degree of bulk and the market appeal of false-twist yarns.

The exact shape of the reversing helix has so far defied all attempts to describe it in mathematical terms. All one can say with certainty is that, within any length of yarn whose ends cannot rotate relative to each other, the total number of S-turns must be equal to the total number of Z-turns, since there cannot be any real twist in the yarn. The length and frequency of the S- and Z-helices is virtually unpredictable, although some light can be shed on this problem on the basis of filament migration.

The false-twist process thus begins with a very clearly defined deformation of the yarn, which can be expressed very accurately in terms of the temporary twist, and it ends with a semi-random deformation, which, on the face of it, bears little relation to the original one. This apparent contradiction, however, does not mean that the control of the temporary twist on the machine serves no useful purpose. Practical experience, extending over nearly three decades and over millions of tons of yarn, has shown that there is a very close correlation between the temporary twist on the false-twist machine and the ultimate yarn and fabric properties.

For this reason, Heberlein, as the pioneers of the false-twist process and licensers of the Helanca trade mark, had to enforce strict quality-control procedures to ensure that the Helanca quality should not be debased by temptations to reduce twist and thus cheapen the process.

In the recent past, the false-twist process has entered a period of profound changes with regard to the raw material, the machine, and the end-product. The conventional fully drawn continuous-filament yarns are being replaced as parent yarns by partly drawn (POY) yarns, which are the result of higher spinning speeds and the elimination of draw-twisting. The conventional pin twister has reached a speed of 800,000 rev/min in commercial practice, and, with friction twisters, the rotational speed of the yarn has reached several million rev/min. Most important of all, the final user of the yarn is demanding a greater variety of products, and certain yarn characteristics that in the past were considered unacceptable are now becoming the fashion.

The purpose of this paper is to describe some of the yarn characteristics that can be obtained on a false-twist machine and to discuss some special problems that arise in modern high-speed texturing.

2. EFFECTS OBTAINABLE WITH THE FALSE-TWIST PROCESS

2.1 Processing Parameters

The false-twist process imparts both bulk and stretch to the continuous-filament yarn. In the early days of the process, the emphasis was more on stretch, and this property was particularly pronounced in the yarns produced by the three-stage process (twisting, heat-setting, untwisting). Stretch was obviously desirable in ski-pants and slacks and was also considered important in ladies' stockings. The enthusiasm for stretch probably reached its climax in the early 1960s, when some people were predicting that even men's suits should and would be made from stretch yarns.

During the last decade, however, the emphasis has decisively shifted from stretch to bulk, and the Set yarns of the Crimplene type have taken over a major part of the market. These are produced by subjecting the untwisted yarn on the false-twist machine to a second heat-setting treatment, which largely eliminates the stretch but leaves the bulk.

In the manufacture of a stretch yarn, the main processing parameters are:

  (a) the parent (or feeder) yarn;
  (b) the yarn twist;
  (c) the yarn tension in the processing zone;
  (d) the temperature of the first heater; and
  (e) the overfeed in winding.

In the manufacture of Set yarns, the following two main parameters are added:

  (f) the overfeed in the setting zone; and
  (g) the temperature of the second heater.

Even if one considers only the above five (or seven) main parameters, the number of possible permutations is very large. It becomes very much larger if one includes secondary parameters, such as the position, shape, and material of yarn guides, the temperature profile of the heater, the nature and length of the cooling zone, etc.

For this reason, a comprehensive discussion of the effects of processing parameters is beyond the scope of this paper. The examples discussed below have been chosen merely to illustrate the actual and potential versatility of the false-twist process with regard to yarn characteristics.

2.2 The Effect of Twist

The effect of twist on the characteristics of the end-product is greatly influenced by the structure of the knitted or woven fabric. Rather than give a general discourse on the effect of twist, it is therefore proposed to relate the outcome of one particular experiment, which was designed to test the reaction of 30 experts to changes in twist.

A fully drawn 167-dtex polyester-fibre feeder yarn was texturized at various twist levels, ranging from 1500 to 2700 turns/m in steps of 200 turns/m. The textured yarn was knitted into a double-jersey fabric, which was dyed and finished. The 30 experts were kept in ignorance of the twist levels of the yarn in the various samples and were asked to grade these on the basis of the following point scale:

very good   = 3 points;
good   = 2 points;
satisfactory   = 1 point;
unsatisfactory = 0 points.

An analysis of the results showed that all the experts were able to put the fabric samples in the correct order with regard to twist. In some cases, they were not able to distinguish between adjacent twist values, but none of them placed any samples in the wrong order. In order to facilitate the grading, the experts were instructed to consider the point scale as being synonymous with the twist scale in the sense that higher twist was to be regarded as better than lower twist. In this respect, the judgement of the experts differed from the probable judgement of non-expert users, for whom twist has no meaning and who would judge a fabric purely in relation to the intended end-use.

Table I shows the frequency distribution of the various gradings for each twist level. Although all experts placed the samples in the correct order, there were considerable differences between individual experts with regard to the absolute quality level of the samples. As could be expected, the degree of unanimity was highest at the extreme twist levels and lowest at the intermediate twist levels. This is reflected numerically in the highest number of experts giving the same grading. This highest number is 29 at 1500 turns/m and decreases to 13 at 2300 turns/m. It then rises again to 18 at 2700 turns/m. There was much greater agreement in calling the lowest-twist fabric 'unsatisfactory' than there was in calling the high-twist fabric 'very good'.

Table I
Frequency Distribution of Gradings

Twist (turns/m)	Number of Gradings			
	Very Good	Good	Satisfactory	Unsatisfactory
1500	0	0	1	29
1700	0	0	6	24
1900	0	0	10	20
2100	6	6	16	2
2300	5	12	13	0
2500	17	9	4	0
2700	18	7	5	0

Table II shows the average ratings of the samples, and it is clear that the relation between the twist and the average rating is not continuous. Large changes in the average rating occurred between 1900 and 2100 turns/m and between 2300 and 2500 turns/m. At the other twist levels, the same increment in twist caused only small changes in the average rating.

Table II also shows the percentage of experts who gave a particular 'threshold grading' to the various samples. A threshold grading is any grading that is equal to or better than the particular grading quoted in Table II. Thus, the percentage of experts giving a threshold grading of 'satisfactory' includes all those who graded the sample as satisfactory or better (good or very good).

Table II
Average Gradings and Distribution of Threshold Gradings

Twist (turns/m)	Average Grading	Percentage of Threshold Gradings		
		Very Good	Good	Satisfactory
1500 ..	0·0 Unsatisfactory	0	0	3
1700 .. 1900 ..	0·2 0·3 } Nearly unsatisfactory {	0 0	0 0	20 33
2100 .. 2300 ..	1·6 1·7 } Satisfactory–good {	20 17	40 57	93 100
2500 .. 2700 ..	2·4 2·4 } Good–very good {	57 60	87 83	100 100

Perhaps the most significant fact emerging from this survey is that even the low twist level of 1700 turns/m was considered satisfactory by 20% of the experts, whereas, at the other end of the scale, the high twist level of 2700 turns/m was considered no more than satisfactory by 17%. This fact is all the more significant because the experts had been instructed to regard higher twist as an advantage. In an average panel of users of fabrics produced from the yarns, these two figures would probably have been much higher. This tends to show that it is to-day neither possible nor indeed necessary to lay down general standards with regard to twist. *Different twist levels produce different effects and appeal to different sections of the market.*

In the early days of the Helanca process, Heberlein prescribed a minimum twist level based on the formula:

$$\text{minimum twist (turns/m)} = \frac{306,000}{N + 67} + 800,$$

where N is the linear density in dtex.

This formula, however, was developed at a time when the bouclé-type crimp structure caused by lower twist levels was generally disliked, and any downward deviation from the twist as given by the formula would have lessened the market appeal of Helanca-yarn fabrics.

This formula has now become largely obsolete. On the one hand, the twist used in draw-texturing tends to be higher. For 167-dtex yarn, the formula leads to approximately 2100 turns/m, whereas in the draw-texturing of such yarns it is not uncommon to use twist levels between 2400 and 2800 turns/m. On the other hand, certain effects due to low twist have become not only accepted but positively desired. For example, the Helanca RE type of yarn was developed specially for its bouclé-type character, which can be further enhanced by doubling with a stretch component. The application of low twist tends to be particularly advantageous with trilobal and multilobal fibres, for which too high a twist level may excessively deform the fibre cross-section and thus diminish the desired effect.

The important thing is to find the twist level most appropriate for a particular end-use and then to ensure that this twist is obtained and maintained.

2.3 Effect of Heater Temperature

As with twist, the recent past has seen a greater readiness to depart from fixed rules with regard to heater temperature. Broadly speaking, POY yarns can be texturized at significantly lower temperatures than fully drawn yarns because of the internal heat developed by the drawing process. On the other hand, many high-speed machines are approaching a speed limit dictated by the length of the heater, and there is a tendency to compensate for this by the use of slightly raised heater temperatures.

From the point of view of yarn properties, it can be regarded as a general rule that higher temperatures lead to greater bulk and better texture and to a stiffer handle. If one compares, for instance, fabrics made from Helanca RE yarn texturized at 215 and 175°C, respectively, one finds that the lower temperature produces a somewhat leaner fabric, which, however, has a pleasing soft handle. Variation of heater temperature thus provides a means of adapting the product to the requirements of the market.

2.4   False-twist Yarns in Woven Fabrics

By the application of tension, any false-twist yarn can be completely, but only temporarily, robbed of its texture. This may give rise to the idea that, in woven fabrics, in which the yarn is under a certain tension even when the fabric itself is relaxed, the intensive crimp imparted by the false-twist process is largely wasted. Practical experience shows, however, that this is not so.

The yarn stresses in a woven fabric depend on the weave and are highest in the plain weave, but, as Fig. 1 illustrates, even in this weave, the texture of the yarn is to a large extent maintained and is certainly very different from the structure of the untexturized yarn, which is shown in the upper part of Fig. 1. The retention of crimp and texture under a certain degree of yarn tension can be explained by the fact that there is a measure of non-uniformity from filament to filament and along each filament, so that each small section of the yarn contains some straight filaments and some that are strongly crimped. This effect is the greater the longer the float of the weave, and this is illustrated in Fig. 2, which shows textured yarn in a twill weave.

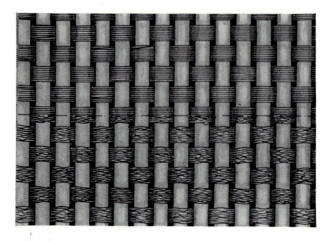

Fig. 1

Comparison of untextured and textured yarns in a plain weave

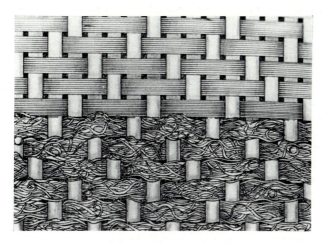

Fig. 2
Comparison of untextured and textured yarns in a twill weave

2.5 False-twist Staple-fibre Yarns Produced from Fibre Blends

Although every throwster knows that the choice of the feeder yarn is the most important processing parameter, it is not generally realized that this choice is not necessarily confined to continuous-filament yarns. Considerable improvements in the quality of staple-fibre yarns can be obtained by subjecting them to a false-twist process, provided that the yarn contains a thermoplastic component, such as polyester fibre or nylon.

Experiments with 50–50% and 67–33% polyester-fibre–cotton blends have shown that false-twisting produces in these yarns not only stretch but also increased bulk and a very pleasing soft handle in the fabric. To the best of the authors' knowledge, there is at present no significant commercial production of such yarns, probably because of the economics of the process. Nevertheless, the false-twisting of staple-fibre blends is an exciting technical possibility that could be of interest in the production of fitted sheets, stretch covers, etc.

2.6 Conversion of Continuous Filaments into Staple-fibre Yarns

The problem of converting continuous filaments into a staple-fibre yarn by a shorter route than chopping them into short staple fibres and then putting them through a conventional spinning sequence has been approached and solved by a variety of methods. In one form or another, the existing methods start with a continuous-filament tow, which is converted into a staple-fibre sliver by stretch-breaking or cutting the filaments. The final yarn linear density is obtained by a more-or-less conventional drafting sequence, usually involving a high draft.

The false-twist process offers a different route, by which the yarn reaches its final linear density in continuous-filament form and is then converted into a staple-fibre yarn by abrasion of the filaments. The procedure is to give the feeder yarn initially the twist that is required in the staple-fibre yarn. The amount of twist required depends on the ultimate staple length and can be fairly low because, by abrasion, an average staple length of 10 cm or more can be obtained. The twisted yarn is then put through the false-twist machine where it is temporarily twisted in the same direction as the initial twist but to a much higher level. In this highly twisted state, the yarn is presented to a rotating abrasion surface, which abrades and breaks the individual filaments. The very marked filament migration from the centre to the surface of the yarn and vice versa, which is characteristic of the false-twist process, ensures that each filament in turn is in contact with the abrading surface, so that no filaments remain unbroken and none are broken too frequently.

Experiments with this process have shown that it produces a surprisingly uniform staple length. Pullovers, socks, and other articles produced from the abraded yarn have a very pleasing appearance and handle. Several technical and economic problems would have to be solved, however, before this process could be put to commercial use.

If one wanted to be unkind to some of the friction twisters that are currently being offered for sale, one might say that they have gone some way towards the conversion of continuous filaments into staple-fibre yarns. However, since their purpose is to produce a textured continuous-filament yarn, the broken filaments they produce are regarded as a fault. If their number were increased by a few orders of magnitude, this fault might well turn into a virtue.

2.7   Texturing of Warps

Although this topic does not fall directly under the heading of this paper, it may be of interest to mention the possibility of texturing whole warps, either while they are being assembled or even perhaps on the loom or warp-knitting machine. The procedure is to pass the warp through a type of schreiner calender. The pressure in the nip of the rollers and the fine fluting of the heated roller lead to a deformation of the cross-section of the filaments and produce in the fabric a distinct textured effect. This effect is considerably less intensive than the effect of false-twisting but may be adequate for some end-uses.

3.   FALSE-TWIST MACHINES

3.1   Functions of the Machines

The three main functions of a false-twist machine are to twist the yarn, to heat-set it, and to wind it onto a package. Each of these functions poses its own problems, but the relative importance of these problems depends on the type of machine under consideration. It is therefore useful to give a broad classification of the false-twist machines that are on the market at present.

3.2   Classification of Machines

Existing false-twist machines can be classified according to the scheme shown in Table III. In interpreting this table, it would be mistaken to regard the standard machines as the machines of the past, the first-generation high-speed (h.s.) machines as the machines of to-day, and the second-generation h.s. machines as the machines of the future. To do this would be similar to saying that the motor car is the vehicle of the past, the aeroplane the vehicle of the present, and the rocket the vehicle of the future. Clearly, these three types of vehicle have different functions and are likely to exist side by side for as long as one can foresee.

Table III
Classification of False-twist Machines

Type of Machine	Maximum Take-up Speed
Standard machines	150–180 m/min
First-generation high-speed draw-texturing machines	400 m/min
Second-generation high-speed draw-texturing machines	600–700 m/min

Similarly, the three types of false-twist machine are not mutually exclusive. The standard machine is eminently suitable for the throwsters who produce a great variety of yarns for a broad spectrum of the market. Some of the largest firms in Europe, the U.S.A., and Japan are not only still using standard machines but are also installing new ones. Furthermore, these machines are obviously very suitable for the developing countries, where neither the quality of the feeder yarn nor the level of technology is ripe for high-speed operation.

The h.s. machines of the first and even more so of the second generation are primarily suited for the needs of larger-scale production and for firms whose yarn quality and technology are at the required level.

It must be emphasized that the machine speeds quoted in Table III are merely the mechanical speeds of the machines. Particularly in the polyester-fibre sector, machine speeds in excess of 400 m/min are still fraught with processing problems, and the speeds used in large-scale commercial production are therefore rarely above that figure.

3.3   Basic Machine Concepts

In the early days of false-twisting, it was regarded as essential that the yarn should traverse the processing zone in a straight line. As long as processing speeds were low, this created no problems because, even with short heaters, the dwell time of the yarn in the heater was long enough to ensure adequate heat-setting.

As take-up speeds increased, however, the 'straight-line' concept increasingly became a stumbling block to progress because heater lengths and therefore machine heights had to increase *pro rata*. Some of the latest high-speed machines have reached heights of 5 m (17 ft), and this seems to indicate that the builders of false-twist machines have reached the cross roads, where they must either forsake the straight-line philosophy or abandon all hopes of higher speeds.

Heberlein have studied this problem in great depth and have come to the conclusion that, by proper machine design, the straight yarn path can be dispensed with without detriment to yarn quality or machine efficiency. This has enabled Heberlein to build their 600 m/min machine (Fig. 3) as a low-profile machine with a height of less than 3 m (10 ft). This low height makes threading-up very much easier and also eliminates possible problems with regard to buildings. Furthermore, the break with the straight-line tradition gives the Heberlein h.s. machine a potential for higher speeds than those currently quoted.

Fig. 3
The Heberlein FZ 42/11 False-twist Machine

3.4   Materials-handling Problems

The introduction of partly drawn and undrawn feeder yarns, which are supplied on packages weighing up to 30 kg, and the economic pressures towards larger take-off packages have created serious handling problems, particularly where female staff are employed. Whereas in the past it was reasonable to leave it to the individual throwster to solve his materials-handling problems, it is now up to the machine builder to pay careful attention to the design of creels and to the introduction of suitable handling aids. Heberlein have given close attention to this aspect of machine design and have borne in mind the fact that a measure of flexibility is necessary to integrate the false-twist machine in the optimal way into the materials-flow concept of individual firms.

3.5   Energy Problems

Rising energy costs, together with the increased energy requirements of h.s. machines and, by no means the least-important aspect, a growing concern for the working environment of operatives, have made it imperative to pay attention to the problem of energy conservation.

Heberlein have very largely solved this problem, together with those of noise and fume extraction, by means of the HemaTherm system, which provides for the almost complete insulation of the whole machine and which converts the space between the two sides of the machine into a central heat store. The general principle of the HemaTherm system is to utilize the heat gained from cooling the yarn and the spindles, together with conserved heat from the fume-extraction system, for minimizing the heat requirements of the heaters. The insulation of the machine also protects operatives against noise and reduces substantially the load on the general air-conditioning system of the plant. Furthermore, the air-circulating and filtration elements of Hema Therm prevent any contamination of the working areas by fumes from the machine.

4. TWISTING ELEMENTS

4.1 Introduction

A great deal has been said and written in the recent past about friction twisters, and it is therefore sufficient here to deal with recent developments in pin-twisting and to confine the discussion of friction twisters to the Heberlein TwistMaster, which, at the last International Textile Machinery and Accessories (ITMA) Exhibition, was the only really new type of friction twister on show. In addition, certain points of theory will be dealt with and a comparison made of the relative merits of pin and friction twisters.

4.2 Recent Developments in Pin-twisting

With regard to false-twist spindles in general, the view is often expressed that the pin twister is a thing of the past and that the future belongs to friction-twisting. There is undoubtedly an element of truth in this, but it must be borne in mind that most judgements about pin twisters are based on the fact that, until recently, pin-twisting was done at speeds in the region of 350,000–450,000 rev/min. The figure of 800,000 rev/min was frequently quoted as the limiting speed of pin twisters but with the implication that—like the speed of light—it can never be reached in practice.

In this respect, the year 1975 saw a revolutionary development in the form of the Heberlein Magnetic Pin Twister, which, at the ITMA Exhibition of that year, was shown operating at 1,000,000 rev/min and which, in industrial practice, is operating at 800,000 rev/min. The new pin twister is shown in Fig. 4, and technical details are discussed in a recent paper by one of the present authors[2].

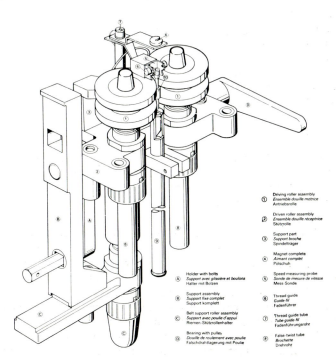

①	Driving roller assembly *Ensemble douille motrice* Antriebsrolle		⑤	Speed-measuring probe *Sonde de mesure de vitesse* Mess-Sonde
②	Driven roller assembly *Ensemble douille réceptrice* Stützrolle		⑥	Thread guide *Guide-fil* Fadenführrer
③	Support part *Support broche* Spindelträger		⑦	Thread guide tube *Tube guide-fil* Fadenführungsrohr
④	Magnet complete *Aimant complet* Polschuh		⑧	False-twist tube *Brochette* Drehrohr
Ⓐ	Holder with bolts *Support avec glissière et boulons* Halter mit Bolzen			
Ⓑ	Support assembly *Support fixe complet* Support komplett			
Ⓒ	Belt support roller assembly *Support avec poulie d'appui* Riemen-Stützrollenhalter			
Ⓓ	Bearing with pulley *Douille de roulement avec poulie* Falschdrahtlagerung mit Poulie			

Fig. 4

The Heberlein Pin Twister operating at 800,000 rev/min

As long as friction-twisting requires special skills with regard to machine settings and special yarn finishes, there will always be a place for pin twisters, and this is borne out by Heberlein's experience over the last year and particularly at the recent ITMA Exhibition. In spite of adverse economic conditions and contrary to current trends in textile engineering, Heberlein have been able to increase their order book for pin twisters, and their list of customers includes several large throwsters who have been experimenting with friction-twisting for a long time.

4.3 The Heberlein TwistMaster Friction Twister

Before the 1975 ITMA Exhibition, it seemed that the industry had standardized on two basic types of friction twister, the bush type and the stacked-disc type. It therefore came as a surprise when, at the Exhibition, Heberlein launched a completely new system in the form of the TwistMaster, which is shown in Fig. 5. The new twister consists of one main twisting element—a slotted sphere—and one secondary element, a friction disc, which penetrates into the slot of the sphere.

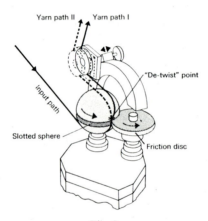

Fig. 5
The Heberlein TwistMaster Friction Twister

Apart from the simplicity of this design, which makes for particularly easy threading-up, the new twister incorporates two basic features that distinguish it from other friction twisters on the market.

The first of these is the distinct asymmetry of the system. Whereas all previous systems aimed at a very nearly equal distribution of the work done in twisting over all friction elements, the TwistMaster clearly allocates the main function of twisting to one element—the sphere—with the disc fulfilling only an auxiliary function. A variety of theoretical arguments can be put forward to explain the advantages of this system, but the ultimate proof of the pudding is in the eating, and the TwistMaster has performed very well indeed in extensive industrial trials. It may well be that in friction-twisting the old saying applies that 'too many cooks spoil the broth'. The TwistMaster has only one 'cook' and one assistant, and this may well be the reason for its success.

A second distinguishing feature of the TwistMaster is the yarn path, which is such that the yarn first makes contact with the sphere at its pole, where the circumferential speed is zero. The yarn then follows roughly the line of a meridian until it reaches the equator, i.e., the slot that contains the disc. Between the pole and the equator, the yarn passes through a region of increasing circumferential speed of the friction surface while its own circumferential speed remains virtually constant. The twister surface therefore initially lags behind the yarn surface (negative slip), and later it runs ahead of the yarn (positive slip). At the change-over from negative to positive slip, the yarn passes through a point of zero slip.

Clearly, the twisting of the yarn can only occur in the region of positive slip, but the existence of a change-over point to negative slip has a self-regulating influence on the system. If, for instance, the yarn twist diminishes, the point of zero slip moves towards the pole and thus increases the region of positive slip. This increases the twisting action and therefore compensates for the reduction in twist. This mechanism may explain why, with the TwistMaster, it is comparatively easy to avoid the periodic twist variations that are known as 'surging' and are the curse of many friction twisters.

4.4 Some Points on Friction-twisting Theory (the Tension Ratio)

One great advantage of friction twisters is the possibility of varying the ratio between the output and input tensions (T_2/T_1) over a wide range on either side of unity so that the output tension can be higher or lower than the input tension or equal to it. The method for adjusting the tension ratio is to vary the ratio between the twister speed and yarn speed (the D/Y ratio). The higher the D/Y ratio, the lower is the tension ratio.

The variation of the tension ratio can take different forms. One of these is to keep the input tension constant and to vary only the output tension. Thwaites[3] has considered this case and has shown that this form of varying the tension ratio also leads to a variation in twist.

In commercial practice, the twist must be kept constant if a particular yarn quality is to be achieved. In order to maintain constant twist while varying the tension ratio, any lowering of the output tension must be accompanied by an increase in the input tension (and *vice versa*). The sum (or average) of the two tensions, however, is at its lowest level when the two tensions are equal ($T_2/T_1 = 1$). It is therefore of considerable advantage to operate with a tension ratio in the vicinity of unity, and this requires a friction twister that can produce this tension ratio.

Denton[4] has dealt with this problem and has shown that the ability of a friction twister to produce a tension ratio of unity is primarily dependent on the angle φ between the yarn axis and the direction of movement of the twister surface. He also showed that, for any particular value of φ, there is a value of the D/Y ratio that leads to a tension ratio of $T_2/T_1 = 1$. This value will be denoted here by D_1/Y. Finally, Denton arrived at certain mathematical relations between D_1/Y_1 and φ that led to the conclusion that D_1/Y has its lowest value when φ is equal to the yarn-helix angle and approaches infinity as φ approaches 90°.

If Denton's final conclusions are correct, this means that a tension ratio of unity cannot be obtained with a friction twister in which the twister surface moves approximately at right angles to the yarn axis. Denton's arguments, however, seem to take insufficient account of the effect of twist contraction. When this effect is fully considered, it is found that, even when $\varphi = 90°$, it is possible to obtain equality of input and output tensions with a finite, and not unreasonably high, value of the D/Y ratio. This is discussed in the Appendix to this paper.

The analysis presented in the Appendix agrees with Denton's analysis in that it also shows that D_1/Y has its lowest value when φ equals the yarn-helix angle and increases with increasing values of φ. This does not mean, however, that it is desirable to make φ as nearly as possible equal to the yarn-helix angle. To do this has the effect of reducing the slip between the yarn and the twister, but both theory and practice show that a certain amount of slip is necessary to ensure the stable operation of the twister. The problem is therefore to choose not the lowest possible value of φ but a value that represents the best compromise between the conflicting requirements of twister wear and yarn abrasion on the one hand (low slip) and operating stability on the other hand (high slip).

Irrespective of whether the analysis presented in the Appendix is correct or not, practical experience with the TwistMaster, for which φ is approximately 90°, has shown that it is possible to obtain equality of input and output tensions with a D/Y ratio that is high enough to ensure stable running conditions but not so high as to cause significant twister wear or yarn damage. This is a matter not only of twister geometry but also of the correct choice of materials and good design work.

4.5   The Relative Merits of Pin and Friction Twisters

4.5.1   Factors Affecting the Choice of Twister

As a company whose development and production programme includes both pin and friction twisters, Heberlein are in a position to take an objective view of the two types of twister and to advise their customers accordingly. The usual procedure is for the customer to carry out trials with his own yarns on both twisters and make his own decision, which is never based entirely on technical considerations but must invariably be influenced by economic aspects, such as the scale of the intended investment, the relation between yarn quality and selling price, etc.

If, for instance, a customer has an installation of machines of any make that are capable of a mechanical speed of 400 m/min but are fitted with out-dated pin twisters, which limit the actual production speed to 250 m/min, he can achieve a very large increase in productivity with a modest investment by fitting his existing machines with a pin twister for texturing coarser yarns and a bush-type friction twister (see Fig. 6) for texturing finer yarns.

If, however, a major investment in new machines is planned, then the question would have to be asked as to whether the customer is content with a take-up speed of 400 m/min or requires higher speeds. In the former case, he could choose between pin twisters and friction twisters on purely technical grounds. In the latter case, his choice would be limited to the TwistMaster, since the pin twister cannot give speeds in excess of 320–350 m/min, the actual speed depending on the desired yarn quality.

The outcome of any particular trial with customers' yarn is greatly influenced by the quality of the raw material and by the desired quality standards of the end-products. At the same take-up speeds, some yarns give better results with a pin twister and some with a friction twister. There are, however, certain basic avdantages and disadvantages inherent in both types of twister that can be discussed in a more general way.

Fig. 6
The Heberlein Bush-type Friction Twister

4.5.2   Take-up Speed

Friction twisters permit considerably higher take-up speeds than pin twisters. With pin twisters, the take-up speed has to be drastically reduced when finer yarns are texturized. With friction twisters, the attainable take-up speeds are less sensitive to linear density and tend to be higher with finer yarns. The speed advantage of friction twisters is therefore particularly great with hosiery and other fine yarns.

4.5.3   Twist Control

Pin twisters permit a very easy and accurate control of yarn twist by appropriate adjustment of the ratio between yarn speed and spindle speed. The twist imparted by a pin twister is not influenced by other factors, such as yarn tension, heater temperature, yarn finish, etc. The yarn twist can easily be monitored by electronic spindle-speed indicators.

The twist imparted to the yarn by a friction twister depends essentially on the balance between the torque applied to the yarn and the torque required by the yarn at a particular twist level. The applied torque depends on the yarn tension, coefficient of friction (yarn finish), twister speed, and angle of wrap. The required torque depends on the yarn tension and temperature. To obtain any particular twist value, all these parameters have to be adjusted, and this is difficult because there is no established commercial method for monitoring twist. For this reason, the use of twist as a yardstick of yarn quality has largely been abandoned in friction-twisting. It has been replaced to some extent by the D/Y ratio, but the relation between yarn quality and this ratio is very tenuous.

4.5.4 Twist Stability

With pin twisters, variations in twist can, in practice, only be caused by variations in spindle speed, which are readily detected. With friction twisters, a variation in any of the parameters listed in Section 4.5.3 can cause twist variations. In addition, as mentioned in Section 4.3, friction twisters are liable to periodic twist variations, known as surging. These are probably caused by the interrelation between twist and tension. Any increase in tension can cause an increase in twist, which, in turn, can cause a further increase in tension. Once this chain reaction has set in, it continues until the twist cannot increase further. As soon as the twist ceases to increase, however, the yarn tension begins to fall and thus starts a chain reaction in the opposite direction. Surging is more likely to occur at higher twist levels and at higher take-up speeds and represents probably the main speed barrier in friction-twisting. It can be avoided by appropriate twister settings.

In general, twist stability tends to be better with pin twisters.

4.5.5 Yarn Tension

With pin twisters, the output tension is always higher than the input tension. With friction twisters, it can be higher than, lower than, or equal to the input tension. Broadly speaking, the input tension (i.e., the tension in the processing zone) tends to increase the texture of the yarn, whereas the output tension tends to reduce it. A low tension ratio also seems to be particularly desirable in simultaneous draw-texturing.

For these reasons, the tension conditions tend to be better with friction twisters than with pin twisters.

4.5.6 Threading-up and Passage of Knots

The general lay-out of friction twisters is more open than that of pin twisters, and this tends to facilitate both threading-up and the passage of knots.

4.5.7 Dye Uniformity

This tends to be marginally better with pin twisters, mainly because of the better twist stability.

4.5.8 Noise

Because of the much lower rotational speeds, friction twisters tend to produce less noise than pin twisters.

4.5.9 Summary of Relative Merits

The above considerations can be summed up as follows:

pin twisters are likely to be better with regard to:

twist control;
twist stability; and
dye uniformity;

friction twisters are likely to be better with regard to:

take-up speeds;
yarn tension;
threading-up and the passage of knots; and
noise.

If equal weight were attached to each of the above points, the result of this comparison could be regarded as a marginal victory for friction twisters. This is not possible, however, because the importance attached to each of the points must depend on many technical and economic factors, which vary from firm to firm and from time to time. The choice between the two types of twister is therefore a highly individual one as far as the throwster is concerned. The position is somewhat different for those machinery manufacturers who have thrown their whole weight behind friction-twisting. Fortunately, Heberlein are in a position in which their own commercial interest coincides with that of the throwster.

5. CONCLUSION

At the present time, friction-twisting is undoubtedly the key problem in texturizing. On looking at the relative merits of pin- and friction-twisting, it is clear that the control of the twisting operation, which, after all, is the main function of a twister, is probably the main factor that mitigates against a rapid change-over from pin- to friction-twisting. For this reason, pin-twisting is still going strong. It is not impossible, however, that a synthesis of the two techniques can and will be achieved whereby the many advantages of friction twisters are combined with the easy and accurate control of twist of the pin twister. The next few years will show whether this can be done in a practical and economic way.

REFERENCES

1 M. J. Denton. *J. Text. Inst.,* 1968, **59,** 550.
2 K. Greenwood. *J. Text. Inst.,* 1975, **66,** 420.
3 J. J. Thwaites. *J. Text. Inst.,* 1970, **61,** 116.
4 M. J. Denton. *J. Text. Inst.,* 1975, **66,** 303.

APPENDIX

THE CONDITIONS REQUIRED TO EQUALIZE INPUT AND OUTPUT TENSIONS ON A FRICTION TWISTER

The present analysis is based on Fig. 7, which shows the direction and magnitude of the velocities and forces at a point of contact between the yarn and the twister. The various symbols used are defined as follows.

T_1 = Input tension
T_2 = Output tension
Y = Forward velocity of untwisted yarn
v_1 = Forward velocity of twisted yarn (smaller than Y because of twist contraction and decreases with increasing twist)
v_2 = Circumferential velocity of twisted yarn (increases with increasing twist)
v_R = Resultant surface velocity of yarn (resulting from v_1 and v_2)
θ = Yarn-helix angle (angle between direction of v_R and the yarn axis)
D = Surface velocity of twister (general)
D_1 = Surface velocity of twister when $T_2 = T_1$
φ = Twister angle (angle between direction of D and the yarn axis)
U = Untwisting force due to the torsional rigidity of the yarn
δ = Escape angle (angle between U and the yarn axis)
F = Frictional force between the yarn and the twister

F_1 = Component of F along the yarn axis

γ = Drag angle (angle between F and the yarn axis)

s = Slip velocity (velocity of twister relative to yarn)

s_1 = Slip velocity when $D = D_1$ $(T_2 = T_1)$

With reference to the parameters listed above, the choice of the yarn-helix angle, θ, and the yarn take-up speed, Y, fully determines the values of v_1, v_2, and v_R. The required relations have been developed by Denton[4] and other workers. They must include some relation between twist contraction and the helix angle, such as, for instance, the Morton–Hearle equation used by Denton. Since both v_1 and v_2 are functions of θ, it is possible to establish a direct relation between these two velocities. The corresponding curve is shown in Fig. 7. This curve is virtually identical with the path that any point on the yarn surface describes during the twisting or untwisting of the yarn. The curve is unique for any particular yarn.

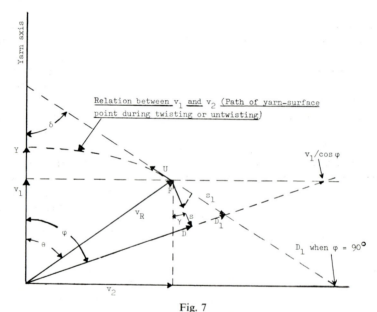

Fig. 7

The forces acting on the yarn surface

The choice of θ also determines the value of the untwisting force, U, but the present analysis does not require any mathematical relation between U and θ.

The twister angle, φ, can, in theory, have any value greater than zero and smaller than $180°$, but the practical range of φ is much narrower and lies between θ and $90°$. The example of φ shown in Fig. 7 lies within that range.

For any particular combination of φ and θ, the value of D can vary between a minimum, which is a function of φ and θ, and infinity. The value of D determines the ratio T_2/T_1 in a manner that will be discussed. The purpose of the present analysis is to find D_1, which is the value of D resulting in a tension ratio of unity $(T_2/T_1 = 1)$. The value of D also determines the magnitude of the slip velocity, s, and this analysis sets out to find s_1, which is the value of s corresponding to D_1.

So far as a repetition of Denton's arguments[4] is necessary for the present discussion, these will be dealt with very briefly. A fuller discussion is only required where new aspects are introduced.

Denton[4] has shown that the drag angle, γ, which defines the direction of the slip velocity, s, is given by:

$$\tan \gamma = \frac{D\sin \varphi - v_2}{v_1 - D\cos \varphi}. \qquad \dots \dots (1)$$

The angle γ also defines the direction of the frictional force, F. The magnitude of F must be such as to balance the untwisting force, U. The force F has a component F_1, which acts along the yarn axis and is given by:

$$F_1 = F\cos \gamma. \qquad \dots \dots (2)$$

When F_1 is positive, it acts in a direction opposite to the running direction of the yarn and tends to cause a rise in tension across the twister. If F_1 is negative, it acts in the running direction of the yarn and tends to cause a fall in yarn tension across the twister. Finally, if F is zero, it has no influence on the yarn tension.

All these conclusions are due to Denton and other workers. Denton made the implicit assumption, however, that F is the only force present that can have a component along the yarn axis. Starting from this assumption, he concluded that, when $F_1 = 0$, there is no change in tension across the twister. This, according to Equation (2), is the case when $\gamma = 90°$. Inserting this condition into Equation (1), one obtains $D_1 = v_1/\cos \varphi$.

If this expression for D_1 were correct, it would mean that $D_1 = \infty$ when $\varphi = 90°$, so that a tension ratio of T_2/T_1 could not be obtained with a friction twister moving at right angles to the yarn axis.

Although Denton's conclusions in this respect agree with those of earlier workers, they cannot be sustained if one considers the direction of the untwisting force, U. The existence of this force, which is due to the torsional rigidity of the yarn, was implicit in Denton's argument, but there was also an implied assumption that the force acts at right angles to the yarn axis and can therefore have no influence on the yarn tension.

The latter assumption would only be correct if the yarn could untwist without changing its length. In this case, v_1 would be identical with Y, irrespective of the value of θ, and the curve shown in Fig. 7 would be a horizontal straight line. This is obviously not the case and has never even been suggested as a simplifying assumption. As the yarn untwists, a point on the yarn surface must follow the curved path shown in Fig. 7, and the direction of the untwisting force is therefore the direction of the tangent to the curve at that point. This tangent cannot be at right angles to the yarn axis except in the limiting case when $\theta = 0$. In all practical cases, where θ lies between 55 and 70°, the angle between the tangent and the yarn axis is the region of 65–70°. This angle will be referred to as the 'escape angle', δ, because it defines the direction in which the yarn 'wishes' to escape from the grip of the twister.

From Fig. 7, it can be deduced that δ is given by:

$$\delta = 90° + \tan^{-1}\left(\frac{dv_1}{dv_2}\right). \qquad \dots \dots (3)$$

Since the slope of the curve of v_1 against v_2 must always be negative, Equation (3) shows that δ must always be an acute angle. The value of dv_1/dv_2 can be found on the basis of the Morton–Hearle equation or any other relation between the twist contraction and helix angle.

With U acting at an acute angle to the yarn axis, it has a component U_1 along the yarn axis, which always acts in the running direction of the yarn and tends to cause a fall in tension across the twister. Whether there is an actual rise or fall in tension across the twister or no change in tension will thus depend on the relative magnitudes of U_1 and F_1 and on the direction of F_1 (positive or negative). This analysis is concerned with the condition in which there is no change in yarn tension across the twister, and this condition exists when $U_1 = F_1$, which the case when:

$$F\cos\gamma = U\cos\delta. \qquad \dots\dots(4)$$

Equilibrium further requires that:

$$F\cos(\delta - \gamma) = U. \qquad \dots\dots(5)$$

When Equations (4) and (5) are solved for γ, it is found that a tension ratio of $T_2/T_1 = 1$ requires γ to be equal to δ. In order to find the value of D_1, it is therefore only necessary to replace γ by δ in Equation (1) and to solve this equation for D. This leads to:

$$D_1 = \frac{v_1\sin\delta + v_2\cos\delta}{\sin(\delta + \varphi)}. \qquad \dots\dots(6)$$

This value is indicated in Fig. 7, which, for comparison purposes, also shows the value of $v_1/\cos\varphi$, which was suggested by Denton[4] as the expression for D_1.

Geometrically, the value of D_1 given by Equation (6) is found by intersecting the line of D with the line of U. Fig. 7 shows that, even when $\varphi = 90°$, this intersection leads to a finite value of D_1, which means that a tension ratio of unity can be achieved with a friction twister moving at right angles to the yarn axis.

It will be seen that Equations (4)–(6) reduce to the forms used by Denton if one assumes that $\delta = 90°$.

In order to find the slip velocity, s, it is only necessary to apply the cosine rule to Fig. 7. This leads to:

$$s_1^2 = v_R^2 + D_1^2 - 2v_R D_1\cos(\varphi - \theta). \qquad \dots\dots(7)$$

This equation shows that, when D_1 is finite, then s_1 is also finite, so that, even when $\varphi = 90°$, the amount of slip existing when the tension ratio equals unity is finite.

The present analysis is no more conclusively proved than any other theoretical treatment of friction twisters. It offers an explanation, however, for the observed fact that a twister moving at right angles to the yarn axis can produce a tension ratio of unity with a finite, and not unreasonably high, D/Y ratio and with a modest amount of slip. The essence of the present analysis is the statement that the escape angle, δ, is substantially less than $90°$. This leads to an approach that appears to be more consistent than earlier analyses, which allowed for twist contraction in relation to the velocities v_1 and v_2 but ignored it in relation to the direction of the untwisting force.

The present approach also resolves certain inconsistencies in Denton's treatment of a friction twister operating without slip. This aspect will be the subject of a separate paper.

Heberlein Maschinenfabrik A.G.,
Wattwil,
Switzerland.

11—THE USE OF TEXTURIZED YARNS IN CARPET MANUFACTURE

By W. G. Martin and W. G. A. Cook

After a review of the many uses for texturized continuous-filament yarns in the manufacture of carpets, the development of the more sophisticated effects that can be obtained by the use of processed texturized yarns is discussed. The use of twisted heat-set and other processed continuous-filament yarns in making carpets is covered by outlining the various methods available for producing such yarns, ranging from conventional autoclaving to continuous methods, and discussing the end-uses into which such yarns go and the effects that can be obtained by utilizing these processed yarns in the various methods of carpet manufacture.

1. INTRODUCTION

In this paper, the various end-uses for bulked continuous-filament (bcf) yarns in carpet manufacture will be considered, and in this context the use of these yarns in both loop-pile and cut-pile constructions will be covered. The use of texturized yarns in cut-pile carpets will be considered in detail, with particular attention given to processed bcf yarns. This subject is perhaps best described as 'yarn-engineering', which allows the construction of a wide range of yarns by paying particular attention to the ultimate end-uses and, in essence, by producing a specific yarn for a specific end-use. The advantages to manufacturer and consumer alike are readily apparent in that the designer has available to him a product with which his own handwriting can be seen in the final carpet and the consumer can be assured of improved quality and performance, together with all the aesthetic properties that have come to be accepted in modern floorcoverings. Such yarns have to date found their major end-uses in the medium of tufted carpets but should not be considered as being limited to this method of manufacture alone.

The principal synthetic-fibre continuous-filament yarns available in textured form are those of polyamide and polypropylene fibres. Polyamide-fibre yarns are available as both nylon 6.6 and nylon 6 in a wide range of products differing in linear density and dyeing characteristics. The principal linear densities available are generally in the following ranges:

1200–1500 dtex,
1800–2000 dtex,
2500–2800 dtex,
4000–4500 dtex.

With regard to differential-dyeing characteristics, most fibre producers have a range of products covering all or most of the following types, which are available for piece-dyeing:

regular acid-dyeing,
deep (or ultra-deep) acid-dyeing,
low acid-dyeing
basic (cationic) dyeing.

These differential effects can either be used in straight yarns or combined together to give a range of marl yarns. As well as these undyed yarns, there are also available various ranges of solution-dyed yarns.

Polypropylene-fibre yarn is available as a texturized yarn in a similar range of linear densities and solution-dyed colours, and piece-dyeable variants have recently become available.

2. CARPET MANUFACTURE

Carpet manufacture generally falls into two categories, loop-pile and cut-pile, and this is perhaps the best basis on which to discuss the uses of texturized yarns.

Initially, bcf yarns were used in the manufacture of loop-pile carpets, yarns of high linear density being used on coarse-gauge tufting machinery, i.e., 4000-dtex yarns on a 3/6-gauge machine. Their main use was either as solution-dyed yarns or to give piece-dyed effects in plain-coloured carpets This was quickly followed by the use of marl yarns to give simple multi-colour effects.

With the advent of differential-dyeing yarns, together with a greater acceptance of piece-dyeing, and with the more sophisticated patterning attachments that were being developed in tufting, it was possible to advance to simple tone-on-tone effects in high–low tufted constructions. These were to be followed by more contrasting effects with the introduction of basic-dyeable yarns.

At the same time, finer-gauge tufting machines were emerging, which led to a demand for finer yarns, the linear density being reduced from 4000 to 2720 dtex and ultimately to 1360 dtex. These lower linear densities allowed differential marl combinations to be used and lighter-weight carpets with good performance characteristics to be developed.

As well as plain and simple two- or three-colour combination effects, a growing demand was arising for multicolour carpets made on tufting equipment. These were first satisfied by the use of space-dyed or printed yarns to give simple random multicolour carpets, the aim for these yarns being randomness rather than any uncontrollable patterning, which the use of these yarns can give. More sophisticated effects were possible by the use of combinations of space-dyed yarns or space-dyed and solution-dyed yarns on the high–low pattern attachments.

The biggest advance in multicoloured effects came with the perfection of full-width carpet-printing, and very rapidly machine development progressed from simple prints to the superb prints that have become well known to-day.

At the same time as the manufacture of loop-pile carpets was being perfected, the development of cut-pile carpeting was also taking place. Colour effects were originally obtained by using spun yarns made from stock-dyed fibres and as such were restricted to plain colours, marls, or simple heather mixtures. However, the basic tufting process did not allow patterning in the cut-pile area comparable with that possible in the loop-pile high–low area, and, with the progress being made in texturized yarns, together with a lowering of linear densities, a new concept of processed yarns began to emerge, initially made up of twisted marls but rapidly developing in twisted and plied heat-set yarns. Such yarns, while retaining all the advantages of bcf yarns such as uniformity and strength, added new dimensions to carpet manufacture by allowing the introduction of cut-pile effects in both long and short pile that would retain their twist and tuft definition through subsequent colouring and finishing operations and thus eliminate the problem of the felty appearance experienced when unset yarns were used in cut-pile constructions. These effects were initially concentrated in developing the very successful ranges of shag or luxury long-pile effects, but the advent of printing allowed the manufacture of multicolour cut-pile tufted carpets that could at last compete with the traditional Axminster and Wilton carpets in colour effects, appearance, and performance. By taking into account the properties of the original bcf yarn, it is possible, by the correct combination of bulk, twist, and heat-setting conditions, to produce a yarn suitable for any particular end-use. This development of 'yarn-engineering' is the one that will be covered in detail by describing first the methods of manufacture and then the uses and properties of the yarns.

3. METHODS OF YARN-PROCESSING

3.1 Twisting

If one starts with a texturized continuous-filament yarn, the basic method of yarn manufacture covers twisting and setting. The twisting operation usually embraces the twisting of a singles component before being folded, although in some cases a single uptwisted yarn can be used.

The singles-twisting operation can be carried out on various twisting machines, the most commonly used method being that of uptwisting on standard 2:1 twisting machines. These machines have advantages over, say, ring-twisting machines, which can also be used, in that they have high through-puts with consistent quality. By using either twisting method, it is possible to insert the level of twist required in either the S or the Z direction ready for fold-twisting.

Fold-twisting can be done on ring doublers, on which two or more ends of singles-twisted yarn can be brought together from a stand-off creel and twisted on the bobbin on a rotating spindle. Alternative methods are to use 2:1 twisting, but this requires an additional assembly-winding operation, which can be done during the original singles-twisting by winding two or more ends onto the take-up package. In general, ring-doubling is considered the most satisfactory route because of its versatility, since it gives a regular yarn with little variation in twist and eliminates potential problems caused by uneven tension in assembly-winding.

By using these twisting methods, it is possible to 'engineer' any yarn construction from two-fold upwards by using yarn of any input linear density and ranging from balanced to high-twist constructions. In all cases, the direction of twist in singles and folded yarns is opposite, the final twist direction depending on the tufting machine being used in carpet-making.

The most recent development in twisting has been aimed at carrying out the two twisting stages in a single operation. Such methods are known as *direct cabling* and are now available from machine makers. These twisting methods are very competitive, since they allow continuous cording from two supply packages to produce two-fold yarns of equal and opposite twist. This is accomplished by feeding yarn from an outboard creel to the base of a spindle and passing it up the centre of a spindle and out through the spinner plate. This yarn is then ballooned around a stationary second package, situated in the twister bucket in the normal 2:1 position. Yarn from the second package is withdrawn through a pre-tensioner and meets the ballooning yarn at the balloon eyelet. This is the point at which cording takes place. The twisted yarn then passes round tension rolls to the overfeed and the take-up package. As previously stated, the process is limited to two-fold yarns of equal and opposite twists but does have the advantage of being a one-stage process using less labour and eliminating considerable yarn-handling.

3.2   Heat-setting

3.2.1   *Autoclave-setting*

Heat-setting is best considered by covering the conventional autoclave route first and then discussing the more modern continuous alternatives that have been developed.

Conventional autoclave-setting is a batch process in which the yarn is steamed in a pressure vessel in order to set or fix the twist. To arrange the yarn in a suitable package for setting, it is wound into jumbo hanks of, say, 4 kg in mass and 3 m in circumference. The hanks are then loaded into a suitable container and heat-set in an autoclave by using a multiple-pressure-steaming cycle in order to effect uniform treatment. In some cases, the yarn is tumbled before being autoclaved to bulk it and develop the twist. On removal from the pressure vessel, the yarn is cooled and conditioned and then backwound onto a cone ready for tufting.

This is a well-proved method of heat-setting and produces an excellent yarn, giving good bulk development and tuft definition in the finished carpet, provided that strict process controls are instituted in order to eliminate batch-to-batch variations. The process does, however, involve a high labour content, with considerable yarn-handling.

To move away from batch-processing by means of labour-intensive methods, various continuous processes have been developed, of which the ones discussed below are significant.

3.2.2   *The Superba Process*

In this process, the yarn is coiled onto a brattice, which travels through a processing chamber. The yarn is first relaxed and then fed into the setting zone, which is really a form of continuous-pressure steamer, and finally cooled and wound onto a package ready for tufting. Temperatures of up to 138°C are used, with the setting time reduced from 30–40 min in an autoclave to about 2 min in the Superba machine.

The advantages are obvious in that it is a continuous process replacing a batch process, with all the subsequent saving of labour and handling. The labour-saving is significant in that it is claimed that two operatives can easily run three machines, but the capital cost is high. The quality of the set yarn is regarded as being the nearest to that of autoclave-set yarn so far achieved.

3.2.3   *The Relset Process*

This is a process involving the use of dry heat rather than steam. The yarn is blown at high temperatures by compressed hot air through heated coils. The yarn bulks as it is blown through the coil, and, set by the temperature of the heated coils, it is collected in sliver cans and then rewound onto a package ready for tufting.

The advantage is that the Relset process is a semi-continuous process of low capital cost, with lower labour content than the conventional route. However, the results are not directly comparable with steam-set yarns. The process is claimed to produce straight yarns suitable for piece-dyeing.

This principle has also been considered as a means of relaxing yarn before autoclaving, as an alternative to putting yarn into hank form. The process known as Rebulk relaxes the yarn through tubes of lower temperatures, it is collected in bags or perforated cans, and these are heat-set in the autoclave in the normal way before the yarn is wound back onto a package. The very nature of coiling and setting in coiled form gives a lively yarn, with the result that the yarn is kinky rather than straight in carpets made from it.

3.2.4   The Horauf Process

This method carries the yarn through a steam chamber in the form of coils wound on moving tapes, supported on a central horizontal pillar. The yarn passes through a relaxing zone, after which it is steamed in a superheated-steam chamber, rather than a pressure chamber, and is cooled before being directly wound onto a tufting package.

This system is fully continuous, with obvious labour-saving advantages, but, whereas it is claimed to be wholly satisfactory for spun yarns, it does not give heat-set continuous-filament yarns capable of direct comparison with autoclaved yarns.

4.   ADVANTAGES OF USING TEXTURIZED YARNS FOR CARPET PILE

Those who are not familiar in detail with the carpet trade may wonder why such relatively complicated and expensive steps as yarn-twisting and heat-setting are being proposed for the carpet pile when the only real effect is one of appearance. By twisting and heat-setting nylon staple-fibre and continuous-filament yarn before using it as a carpet pile, the cost is increased by at least 30 or 40%, and, indeed, the real cost in terms of the amount of yarn required to cover a given area of carpet will be even higher, since the twisting process inevitably results in the yarn's losing some of its bulk.

As in so many other areas of textiles, the answer lies essentially in the customer's requirement of a familiar handle and appearance. For decades, the British carpet-buying public has relied on Axminster and Wilton looms to provide it with the carpets that it requires. These machines have used yarns made from wool or blends of wool and other fibres to produce cut-pile carpets (whose appearance is sometimes plain but more often multicoloured) that have become established as the norm in the market. A critical factor, particularly with the numerous Axminster styles, has been the clearly defined tuft appearance, which in turn comes from the hank-dyeing opera-tion. Virtually all yarns for the Axminster process and many for the Wilton process are hank-dyed under atmospheric conditions, and this is sufficient to set the wool in such a manner that, when the tuft is cut in the loom, it retains an essentially tubular shape at its tip.

Economic pressures on carpet-weaving dictate that it will in the future be responsible for a smaller and reducing proportion of the total British carpet market. However, the retail purchaser's basic requirement is clear: the carpets that replace the woven ones will meet with greatest approval when they duplicate the traditional appearance as closely as possible in colour, design, and surface texture. Unfortunately, the colouring processes that are primarily involved in the new routes to competitively priced carpets in the 1970s are piece-dyeing and printing, and these processes, which involve hot and wet operations after the tuft has been cut, tend to lead to disintegration of the tubular shape of the tuft.

The yarn-twisting and setting processes described earlier made their first penetration in the British carpet market during the late 1960s, when the American taste for long-pile or shag carpets reached Europe. A shag carpet may be defined as one in which the tuft is long enough and the tuft density low enough for the pile to lie horizontal in a generally random manner. Obviously, since the sides of the tufts in such a carpet are visible on the surface to a great extent, the degree of twisting and the efficiency of the heat-setting are all-important. However, the demand for carpets of this type, although healthy, has never reached the 'craze' proportion of the U.S.A., where, in certain parts of the market, two out of every three carpets sold have been of this type. The British market still prefers multi-colour designs on its floorcoverings, and the shag style does not lend itself readily to traditional detailed-design effects.

5. THE INCREASED PRODUCTION OF PRINTED CARPETS

The real expansion in demand for heat-set yarns has followed the vast increase in the production of printed carpets in Britain over the last few years. By the end of the 1960s, about 5 million m² per annum of printed carpets were sold in the U.K. by three manufacturers. To-day, the figures are of the order of 70 million m² from a total of 15 manufacturers. When it is remembered that the total British market for all soft floorcoverings is of the order of 180 million m², it can be seen that carpet-printing now dominates the industry in a quite remarkable manner.

However, it would be wrong to suggest that the production of this massive quantity of printed carpet is based on the use of heat-set continuous-filament yarns. Most of it is produced by using loop-pile tufted print-base cloths in order to have the cheapest or most economical base fabric for the printer to exercise his design and colour expertise. Heat-setting and twisting yarns for this loop-pile carpet would have little beneficial effect and would lead simply to higher costs. Where manufacturers have wished to produce a texture more akin to that of the traditional cut-pile Axminster effect, they have tried to do this, with some success, by using variations in pile height in the loops in order to give an impression of texture. In other cases, making a virtue out of necessity, they have instead gone to very tightly packed loops to give a hard-wearing cord-like appearance, allied in many cases to a design that gives a tile effect.

There is no doubt that a major market requirement is still for each major carpet printer to have in his ranges cut-pile printed carpets, which, to the retail customer, are indistinguishable from Axminster carpets but are offered for sale at prices that the Axminster manufacturer finds increasing difficulties in matching.

It is most unfortunate that neither piece-dyeing nor printing generates or even helps to preserve tuft definition, with the interesting exception of the Crawford Pickering Multicolour Unit.

For those who are not familiar with the detailed operations of the carpet industry, the schematic layout in Fig. 1 may be useful.

One can postulate that heating continuous-filament nylon yarn under hot and wet conditions before cutting and forming a cut-pile tuft is a good thing because it helps to set the yarn and retains the tuft's tubular shape after cutting, whereas heating the same continuous-filament yarn under wet conditions after cutting the tuft is bad because it tends to cause the tuft's shape to break up and results in loss of tuft definition in the surface pile. It can be seen from Fig. 1 that the Crawford Pickering Multicolour route therefore appears to have a significant advantage over other printing techniques. However, the setting time and temperature involved in yarn-printing (say, 100°C for 6 min) are much less severe than the conditions used for yarn-setting, and hence it is still necessary to include this process before yarn-printing.

Loop-Pile Print

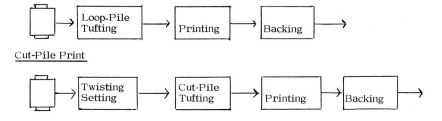

Cut-Pile Print

Crawford Pickering Multicolour Cut-Pile Print

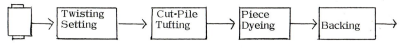

Piece Dyed Filament Cut Pile

Fig. 1

Schematic layout of operations involved in the production of tufted carpets

Corresponding to the U.K. interest in cut-pile printing of the Axminster style is the Continental interest in plain piece-dyed sophisticated pile effects, as typified by the German soft-velour market. Multicoloured carpets have been of less interest in these Continental markets than in the U.K., and the modern tufted soft-velour qualities, predominantly in nylon staple-fibre yarns, are the modern counterpart of older plain Wilton qualities. The need to minimize cost, etc., is pushing many manufacturers of such carpets towards the use of continuous-filament yarn, and once again it can be seen that attractive pile effects from continuous-filament yarn can only be obtained from heat-set yarns. Once such qualities are installed in the Continental markets, they will also provide attractive print-base cloths in their own right within these markets.

6. CONCLUSION

In deciding on ideal or preferred routes to heat-set continuous-filament yarns, it is tempting simply to survey the steaming-temperature conditions and steaming durations during the various yarn-setting and carpet-printing operations, as well as the hot, moist conditions found during carpet-backing, in order to define the ideal yarn. Unfortunately, evaluations of this type ignore the vital influence of such matters as the mechanical pressure exerted during printing, the number of printing stages used, the carpet-pile constructions, and the heat history of the yarns originally chosen for the work. Where carpets are to be piece-dyed rather than printed, the vital factors include the choice between winch-dyeing, with its agitation, and continuous dyeing, with its physical pressures.

In practice, the range of equipment likely to be used on a given yarn and the variety of operating conditions that it may encounter mean that in practice there is no such thing as the ideal yarn for cut-pile use.

The authors' own surveys, carried out by making carpets from a wide variety of yarns heat-set in different ways, by both batch and continuous processes, certainly suggest that the autoclave route is still the most flexible.

On the other hand, the continuous processes can give yarns entirely suitable for certain market areas, and the probability is that, over the next few years, they will gain an increasing part of the market below the auto-clave-set market in cost.

As was mentioned above, the woven-carpet section of the textile industry will in future account for a smaller part of the total carpet market in the U.K., in line with similar trends in other countries. It should not be forgotten, however, that the woven-carpet sector in the U.K. has great historical strength, and the probability is that, as set continuous-filament yarns for cut-pile tufted carpets become more widely available in a range of qualities, some will be used by the technically advanced weavers in certain market areas, where use will be made of either their considerable bulk or their performance, or of both.

(W.G.M.) Lontex Industries Ltd,
Fernbank,
Barnoldswick,
Colne,
Lancs.
(W.G.A.C.) Carpet Centre,
ICI Europa Fibres,
Oestringen,
Germany (B.R.D.).

12—THE PRODUCTION OF WOVEN FABRICS FROM TEXTURED POLYESTER-FIBRE YARNS

By M. J. D. DYER

The rapid growth in recent years in the development of woven fabrics produced from textured polyester-fibre yarns is outlined. The desirable yarn properties for these fabrics are discussed, and it is shown that, to benefit fully from the opportunities offered by the yarns, certain basic principles of processing and fabric construction must be followed. The methods used in warp preparation, weaving, and finishing are considered, and the optimum requirements for fabric construction are outlined. Some predictions of likely future trends are made.

1. INTRODUCTION

Textured polyester-fibre yarns, with their inherent properties of crease-recovery and dimensional stability, offer the potential for fabrics to be produced with pleasing aesthetics and good performance characteristics. The opportunities offered by these yarns were first recognized in the knitting section of the textile industry with spectacular results, but early efforts by weavers to produce fabrics from the same yarns were unsuccessful. Not until it was realized that woven constructions required yarns designed and texturized for the intended end-use did any significant penetration of the market occur. Before discussing processing and weaving techniques, therefore, it is worth while to outline briefly the characteristics of textured polyester-fibre yarns used in woven-fabric production.

2. YARN PROPERTIES

The majority of woven cloths are produced from single-heater false-twist yarns, although in the higher linear densities—167 dtex and 167 dtex $\times$ 2— some partly stabilized twin-heater yarns are used. This is in contrast to the use of fully stabilized yarns in knitting. Unstabilized yarns are necessary because of the inherently rigid structure of woven fabrics, and, as will be seen later, the relatively high and irregular tensions used in the weaving process. During processing, yarn bulk is lost, and, unless the yarn has sufficient shrinkage force to overcome the resistance of the fabric structure during finishing, the bulk cannot be developed, and a lean, rigid cloth will result. This was the basic problem in the early days of development of woven fabrics from textured yarns when fully stabilized knitting yarns were used; the introduction of single-heater yarns into woven constructions enabled the yarn bulk to be developed in finishing, which resulted in the full, soft handle characteristic of present-day woven textured polyester-fibre fabrics.

It is usual to post-twist the single-heater yarns, both to reduce liveliness or torque and to improve the mechanical performance through the weaving process. The liveliness or torque is reduced when post-twist is added in the same direction as the false twist, but too high a twist level will reduce the yarn bulk. The average level of post-twist will decrease with increase in linear density, but the following general twist levels are operative at present:

   50 dtex: 150–200 turns/m;
   84 dtex: 120–150 turns/m;
  167 dtex: 80–120 turns/m.

There is, however, a rapid increase in the use of yarns without post-twist for weft.

Where two-fold yarns are used—primarily those of 167 dtex × 2—it is usual for the singles yarn not to have post-twist. If two singles yarns of opposing false twist are doubled at low doubling-twist levels, the resultant yarn will tend to be balanced. If, however, the doubling twist is increased, the twist will eventually favour the false-twist direction of one of the singles yarns, and the two-fold yarn will become unbalanced. For 167-dtex × 2 yarns, the best balancing twist is in the region of 80–120 turns/m. At higher levels of post-twist, yarns of the same false-twist direction as the doubling twist tend to give a more balanced yarn, but it should be remembered that, as the twist level is increased, the yarn bulk is decreased. Optimum post-twist levels will vary with texturizing conditions and twisting or doubling tensions.

In contrast to the procedure in warp- or weft-knitting, it is necessary to subject the yarns to several intermediate processes before being woven, and every process will develop the faults existing in the incoming textured polyester-fibre yarns. It is therefore imperative that textured yarn supplied for weaving is of first-grade mechanical quality and that the physical properties are adjusted to suit the processing requirements. Mechanically, the yarn must be free from looped and broken filaments and knots to prevent weaving problems and fabric faults. The physical properties must be uniform both within and between packages to prevent dye-uptake, shrinkage, and bulk differences in the finished cloth.

3. PROCESSING

3.1   General Principles

From the outset, it must be stated that the production of woven fabric from textured polyester-fibre yarns does not require specialized equipment or additional skills beyond those required for handling normal continuous-filament yarns. The techniques and practices necessary for producing first-grade fabrics from textured polyester-fibre yarns are essentially the same as those required for weaving cloths from normal continuous-filament polyester-fibre yarns. What must be stressed, however, is the need for a clear understanding of the textured-yarn characteristics, strict quality-control standards at all stages, and meticulous attention to detail.

Because of the sensitivity of textured yarns to tension variations during processing and the effect of tension variation on cloth appearance and handle, it is essential that tight control is kept on all operations at all times. Once the optimum settings have been found for an individual process, a control procedure must be introduced to ensure that they are kept within a fine tolerance. The margin of error is extremely small, and the difference between operating within and operating outside strict control specifications will be the difference between first-grade and reject fabric.

The most important factor in handling textured polyester-fibre yarns is to ensure low and constant tensions. Irregular tension will cause changes in bulk level, which will show as either warp stripes or weft barré. To avoid stretching the yarn, it is recommended that all running tensions in all processes are controlled at around 0·1 gf/den (8·8 mN/tex), and, to prevent tension variation, all running surfaces should be matt chrome or ceramic.

3.2   Warp Preparation

Weaving efficiency and cloth quality depend primarily on well-prepared weaver's beams. It is therefore essential that careful consideration be given to warping and sizing techniques and conditions to ensure that the weaving shed is presented with first-grade warps. Whether weaver's beams should be sized depends on the yarn linear density, the linear density per filament, the level of post-twist, the number of ends/cm in the fabric, and the loom type. As a general guide, however, it is usual to size all yarns with a linear density below 167 dtex. Both sized and unsized 167-dtex warps are used, depending on the loom type and fabric construction. Yarn of 167 dtex × 2 is invariably woven unsized.

The choice of processing route is as follows:

(i) section-warping, followed by beam-to-beam sizing;

(ii) full-width back-beaming, followed by sizing of the assembled back beams;

(iii) full-width back-beaming, sizing of individual back beams, and assembly of sized back beams onto weaver's beam; or

(iv) sizing directly from the creel, followed by assembly of sized back beams onto weaver's beam.

The sizing process itself is the most critical operation, and it is at this stage that the four systems vary, so that, before discussing the relative merits or otherwise of the different routes, it is necessary to review the object and principles of sizing continuous-filament yarns. The object of sizing is to protect the yarn from the abrasive action of the loom, but the requirements of sizing are inherently incompatible in that it is necessary to stick together adjacent filaments in individual threads without, at the same time, causing adhesion between individual filaments of adjacent threads. The sizing of continuous-filament or textured yarn is unlike spun-yarn sizing, where size is soaked into the fibre and also coats the thread in a protective sheath; it is more akin to spot-welding. Low size concentrations are used, and adjacent filaments are stuck together at intervals by size, not so much to protect the filaments from breaking but rather to stop already-broken filaments from peeling back and causing large slubs.

If adjacent threads are allowed to touch during sizing, or after sizing while in a tacky state, individual filaments from adjacent ends will 'weld' together in the same way as adjacent filaments from one end. When adjacent threads are subsequently split, broken filaments will be produced. For this reason, sizing directly from the creel (the direct warper–sizer method, e.g., on the Tsudakoma machine) is considered to be the best method of sizing textured polyester-fibre yarn in that, at all stages of drying, the sized threads are kept completely separate. If conventional sizing is used, wet splitting is required immediately after sizing to separate the total number of threads into several warp sheets, and some form of infra-red drying is needed to ensure that the size is dried past the tacky stage before the yarns run onto the drying cylinders, where the ends will roll together.

Both method (ii) and method (iii) above, which are based on back-beaming, can produce satisfactorily sized warps provided that infra-red drying and wet splitting are used in sizing, but method (iii)—the sizing of individual back beams — is preferred, since only a relatively small number of threads are sized at any one time.

Whereas section-warping and beam-to-beam sizing can at times produce good warps, it is extremely difficult to incorporate a suitable wet-splitting and infra-red-drying system, and one is therefore dependent on splitting the sized sheet into individual threads only after drying, which will result in broken filaments. Such a system will produce weaver's beams of variable quality.

Sizing conditions and settings will vary from yarn to yarn, but the standard procedures applied to normal continuous-filament polyester-fibre yarns should automatically be used for textured polyester-fibre yarns. The sizes used for normal continuous-filament polyester-fibre yarns are suitable, although, because of the inherent bulky nature of textured yarn, the amount of size on yarn required for high weaving performance should average between 6 and 8%, and a pick-up of 80–100% can be expected. It is, however, important in the sizing of textured yarn to avoid a combination of high heat and tension, which will set the yarn and produce bulk and dye-uptake problems in the fabric.

If unsized weaver's beams are required, satisfactory warps can be made by either the section-warper or back-beam method, and the choice of system is based more on economic than technical grounds. The standard settings used for normal continuous-filament polyester-fibre yarns can be applied, but care must be taken to avoid snarling, particularly during slow-speed running. Surrounding individual packages with a polythene bag or skirt has proved to be effective, but a more sophisticated method, particularly where yarns of high torque are processed, is to use an anti-snarl device between the package and first guide eye.

3.3 Weaving

Provided that the beams have been prepared correctly, warps of textured polyester-fibre yarns can be woven satisfactorily on a wide range of loom types without any additional procedures other than those necessary for weaving normal flat-filament polyester-fibre yarns. The main problems with textured polyester-fibre yarns are in the weft, particularly when conventional shuttle looms are used on which the yarn is first wound onto a pirn and then unwound from a shuttle during weaving. Both operations are extremely variable, and great care must be taken to ensure that the correct settings are used and strictly maintained.

Conventional pirn-winding is not ideal. Textured polyester-fibre yarns are very sensitive to tension variation, and it is not possible to maintain an identical tension across several pirning heads. If conventional pirn-winding is to be used, it is essential to use sequential pirning. In this method, all the pirns from an individual spindle are confined to one loom and are used in the exact order of winding from the supply package, although a preferred system, requiring even more control, is to reverse the weaving sequence of the pirns from alternate packages to minimize the possibility of package-change bars.

It is strongly recommended that pirn-winding be done at the loom on Unifil winders to ensure complete control of pirning conditions and pirn-tube quality. It is advisable to reject the last part-pirn wound from the inside of each supply package to minimize package-change barré in the fabric.

The most common fault in weaving textured yarns on conventional looms is pirn-change barré caused by high and variable unwinding tensions during winding-off from the pirn base in weaving. Because of the characteristics of the pirn tube, it is not possible to produce an even unwinding tension from nose to base, but consideration of the following points will minimize the fault:

(i) pirn tubes should be made of hard impregnated wood; varnished wood is not acceptable;

(ii) the surface should be undulated or finely grooved; a smooth surface is not acceptable;

(iii) the tube length should not exceed 185 mm and the diameter at the nose should be around 10 mm;

(iv) a conical base is preferred, but this is not entirely practicable on tubes that are to be used on Unifil winders;

(v) the diameter of the full pirn should not exceed 23 mm, and the wind ratio should be 14–16 on an initial traverse of the order of 40 mm;

(vi) the unwinding tension in the shuttle should be the minimum to ensure correct threading and a tension of 5–6 gf (49–59 mN) is recommended for the full pirn.

Whereas unconventional looms, on which the weft is taken directly from the cone or tube, do not present the weftway problems associated with conventional looms, they are extremely critical with regard to the incoming-yarn quality. It is necessary that the supply package be capable of unwinding speeds of 800–1000 m/min without giving rise to major tension fluctuations that will be translated directly into the fabric as streaky or barré weft.

3.4   Finishing

It is not intended to discuss detailed finishing routines for fabrics woven from textured polyester-fibre yarns, which would be the subject of a separate paper, but it must be generally stated that the dyeing and finishing routine and conditions are critical in producing fabric that is commercially acceptable in terms of aesthetic appeal and performance. The machinery and techniques used must enable the yarn bulk to develop, and for this reason it is essential that some method of fully relaxing the cloth is used as the first operation. Jet-dyeing is preferred, since cloth bulk can be further developed and retained during dyeing. As mentioned previously, textured yarn is prone to small tension changes, which can lead to dye-uptake variation, and dye selection can therefore make the difference between commercially acceptable fabric and cloth showing stripiness or barré or both.

4.   FABRIC CONSTRUCTION

Many woven fabrics incorporating textured polyester-fibre yarns are now on the market in both men's and women's apparel, in a variety of weights ranging from lightweight blouse cloths to men's trouserings and suitings, and these are made from the following yarn combinations:

(i) standard continuous-filament-yarn warp and textured-yarn weft;

(ii) textured-yarn warp and textured-yarn weft; and

(iii) textured-yarn warp and spun-yarn weft.

The use of continuous-filament warps tends to be confined to the lighter-weight cloths, particularly in the blouse and dress area for print-base fabrics. Fabrics made entirely from textured yarns cover the full weight range from piece-dyed and printed lightweight blouse fabrics, in which cloths of a full, soft handle are required, to women's and men's trouserings, in which durability and high performance standards are essential. Combinations of textured polyester-fibre and spun yarns are also available in a range of weights from lightweight fabrics incorporating blends of polyester fibre and cotton for blouses or shirtings to medium- or heavy-weight fabrics with polyester-fibre–viscose or polyester-fibre–wool yarns for trousering.

To produce the full handle associated with fabrics woven from textured polyester-fibre yarns, it is necessary to obtain the correct relationship between loom sett, finished sett, and finishing routine. The loom sett must be calculated to allow room for the yarns to bulk sufficiently during finishing to produce an aesthetically appealing fabric with good performance characteristics. If the loom sett is too high, the finished cloth will be too harsh and 'boardy', and if it is too low the fabric performance will be poor. The finished-fabric construction will depend on the linear density and linear density per filament of the warp and weft, the weave, and the intended outlet, but the fabric shrinkage in warp and weft between the grey and finished states should never be less than 10%. It is more usual to use shrinkages in the range of 14–18%, although, where high stretch characteristics are required, a shrinkage of 22–24% may be used.

Apart from giving bulk or loft to the finished fabric, shrinkage is related to cloth stretch, which is essential if the comfort factor associated with woven fabrics made from textured polyester-fibre yarns, particularly trouserings, is to be achieved. As a general guide, the percentage stretch is approximately half the percentage at shrinkage levels of 12% and under, but, as the shrinkage increases, the percentage stretch at a given shrinkage level increases, so that, for a shrinkage of 22%, a stretch of about 15% can be achieved. A 15% stretch in both warp and weft is the maximum that can be achieved with conventional single-heater false-twist yarns, and, whereas some American cloths have been produced at this level, it is more usual for fabrics to have an over-all stretch (of warp plus weft) of 15–20%.

5. FUTURE TRENDS

Over the last three or four years, a significant increase has been observed in the penetration of fabrics woven from textured polyester-fibre yarns into the markets for both men's and, particularly, women's wear, and this trend is expected to continue into the foreseeable future. The majority of fabrics currently on sale have been produced from conventionally texturized single-heater false-twist yarns with post-twist. However, with the advances currently taking place in all areas of textile technology, from yarn to finished fabric, one can expect to see a rapid widening of product ranges to give a new generation of woven fabrics for both apparel and semi-industrial end-uses. The introduction of draw-textured yarn allied to modern weaving technology could see yarns woven on high-speed looms without size or post-twist, which would enable a wide range of basic fabrics to be produced at very competitive prices.

Present-day fabrics containing textured polyester-fibre yarns tend to have some surface lustre, and, whereas this has been accepted in the women's-wear market, for men's wear, a deadening of the lustre is desirable. Most fibre producers are currently developing multilobal yarns for this purpose (and, indeed, for some time, du Pont have offered an octolobal Dacron yarn, Type 242), and their introduction will enable a range of woven fabrics to be produced without lustre to make them suitable for men's wear.

Whereas the majority of fabrics currently on sale are solid-dyed, and this is likely to remain so, an increasing number of fabrics with a surface design are being introduced. Design can be achieved in two ways: highly sophisticated designs based on coloured yarns, or simple classical effects obtained by using dye-variant yarns. To use coloured yarns requires a highly flexible production set-up, based on short runs and the ability to offer a wide range of designs and colourways. For this reason, the cloths tend to sell on design flair in the higher price bracket. To achieve long production runs at bulk-market prices, it is necessary to look at dye-variant yarns in which the colourways on a design are achieved by piece-dyeing. Such yarns include black, ingrain, minigrain, and basic-dyeable types, disperse- and basic-dyed mixtures, and polyester-fibre and nylon mixtures. However, the impact eventually made on the market by fabrics produced from dye-variant yarns will depend more on the fibre producers' willingness to produce the yarns rather than on the fabric manufacturer.

This paper has been confined to textured polyester-fibre yarns produced by false-twisting, but the rapid development is now taking place of yarns produced by alternative texturizing routes—primarily air-texturizing—and such yarns offer the potential of producing fabrics that are new and exciting in both handle and appearance and possess extremely high performance standards. With the spun-like appearance and handle already being achieved in fabrics produced from air-textured yarns, a new generation of fabrics woven from textured polyester-fibre yarns, specifically designed for the men's-wear market, can be expected.

Carrington Fabrics Ltd,
Eccleston,
Chorley,
Lancashire.

13—THE USE OF TEXTURED YARNS IN KNITTED FABRICS

By R. L. KNIGHT

The advantages claimed for draw-textured yarns in circular knitting are discussed and related to the subsequent processes in the production cycle. It is shown that the much greater package size for draw-textured yarn, when used in the undyed form, can offer a considerable reduction in the number of processes and may also permit a greater allocation of machines per knitter. Appreciable financial savings are shown to be possible when the undyed yarn is processed. Significant improvements arising from the use of draw-textured undyed yarn rather than conventionally textured undyed yarn from a draw-twisted supply are demonstrated. Further advantages discussed include the possibility of using larger direct-knitting packages and increases in production speeds as more yarn is fed per machine revolution. A novel installation of knitting machines and creels is described.

1. DOUBLE-JERSEY KNITTING

1.1 Methods of Producing Coloured Knitted Fabric

There are three basic systems of producing coloured knitted fabric:

(a) the knitting of undyed yarn followed by piece-dyeing of the fabric produced;

(b) the knitting of dyed yarn; and

(c) the knitting of undyed yarn followed by printing of the fabric produced.

For plain fabrics, however, only *(a)* and *(b)* need be considered.

In western countries, such as the U.K., U.S.A., and Germany, the normal method of producing a plain-dyed fabric is to use system *(a)* (undyed yarn) and only to use dyed yarn where different colours are required in the same fabric. To overcome cost and processing problems in the production of dyed yarns (where these are required), determined efforts are being made by both fibre producers and designers to develop and use yarns of different dye affinity or to use spun-dyed colours.

The various systems available are shown in Fig. 1 and will be discussed in greater detail below.

1.2 Number of Processes

Since the number of processes and handling operations is increased by using the dyed-yarn system, a considerably greater quantity of equipment, labour, and floor space is required for an equivalent weight of coloured fabric, even when the requirement for fabric-dyeing equipment is taken into account. There is also an increase in over-all waste, since each process will provide some rejects or waste yarn.

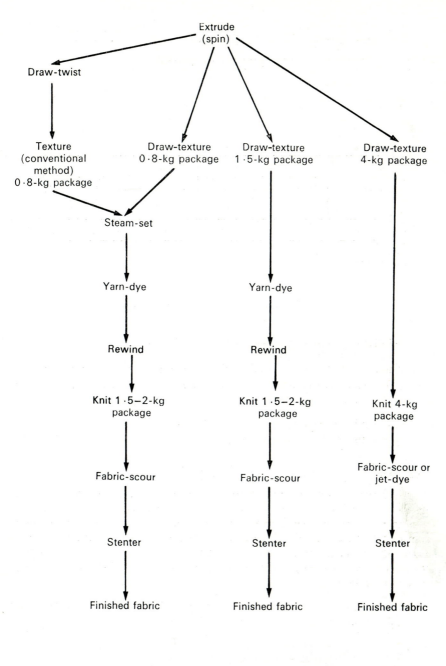

Fig. 1

Process routes for knitted fabrics produced from textured yarn

1.3 Handling

As an example, the handling involved from twisting machine to knitting on a 48-feeder knitting machine is compared in Table I for dyed and undyed yarn. It is assumed that 192 kg of fabric are to be manufactured.

Table I
Handling of Undyed and Dyed Yarn

	Undyed Yarn (4·0 kg)	Dyed Yarn (1·5 kg)
	Yarn	

	48 packages doffed
	48 packages placed on
	    knitting machine
		128 packages doffed
		128 packages dyed
		128 packages rewound
		128 packages placed on
		    knitting machine

Total	96 operations	512 operations
	Fabric	
	2 scour or jet-dye 2 stenter	2 scour 2 stenter
Total	4 operations	4 operations

The amount of handling of yarn will therefore be reduced by a factor of five over-all if undyed yarn is used. The handling would, of course, be greatly increased if a steam-setting route were chosen. The use of larger packages would also enable the knitter to look after at least 50% more machines.

1.4 Yarn Waste before Knitting

Some yarn waste will be created at each process. This will reduce the conversion rate of salable yarn when the dyed-yarn system is used. The extent of the loss will depend on the care taken in processing and handling, but it will be at least 2% higher than that for the undyed system.

1.5 Yarn Waste during Knitting

With magazine creels, there is virtually no waste, since the yarn used in tailing is negligible. With non-magazine systems, $\frac{1}{2}$% waste would normally be expected from the 4-kg undyed package, and 1% for the 1·5–2-kg package.

1.6 Continuity of Yarn

Since modern yarn-dyeing machines have an average capacity of 600 kg, it would be normal to knit this amount of yarn as one batch for a single-shade fabric. This would leave, on average, a residue of 1·5–2% of yarn. Although this yarn residue might be knitted with subsequent dye batches in some non-critical constructions, this would not normally be possible, especially where an even fabric of a critical construction is required.

1.7 Uniformity of Shade

To produce an accurate shade match, the techniques of yarn- and piece-dyeing are very different. In yarn-dyeing, great care must be taken in the shade-matching of textured yarn to ensure that the yarn to be compared is at a similar tension to the standard and that it has the same amount of lubricant. If there are any differences in these respects, the shade appearance in the fabric will be different. An allowance must also be made for some degree of package-to-package variation and inside–outside package variation.

In the piece-dyeing of fabric produced from the same merge of supply yarn (one merge may run for six months), accurate colour matches can be obtained relatively easily. This enables deliveries of fabric to be consistent from month to month. Matching is much easier, since the sample fabric and the standard are compared in the tension-free condition. Rectification is also easier than it is with dyed yarn, which thus reduces waste or reject fabric. This is also assisted by the use of automatic dyeing systems and computer-controlled colour-matching techniques.

The resulting consistency of shade ensures that deliveries of fabric to customers are uniform, and this in its turn considerably assists the making-up process.

1.8 Rejection of Fabric

In the U.K. market, different commercial standards are applied to piece-dyed fabric and yarn-dyed fabric. The easiest way to distinguish this difference in acceptance level is to use the Barriness Scale developed by Hatra (formerly the Hosiery and Allied Trades Research Association). This enables fabrics to be graded on a 1–5 scale, 1 being very bad and 5 nearly perfect. The normal gradings that would be acceptable in commercial practice are:

> piece-dyed: 4 and 5;
> yarn-dyed: 3, 4, and 5.

1.9 Financial Effects of the Process Route

If the cost of undyed yarn ready for knitting is taken as 100 units per kg, the process costs given in Table II are applicable (in the U.K.).

Table II
Comparison of Costs of Piece-dyed and Yarn-dyed Systems

Product or Process	Cost of Piece-dyed System	Cost of Yarn-dyed System
Yarn ready for knitting	100	160
Knitting	33	40
Finishing	57	36
Total	190	236

The costs given in the table assume that the dye-fastness levels are equal in all respects for both systems and that the residual shrinkage of the fabric conforms to international standards. Any reduction in these standards would affect the price levels of both process systems equally.

2. ADVANTAGES OF DRAW-TEXTURED YARN OVER CONVENTIONALLY TEXTURED YARN FROM A DRAW-TWISTED SUPPLY

2.1 Introduction

In Section 1, the use of draw-textured undyed yarn has been compared with that of dyed yarn. There are also significant improvements that arise from the use of draw-textured undyed yarn rather than conventionally textured undyed yarn from a draw-twisted supply. These are detailed below.

2.2 Fabric

Yarn produced on the simultaneous-draw-texturing system dyes to a more level shade than yarn produced by the draw-twist–texture route. This has facilitated the successful production of plain-coloured fabrics with critical constructions and has increased the range of colours able to meet commercial standards of acceptance.

For example, at one time, a very critical fabric in a customer's choice of a wine shade could not be made on a 48-feeder machine because the reject level was too high to allow a commercially acceptable price. This fabric is now made successfully by using draw-textured yarn. A list of shades that could not be used commercially with conventionally textured yarn but can be produced successfully by using draw-textured yarn is given below.

2.3 Fabric Yield

To give the same fabric yield, fabrics made from draw-textured yarn should be knitted 10–15% slacker. The speed of production is therefore increased since 10–15% more yarn is fed per machine revolution.

2.4 Package Size

With the advent of large direct-knitting packages produced on modern draw-texturing equipment, many knitters are installing different systems of operation from those traditionally used in bulk production. A system that has been set up in a mill in a Continental European country and is being currently considered for new plants in England provides a good example of this trend.

The machines are operated in units of twelve and are placed as shown in Fig. 2. By locating the stop motions at the end of the creels, much easier threading and observation by the operative are possible. To ease the viewing of the fabric being knitted and to enable larger rolls of fabric to be produced, the machines are mounted so that the fabric may be seen by the operative at eye level. This enables rolls of up to 45 kg to be knitted, which in its turn reduces handling and waste in finishing. Boxes are used to collect the fabric for transportation.

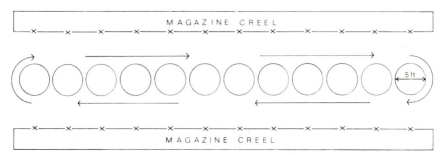

Fig. 2
A novel installation of knitting machines and creels
× Stop motion
➡ Patrol route of operative

This system reduces the labour content normally used; one man per shift with one loader (working only during the day) will be required to staff this installation instead of the usual three shifts of two men. In addition, the use of magazine-creeling reduces yarn waste to an absolute minimum. With the creels separate from the knitting machines, the latter can be placed only 2 ft (0·61 m) apart.

2.5   Creels

If this system is examined in more detail to find what benefits can be derived from its use and then compared with systems that are currently in use in the U.K., it can be seen that there are significant savings to be made.

The average size of knitting mill in this country is approximately 72 machines, and a work load for a knitting operative is generally recognized as being approximately 288 feeders (or six 48-feeder machines). This size of plant would therefore require a knitting staff of 36 persons to operate the plant on a three-shift 120-hr week.

The same number of machines operated from creels with stop motions located in lines, with yarn-loading done independently, would require a knitting staff of eighteen plus six creel loaders, which would represent a saving of $33\frac{1}{3}\%$.

At present-day labour costs, this equates to a saving of approximately £40,000 per annum, which easily offsets the cost of installation. Also to be taken into account is the fact that, in existing plants, service men are employed to deliver yarn to the knitting machines from the yarn store. With the system of creeling described, the creel loader would carry out these duties in addition to the creeling of yarn, which would increase the savings detailed above.

Creeltex Ltd,
Cobden St,
Leicester.

14—FALSE-TWISTED PRE-ORIENTED POLYESTER-FIBRE YARNS AND THEIR USE IN FABRICS

By A. Krieger

The processes of spinning polyester-fibre yarns at high speed (i.e., above 2500 m/min) and of simultaneously draw-texturing this pre-oriented yarn (POY) were accepted all over the world between 1971 (or thereabouts) and 1975 as an optimum from both economic and qualitative aspects. As a consequence of this rather hasty evolution, there exist numerous opinions on the advantages of this product and process that need to be reviewed, such as those relating to dyeability, running efficiency, and productivity. Quantitative correlations for POY-texturizing parameters and textured-yarn properties are dealt with in this paper. Some correlations between textured-yarn characteristics, finishing conditions, and the properties of knitted fabrics are discussed, and remarks on textured polyester-fibre yarns in woven fabrics cover questions relating specifically to textured POY.

1. PRE-ORIENTED YARN: A FOUR-YEAR REVOLUTION?

The present importance of high-speed-spun polyester-fibre continuous-filament yarn (i.e., yarn produced at speeds above 2500 m/min) and its performance in simultaneous draw-texturing may appear to be the result of a revolution. In 1971, there were rumours of new ways of combining drawing and texturing, but hardly any technical papers were published on this subject at that time.

In 1972, it was announced that several fibre producers had started operations in draw-texturing plants[1], and two different new processes were said to be being used:

> (a) using false-twist machines equipped with an additional drawing zone and working with undrawn yarn (i.e., yarn spun at 900–1300 m/min);
>
> (b) spinning at speeds above 2500 m/min and texturing on standard false-twist machines[2].

By 1973, it was evident that the 'political' aspect of the problem was the more important: throwsters were building their own fibre-producing plants[3] and fibre producers were starting to operate their own draw-texturizing machines[4]. Of the two different processes for draw-texturing, both offering economic advantages, only one, the use of pre-oriented, age-stable yarn (POY) is a really practicable way for the fibre producer and throwster to co-operate when their plants are far apart.

At that time, it became clear that the following four processes were available for the production of false-twisted polyester-fibre yarn:

> (a) spinning, draw-twisting, or draw-winding; possibly spin-drawing; false-twisting the drawn yarn in a separate operation;
>
> (b) spinning at low speeds (900–1300 m/min) and draw-texturing this unstable yarn by the simultaneous process;
>
> (c) sequentially draw-texturing this yarn on a texturizing machine with additional drawing equipment;
>
> (d) high-speed spinning (above 2500 m/min) and simultaneously draw-texturing the stable POY.

Processes *(b)* and *(c)* are preferably used in texturizing plants adjoining spinning plants. (The term 'producer-textured' has no technical significance. Fibre producers can use all four processes.)

In 1973, several patent applications for these processes were published. For the ATME-I, eight machine builders brought out their new draw-texturing equipment[5]. Scientific papers, such as one by Lünenschloss[6], opened up discussion on the processes involved. Studies on friction-twisting[7] showed the additional economic potential of POY but mentioned that simultaneous draw-texturing with friction spindles would be very difficult (an opinion that no longer seems valid).

In 1974, the situation was apparently elucidated: the different types of flat yarn were defined[8]; Monsanto published their book 'Draw-textured Yarn Technology'[9]; and numerous papers dealt with the technical and economic aspects of the processes involved[10-13]. Since then, there has been a continuous flow of information: patents, technical bulletins from machine builders, exhibitions such as the ITMA Exhibition in Milan, scientific papers, and so on.

Looking back, one could say that the evolution took about four years to attain the present level of technically and commercially established processes. The main technical conditions were: the general availability of high-speed winders, adequate spin finishes, and essential modifications to texturizing conditions.

However, POY and draw-texturing are clearly not as recent as is commonly believed. Carothers[14] described the method of producing oriented yarns by high-speed spinning as early as 1931. Patents covering the draw-texturing of undrawn or pre-oriented yarn have existed since 1956[15,16]. Furthermore, there is no fundamental barrier to overcome between spinning speeds of 900 and 3500 m/min: the increase in speed was only a logical step in a steady technological evolution.

2.   ADVANTAGES OF POY: ASSERTIONS AND FACTS

There exist to-day some generally accepted views on POY, such as claims that POY can be textured at higher speeds and gives a yarn of better dye-uptake regularity with lower torque and that fabrics made from this yarn have a superior handle. Statements such as these are not strictly correct and must not be taken as the absolute truth. They usually result from experimental work on a few spindles, compared with standard production coming from old spinning, draw-twisting, and texturing equipment. With up-to-date equipment, one can, for example, produce by 'classical' processes a textured polyester-fibre yarn with excellent dyeability and hardly any rejects in many thousands of tons of knitted fabrics dyed by different customers in critical shades. This is real proof that good-quality yarn can be produced by the traditional process. Unfortunately, there is no generally accepted method for judging the regularity of dyeing characteristics. Oversimplification in testing and in interpreting test results to-day causes much confusion. A critical discussion of the subject was presented by Wrye[17], and modern views on fibre structure in draw-textured polyester-fibre yarn in relation to dyeability have been published[18,19].

It is well known that the running efficiency in texturing may vary between pirns of drawn yarn from different sources and sometimes between different merges or even within a merge. The same will be true of POY. With well-adapted yarn types, correct transportation and handling, and optimized texturizing conditions, both POY and fully drawn yarn will give the same excellent running efficiency. Poor results are frequently not very easy to analyse correctly: one or more of several reasons, such as the spin finish, the packaging of bobbins, the creel geometry, or the thread guides, may be the specific cause.

Since drawn yarn and POY need to be textured under their specifically optimized conditions, comparative experiments to prove the existence of a possible intrinsic advantage in the running efficiency of one or other of the two yarn types are difficult and should be made with large quantities over a longer period of time.

That higher productivity is achieved by using higher speeds in texturing is another assertion that ought to be analysed critically. Speed limits in operating plants can be determined by the equipment (the creel quality, the spindle type, the heater length, and the machine construction itself) or by the yarn properties (the unwinding behaviour of the flat yarn, the spin finish, or the textured-yarn properties). It is not very easy to separate these contributions to productivity for a very different new yarn type. If, as is customary in working with POY, the creels, heater temperatures, spin finish, and specifications for textured yarn have recently been optimized, the result may obviously be better than that obtained with products and processing conditions that have been unchanged for a long time.

Statements on textured-POY properties also call for a rather sophisticated analysis. Admittedly, cross-sections of these filaments may be rather deformed circles, but, between textured drawn yarn from pirns, simultaneously draw-textured undrawn yarn, and sequentially draw-textured undrawn yarn, there are more common aspects than real specific differences. Texturizing conditions affect yarn cross-sections in a very broad range within these different processes. Similarly, the amount of torque (twist liveliness and snarling) of the yarn does not simply depend on whether POY or drawn yarn has been textured. As a consequence, the handle and lustre of the fabric may be different for original POY and drawn yarn, but it need not be so. Here—in addition to the influences of texturing conditions just mentioned— conditions of dyeing and finishing are of paramount importance. All this means that, for the knitter or dyer, POY will bring different minor advantages and new possibilities for smaller product modifications. For the throwster, however, POY has one important advantage: it is available in a package size of around 10 kg on bobbins with transfer tails.

3. OPTIMIZATION OF THE PROCESS AND PRODUCT IN THE DRAW-TEXTURING OF POY

If one begins to look very closely at the process and expertise of texturing, one will discover two rather disturbing facts:

> in spite of the many billion pounds of false-twisted yarn produced, the relevant expertise still depends on the actual machines that a producer or researcher uses to such a degree that results published in generalized form (such as the maximum speed, optimum heater temperatures, and yarn characteristics) are usually not valid for other equipment;
>
> for the two decisive yarn characteristics of this process—dyeability and bulk—no scientifically appropriate and correct values exist (from the

point of view of the macromolecular yarn structure and textile application of the yarn) that can be easily measured in practice and are generally accepted.

Despite this, a generalized approach to optimized conditions for texturizing POY is presented (see Fig. 1). The procedure consists of two clearly different phases: firstly, in three nearly independent steps that will give approximately the desired yarn characteristics and process efficiency, the texturizing conditions are determined. Secondly, with minor modifications and with regard to the priority given to the desired yarn properties, the final settings of the machinery are optimized.

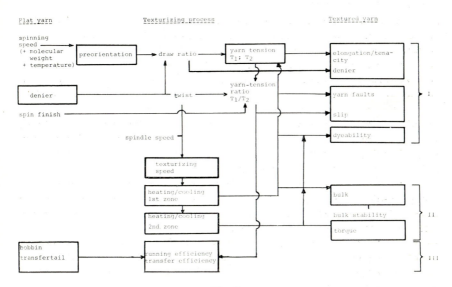

Fig. 1

Draw-texturing polyester-fibre POY: flow chart for optimizing the process and the product

For the first step (I in Fig. 1), a specification will be given for the elongation, tenacity, and linear density of the textured yarn. With a given pre-orientation of the flat yarn and with the permissible yarn tension during draw-texturing, the draw ratio will be fixed. At this stage, the fibre producer has to adjust the linear density of the flat yarn. Once the linear density is given, a provisional twist is also fixed. The draw ratio determines the yarn tension. Obtaining a yarn without slubs and without slip will depend on the spin finish, which in turn determines the yarn-tension ratio. The dye-uptake characteristics of the yarn are partly dependent on the draw ratio.

In the second step, the limits of the spindle speed of the various machines determine the texturizing speed, since the twist level has already been fixed. The temperatures are set to obtain the desired level of bulk for a given heater length in the first and second heater zones and the respective cooling zones. These temperatures will simultaneously give the torque and the final dyeing characteristics. This procedure clearly confirms the statement of Gupta and Kumar[20] that four basic parameters define the process of texturizing: tension, twist, time, and temperature.

The third step is a mechanical check of the yarn path, beginning with the bobbin of flat yarn and ending with the bobbin of textured yarn.

In practice, there will now be produced a quantity of yarn under equilibrium conditions, which should give significant results for running efficiency and yarn characteristics. These results have to be analysed thoroughly. They will give a basis for the second phase of optimizing, a clear priority of the properties to be changed, and a quantitative statement of the changes required. This will allow a final optimization along the same lines as that in the first phase, just described.

The series of graphs in Figures 2–5 may illustrate some aspects of the restricted area for this process of optimizing draw-texturing (the results refer to POY of 270 dtex, spun at 3500 m/min and textured on a Scragg SDS II machine, with a heater length of 1·5 m).

Yarn tension is predominantly determined by the draw ratio, as is shown in Fig. 2. It can be reduced by using a higher twist level[21]; in practice, this usually leads to slightly higher twists than those indicated by the traditional Heberlein formula for drawn yarn. It is well known that raising the temperature of the first heater raises the crimp, whereas raising the temperature of the second heater lowers the crimp. Torque and crimp are

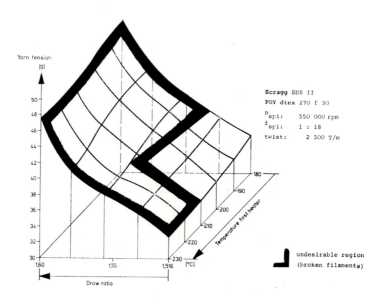

Fig. 2

Yarn tension before the spindle

influenced in the same direction, as is shown in Fig. 3. Figures 4 and 5 demonstrate that, by changing temperatures, draw ratio, and overfeed, only relatively small modifications of torque level can be obtained. If, as will be pointed out later, torque is a very important yarn characteristic in textile operations, additional means apart from texturizing conditions must necessarily be studied to reduce torque.

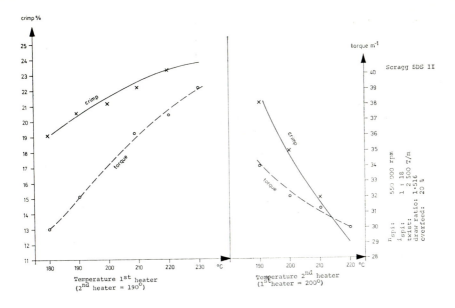

Fig. 3

Crimp and torque as functions of the temperatures of the first and second heater zones

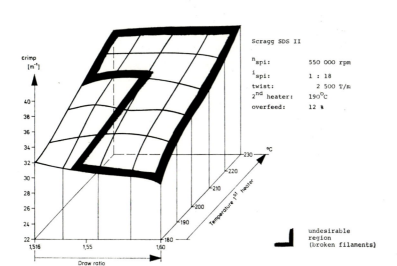

Fig. 4

Crimp in relation to draw ratio and temperature in the texturing zone

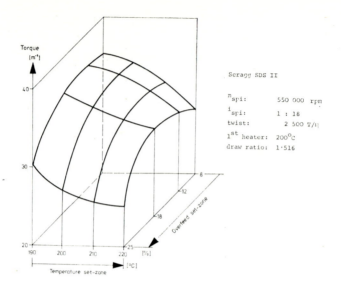

Fig. 5

Torque in relation to temperature and overfeed in the setting zone

It must be stressed that Figures 2–5 should be taken as merely an example. Repeating the same series of experiments on other draw-texturing equipment will give qualitatively the same correlations but may show considerable differences in the absolute values.

4. CORRELATIONS BETWEEN THE PROPERTIES OF TEXTURED YARN AND THOSE OF DYED FABRICS

It has just been mentioned that a few main parameters govern the predominant characteristics of the textured yarn. It is mainly the temperature difference between the first and second heaters that determines crimp and torque. Since, in practice, crimp is not very easy to measure and is difficult to express in illustrative terms, we conclude with the question: is it possible to predict fabric properties from the settings of the texturing (and knitting) equipment?

This subject is at present controversial[22–24]. The sum of the properties of the finished fabrics is so complex that it seems quite unreasonable to give a simple and definite 'yes' to this question. But, within the limits of certain aspects, predictions on dyeability and high–low characteristics (i.e., 'relief' and 'blister' effects) of a double-jersey fabric are possible and can be generalized, as is shown below.

POY (draw ratio 1·7) was draw-textured on a Heberlein FZ 27 machine at 275,000 rev/min and with 2500 turns/m in the yarn. Different temperatures were used for the first and second heaters. Two different fabrics were produced: a plain overknit and a high–low type. After being washed, they were dyed in a jet machine with 0·16% Palanilgelb 3G, 0·052% Palanilblau R, and 0·18% Palanilbrillantblau BGF. The dyed fabrics were treated on a stenter for 30 sec at 165° with 5% underfeed. The fabric weights were between 235 and 255 g/m².

Textured POY can show minor dyeability faults, such as short-length variations (up to a few centimetres of yarn) in dye-uptake (probably due to oscillations in the drawing zone). These defects are only detected in a plain fabric and are not found by the standard test methods. Even the recently published[25] sophisticated method for measuring streaks in dyed fabrics will not enable one to discover this defect. The above visual ratings of a fabric finished under industrial conditions give reproducible results that are of practical use to the knitter and dyer.

On the other hand, the ability of a yarn to give well-structured high–low fabrics cannot be predicted from flat fabrics. Here, too, the visual rating gives reproducible results that are of practical use in industrial production.

From the results in Table I, the following conclusions can be drawn. Yarns with a high crimp dye regularly but give a poor high–low appearance. For a standard yarn, a compromise solution will be found when the temperatures of the first and second heaters are identical. However, in this generalized form, the statement is only true for the Heberlein FZ 27 machine. For a Scragg SDS II, rather different settings give the same result: for the transfer of such results from one type of machine to another, knowledge of the measured yarn property is still indispensable.

5. WOVEN FABRICS OF TEXTURED POLYESTER-FIBRE YARN

There are two main different areas, each with its own specific problems: lightweight, silk-like fabrics on the one hand, and fabrics with comfort stretch, mainly for men's wear, on the other.

The first of these categories is not at present concerned with POY. This is the area of developments in modified cross-sections, speciality fibres such as differential-dyeing types, heather yarns, slub yarns, and so on. A survey of these yarns as produced in Japan was published in 1975[26].

Discussing the area of textured polyester-fibre yarns for men's wear and other outerwear and considering why no worldwide success has so far been registered here as in knitted fabrics, one arrives at a situation as shown in Fig. 6. Firstly, the consumer judges the textile article by comparing it with

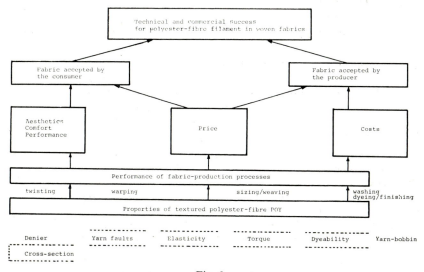

Fig. 6

Flow chart for the technical and commercial success of polyester-fibre yarns in woven fabrics

Table I

Knitted Fabrics of Draw-textured Pre-oriented Polyester-fibre Yarns*

Machine-settings			Textured-yarn Properties		Visual Ratings for Properties of the Finished Fabric	
First, T_1 (°C)	Second, T_2 (°C)	ΔT ($T_2 - T_1$)	Crimp % (Hatra)	Torque (turns/m)	Dyeability†	High–Low Character‡
220	200	-20	11·5	20·7	1·5	3
210	200	-10	10·4	20·3	1·6	3
220	210	-10	9·6	18·9	2	3
200	200	0	9·5	16·1	2·3	3
210	210	0	8·8	16·9	2·5	3
220	220	0	8·6	16·1	2·5	1
210	220	10	7·9	15·9	2·7	1·5
200	210	10	7·9	13·9	2·5	1

*Produced on Heberlein FZ 27 machine.

†Plain fabric, knitted on Mayer OV 36 machine, 30 in. wide, 36 systems, 18-gauge.

Ratings: 1 = evenly dyed, no streaks; 3 = poor regularity.

‡Blister fabric, knitted on Mayer Jacquard OV-JA II machine, 30 in. wide, 24 systems, 18-gauge.

Ratings: 1 = sharp limits between high and low; 3 = unclear, not very high.

a wool or cotton fabric. In his opinion, a polyester-fibre fabric of to-day made from 167-dtex × 2 yarn is, in its over-all characteristics, clearly not as good as a fabric made from natural fibres. This judgement can alter when the price of one of these fibres is drastically changed. Secondly, the sections of the industry that use textured polyester-fibre yarn (weaver, dyer, outfitter) have been familiar with natural fibres for a very long time, obtain them at a reasonable price, and do not have very serious problems in working with them. Changing to synthetic fibres needs minor adaptations of the equipment. It is a vicious circle: as long as the consumer does not ask for this product, there is no great market for a standard fabric sold in large quantities. If it does not exist as a standard item, the weaver is not ready to exploit his own specialized skill, and it is difficult for the fibre producer to develop sophisticated modifications of yarn properties if his customer does not use them under really optimized conditions.

Without modifications of yarn properties and without optimizing the processes of weaving, finishing, and tailoring, there will be no men's wear that satisfies both the consumer and the textile industry. The conditions under which top-quality fabrics of textured polyester-fibre yarn can be produced have been described elsewhere[27, 28], but some key properties of textured POY will nevertheless be discussed here; they will always be the foundation of any technical and commercial success with fabrics made from such yarns. Unlike drawn yarn, for which the fibre producers offer a large selection of linear densities and values of linear density per filament, POY has, up to now, usually been sold in only one linear density and linear density per filament. This may change in the future, but, especially where spinnerets need to be replaced (with those of different numbers of filaments or different cross-sections), it will not happen very quickly. Since it has to be proved by the aesthetic appeal and performance of the finished fabrics which linear density is the best, the choice of novel linear densities is very difficult. This is an additional reason why it is improbable that POY will be available in a wide range of linear densities in the near future.

For the weaving process, the number of yarn faults is the predominant criterion of quality, a situation rather different from that obtaining in the knitting process. Yarn faults cannot be eliminated by any process step (either by twisting or by sizing), so the POY that is the starting material and all subsequent steps and their respective products must be constantly and carefully checked for broken filaments. The spin finish, yarn tension, thread guides, and handling of bobbins are the main points on such a check list.

The elasticity of the textured POY is the property that enables the finisher to optimize the properties of the fabrics. This is the main reason why textured POY for fabrics is used in its high-elasticity, high-bulk form, even though the set fabric shows only comfort stretch. There are numerous papers that discuss this question of setting textured polyester-fibre yarn, and two recent ones are worthy of note[29, 30].

Torque is a yarn property that is frequently very annoying. Since the troublesome loops develop only in the loose yarn, warping is the most critical process: if a yarn that shows very frequent filament breaks has to be warped, it will often be necessary to interrupt the winding process; every stop gives at least the possibility of having no yarn tension. A poor-quality warp will be the result. The loop-forming propensity of the yarn depends on different parameters. The take-off behaviour of the textured-yarn bobbin is a first point; if the yarn falls off the bobbin by itself whenever there is no yarn tension applied, loop-forming will be very probable. This behaviour is caused by the crimp elasticity and the intrinsic torque properties of the textured yarn, by the winding conditions for the textured yarn (the thread tension, hardness of the bobbin, and yarn-crossing angle), and by the yarn surface as modified by lubricants. Finally, the act of unwinding (directions p or q and free or impaired ballooning) can reduce or aggravate the loop-forming tendency. Winding, creeling, and warping of the textured yarn therefore require a very careful and co-ordinated optimization.

Finally, dyeability must be discussed. Although hundreds of papers on this question have been published, no generally accepted test method for judging this decisive aspect of quality exists. There probably never will be one. Dyeability, on the one hand, reflects the entire structure of the poly(ethylene terephthalate) fibre, and it will never be possible to give one single figure that completely describes this structure. On the other hand, dyes, dye auxiliaries, and dyeing conditions have a decisive effect on the result: the visual aspect of the dyed fabric. It is only natural that very misleading results can frequently be drawn from oversimplified tests. In the end, it is the over-all judgement of the visual aspect of the dyed fabric that is decisive, differences in yarn crimp contributing to its appearance.

Only up to a certain degree will it be possible to specify yarn characteristics that are prerequisites for a good fabric; the regularity of all properties is essential[31].

ACKNOWLEDGEMENT

The author is indebted to many engineers in his company's development department and in its production plants who contributed facts and opinions to the view of a many-sided process expressed in this paper.

REFERENCES

1 I. R. Brunet. *Mod. Text.*, 1972, **53**, No. 6, 18.

2 *Chemiefasern/Textilindustrie*, 1972, **22/74**, 860.

3 *Textile Industr.*, 1973, **137**, No. 4, 85.

4 *Text. World*, 1973, **123**, No. 4, 53.

5 *Chemiefasern/Textilindustrie*, 1973, **23/75**, 1094.

6 J. Lünenschloss. *Chemiefasern/Textilindustrie*, 1973, **23/75**, 1067.

7 W. Klein and A. Trummer. *Text. Mfr*, 1973, **100**, No. 1, 16.

8 A. Heierle. Shirley Institute Publication S.12, 1973, 94.

9 Monsanto Co. 'Draw-textured Yarn Technology', 1974.

10 K. Schultz. *Chemiefasern/Textilindustrie*, 1974, **24/76**, 819.

11 M. J. Denton. *Text. Inst. Industr.*, 1974, **12**, 5.

12 O. L. Shealy and R. E. Kitson. *Text. Res. J.*, 1975, **45**, 112; *Mod. Text.*, 1975, **56**, No. 7, 10.

13 J. R. Hardin in Symposium on POY Texturing, Clemson University, Nov., 1974.

14 W. H. Carothers. U.S.P. 2,071,250 (Published 3 July, 1931).

15 Heberlein Maschinenfabrik A.G. B.P. 746,992 (Published 21 March, 1956); French P. 1,098,454.

16 Imperial Chemical Industries Ltd. French P. 1,140,620; B.P. 777,625 (Published 26 June, 1957).

17 R. G. Wrye. 'Thermal History and Dye Uniformity of Textured Polyester' (paper presented at Textile Research Institute Annual Meeting, 1975).

18 V. B. Gupta, M. Kumar, and M. L. Gulrajani. *Text. Res. J.*, 1975, **45**, 463.

19 E. D. Hall and G. D. Rawlings. *Knitt. Times*, 1974, **43**, No. 12, 73; No. 14, 35.

20 V. B. Gupta and M. Kumar. *Text. Res. J.*, 1975, **45**, 382.

[21] H. Weinsdorfer and G. Egbers. *Chemiefasern/Textilindustrie*, 1975, **25**/**77**, 665.

[22] G. Schubert. *Melliand Textilber.*, 1973, **54**, 714.

[23] D. Stockmann. *Chemiefasern*, 1971, **21**, 617.

[24] P. Offermann and R. Sachs. *Dtsch. Textiltech.*, 1972, **22**, 94.

[25] C. J. Kok, P. J. Kruger, R. Lake, R. Turner, and N. van der Vlist. *J. Text. Inst.*, 1975, **66**, 186.

[26] *Japan Text. News*, 1975, Feb., 66.

[27] A. J. Weil. *Mod. Text.*, 1972, **53**, No. 7, 21.

[28] G. M. Anderson. *Mod. Text.*, 1972, **53**, No. 7, 24.

[29] H. J. Berndt. 'Untersuchungen an thermisch-mechanisch vorbehandeltem Polyäthylenterephthalat' (Dissertation, Deutsche Wollforschungsinstitut an der Rheinisch-Westfälischem Technischen Hochschule), Aachen, 1971.

[30] H. J. Berndt, G. Valk, and G. Heidemann. *Melliand Textilber.*, 1975, **56**, 137.

[31] R. P. Hale. *J. Text. Inst.*, 1975, **66**, 62.

Technical Development Department,
Viscosuisse A.G.,
Emmenbrücke,
Switzerland.

15—RECENT RESEARCH AND INDUSTRIAL APPLICATION OF SELF-TWIST SPINNING AND RELATED TECHNIQUES

By G. W. WALLS

By using one alternating twisting unit, or two such units suitably phased, and by adding unidirectional twist where necessary, a series of ten different yarn structures can be made in which staple-fibre strands are combined with fine continuous filaments. Many of the resulting yarn structures are suitable for use in weaving, knitting, or tufting and have considerable advantages compared with ring-spun or 100% continuous-filament yarns. The resulting fabrics also have better stability, strength, abrasion-resistance, and resistance to pilling and snagging.

1. INTRODUCTION

Spinning has always been expensive, and ring-spun yarns have other disadvantages, such as twist liveliness and low strength, especially in fine wool yarns for fine-gauge knitting.

The self-twist system, among other things, improved the economics of spinning, but the yarns produced are essentially two-strand yarns and cannot be spun finely enough or cheaply enough to replace singles yarns in fine-gauge knitting. This paper describes different yarn structures, related to self-twist, that are suitable for various end-uses, including fine-gauge knitting, and discusses these end-uses and the product properties. First, however, it is necessary to describe the two basic developments required before the new yarns could be produced.

2. BASIC DEVELOPMENTS

2.1 Two-stage Machines

Early in the development of self-twist, it was realized that the weakness of the twist-changeover zones could be overcome by using two stages of self-twisting on one machine[1]. Two self-twist yarns from the first stage can then be self-twisted together so that maximum second-stage self-twist occurs at the changeover zones of the first-stage yarns. The final product is thus a four-strand yarn with sufficient strength and abrasion-resistance to be weavable without the addition of unidirectional twist. The properties and potential of these yarns will be discussed later, it being sufficient here to present the concept of two-stage machines.

2.2 The Use of Continuous Filaments

Core yarns and Woolfil yarns (where the filament is on the outside of the yarn) are well known in the industry, and self-twist yarns have been spun by using cores. However, in 1966, it was realized that one component of a two-strand self-twist yarn could be a fine continuous filament (from 1 to 2·2 tex) replacing the second staple-fibre strand. It was later realized that the filament could be joined to the strand on the output side of the twist-rollers since it did not need to be twisted by them. The resulting structure is no longer self-twist, since the filament is *wrapped* around the strand in alternating directions as it is rotated by the twist rollers and fed through them. Fig. 1 is a diagrammatic representation of this structure. The twist-reversal zones are the weakest part of the yarn.

Fig. 1

STm yarn structure: a fine continuous filament wrapped in alternating directions about a staple-fibre strand

2.3 Combination Structures

It is now possible to combine the ideas presented above to produce several yarn structures in which filaments are used as one or two components in a four-strand or three-strand structure. The three-strand structure is possible because at second-stage twisting one component can now be a filament instead of a second self-twist yarn. In all, ten different yarn structures can be produced (Fig. 2). Fig. 2 also includes the shorthand nomenclature developed over the years to describe the various structures. 'S' represents the

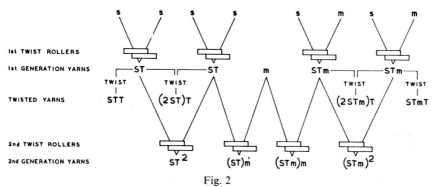

Fig. 2

The ten yarn structures that can be made by using staple-fibre strands and continuous filaments in self-twist and related spinning methods

staple strand, 'm' the monofilament or multifilament synthetic-fibre yarn, and 'T' the twist operation. Briefly, the ten yarns are as follows, the term 'self-twist' being loosely used here to describe not only the self-twist process itself but also the filament wrap about a staple-fibre strand when that strand is rotated in alternating directions:

(1) ST: normal two-strand self-twist staple-fibre yarns;

(2) STT: twisted ST yarn as now used in weaving, two strands;

(3) (2ST)T: two ST yarns plied together, four strands;

(4) STm: one staple-fibre strand self-twisted with one continuous filament;

(5) STmT: twisted STm yarn, one strand and one filament;

(6) (2STm)T: two STm yarns plied together, two strands and two filaments.

The above yarns are made by using only one twisting unit on the spinner; those following need two units:

(7) ST^2: two self-twist yarns self-twisted together, four strands;

(8) (ST)m: one self-twist yarn self-twisted with one filament, two strands and one filament;

(9) (STm)m: one STm yarn self-twisted with a second filament, one strand and two filaments;

(10) $(STm)^2$: two STm yarns self-twisted together, two strands and two filaments.

3. PROPERTIES AND APPLICATIONS

3.1   ST Yarn

This is the basic product of the self-twist-spinning system. It is a two-strand yarn with a consequent spinning limit of about 30 tex for wool. It has low strength and is unsuitable for use as warp in weaving direct from the spinner. However, it has been suggested[2] recently that the yarn can be used in this application after sizing.

The application of tension to the yarns during knitting causes them to rotate, and in the knitted fabric they try to regain their original twist level. This twists the stitch out of shape and can cause an irregular surface appearance. However, this does not happen in warp-knitted fabrics, double-knitted fabrics, and other balanced structures or for bulked yarns. In single-knitted fabrics, it can be minimized by steaming the yarn and knitting a tight structure. Multiple yarn feeds are required for fully fashioned knitting. An end-use that is growing rapidly for this yarn is sock-knitting.

3.2   STT Yarn

The yarn[3] obtained by adding twist to self-twist yarn is the basic weaving yarn, which is still the major end-use for the self-twist system. The yarns and fabrics are directly comparable with two-fold ring-spun yarns and fabrics and have very similar properties.

3.3   (2ST)T Yarn

By plying two self-twist yarns together, a four-strand yarn is obtained, which can be used to make excellent woven fabrics. These again compare favourably with a 2×2-ply ring-spun yarn and fabric. As a four-strand yarn, the linear-density limit is about 60 tex for wool.

3.4   STm Yarn

This yarn, obtained by 'self-twisting' a staple-fibre strand with a continuous filament, is basic to several of the following structures. So far, the yarn in its basic form has not been used in fabric-making.

3.5   (STm)T Yarns

By adding unidirectional twist to STm yarns, usable filament-wrap yarns are produced. However, these yarns are similar to the filament-wrap yarns that can be made on the ringframe, which are cheaper, since they do not need twisting. For this reason, the use of (STm)T yarn in weaving or knitting has not yet been fully investigated. The advantages of the process, such as ease of control of the filament in spinning and the production of large packages suitable for 2-for-1 twisting machines, may encourage the use of this structure in the future. The yarn can be spun to about 17 tex if wool is used.

3.6   (2STm)T Yarn

3.6.1   The Production of (2STm)T Yarn

This yarn has considerable potential for use in weaving. It is made by assembly-winding two STm yarns on the spinning machine and then adding unidirectional twist.

3.6.2 Spinning and Weaving (2STm)T Yarns

In Fig. 3, the strength of these yarns, made by using 60-mm-Hauteur, 21-μm wool and 1·7-tex nylon, is shown as a function of added twist. It can be seen that, in each case, adequate strength (and, in some instances, maximum strength) is obtained at very low levels of folding twist. The high strength enables high twisting speeds to be used and, together with the low twist required, cheapens twisting.

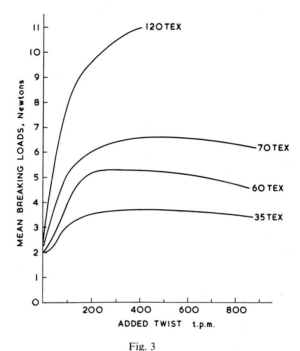

Fig. 3

(2STm)T yarns: the effect of added twist on yarn strength

A series of yarns was spun with the standard 22-cm cycle length and 1·7-tex continuous-monofilament nylon 6.6 with wool of 21-μm diameter, 71-mm Hauteur. The yarns were of R35 tex (9·7% nylon) with 200 turns/m, R60 tex (5·7% nylon) with 175 turns/m, and R120 tex (2·8% nylon) with 100 turns/m. They were twisted at 10,000 rev/min, this being the highest spindle speed available to the author at that time, to give productions of 50, 57, and 100 m/min, respectively, and woven at maximum sett. There were no end-breaks in twisting or weaving. The fabrics were stronger and had higher abrasion-resistance than the equivalent fabrics from ring-spun yarns but were stiff because of the high pick and end density.

3.6.3 Properties of Fabrics Made from (2STm)T Yarns

Two more normal fabrics were made from R50-tex yarns (6·8% nylon), twisted to 200 turns/m, and woven in a plain weave with 16·5 ends/cm and 16·5 picks/cm, and in a twill weave with 22 ends/cm and 22 picks/cm. Fabric properties are given in Table I.

Table I
Properties of Fabrics from (2STm)T Yarns

		Plain	Twill
Abrasion-resistance, Martindale (10^3 rubs)		40	54
Strength, 50-mm strip (kgf)	Warp	45	60
	Weft	41	55
(N)	Warp	441	588
	Weft	402	539
Extension at break (%)	Warp	46	48
	Weft	50	51
30-min Random-tumble pilling		0	0

These fabrics, and a similar fabric made from black and white grandrelle yarns obtained by feeding alternate black and white rovings to the spinner, had excellent handle and appearance. There were no problems in producing high-quality woven fabrics, though exhaustive production trials have not yet been made.

It is appropriate to discuss here the dyeing of yarns and fabrics, which is an important practical factor. Synthetic-fibre continuous filaments are at present available only in white in the fine linear densities used in the process. In light and medium shades, the presence of the small percentage of white filament is not apparent, and top-dyed wools can be used both in solid shades and in grandrelles. In dark shades, however, the white filament causes a speckled effect. Although this is quite attractive, solid shades are also needed. Nylon is the easiest synthetic fibre to dye in combination with wool, and in piece-dyeing or yarn-package dyeing the process is normal. For grandrelles in dark shades, there would need to be twice the number of spinning packages (or half the number of yarns) so that the individual STm yarns could be dyed separately. This has not yet been tried, and it is not known whether the STm yarn can be successfully rewound after dyeing.

3.7 ST^2 Yarns

3.7.1 Introduction

These are the first and most obvious of the yarns made by using two twisting units on the spinning machine and usable direct from that machine (after clearing). As a consequence, a considerable amount of work was done on machine development, yarn parameters, colour effects, weaving performance, etc. A brief description only of the more important factors will be given here.

3.7.2 Spinning ST^2 Yarns

The most important single parameter in spinning is the phasing of the two twisting units so that maximum second-stage twist occurs where first-stage twist is zero. Fig. 4 shows the effect of phasing on yarn tenacity for a 60-tex and a 90-tex yarn made from $20 \cdot 5$-μm wool of 62-mm Hauteur. The stronger yarns give better weaving performance. Similar results are obtained with other linear densities, though the maximum tenacity tends to be higher with finer yarns. Phasing at $\pi/2$ gives higher tenacity than phasing at $-\pi/2$ because of the skewness of the twist distribution[4] and the interactions between the two twisting units.

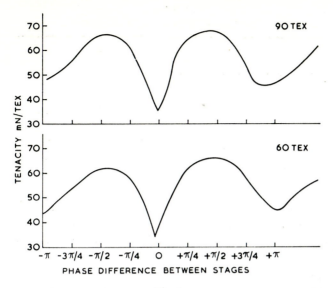

Fig. 4

ST² yarns: the effect of phasing between self-twist stages on yarn strength

Investigation of the effect of the twist level on the yarn strength by altering the amplitude of reciprocation of the twisting rollers and the cycle length showed that a 22-cm cycle length and a 10·0-cm amplitude on each stage were optimum. Longer cycle lengths give weaker yarns, and shorter cycle lengths can result in instability of the second-stage self-twist when tension is applied to the yarn. Lower amplitudes give weaker yarns, and higher amplitudes do not greatly increase strength. Since a 7·5-cm amplitude gave yarns only slightly weaker than 10-cm yarns, and the standard available self-twist roller units have a 7·5-cm amplitude, these units were used for spinning and weaving trials.

Because of the four-strand structure, the linear-density limit for these yarns for wool is about 60 tex, though 50-tex yarns have been spun.

3.7.3 Properties of ST² Yarns

Table II lists typical yarn properties (for 20·5-μm wool of 62-mm Hauteur) for this structure. The yarns are weavable as warp yarns down to the spinning limit, although the yarn-breakage rates in weaving are higher than those for ring-spun yarns of the same linear density. A wide range of fabrics has been made with these yarns used as warp.

Yarn structure and appearance differ considerably from place to place in the second self-twist cycle. In one part of the cycle, the yarn consists of two two-fold yarns lying side by side, whereas in another it is a four-fold yarn. This results in some warp streakiness and diamond barring or diagonal patterning in the weft of fabric. The latter can be avoided by mixing sufficient weft yarns in weaving so that the patterns are broken. The resulting fabric then has an attractive slightly streaky appearance in both directions. If the weft streakiness is eliminated by using a different yarn structure (e.g., STmm: see below), then the warp streakiness becomes objectionable unless hidden by the colour pattern.

Table II
Properties of Typical ST² Yarns

Property	Yarn Linear Density (tex) 50	60	70	80
Self-twist/half-cycle				
First stage	46	42	39	36
Second stage	37	34	31	28
Tenacity (mN/tex)	68	67	67	66
Extension at break (%)	13·6	16·8	18·2	20·3
Weaving breaks* (per 10^4 ends $\times$ 10^4 picks)	4·5	8·0	0·5	0

*Woven to 0·9 compactness[5].

3.7.4 Properties of Fabrics Made from ST² Yarns

Table III gives the physical properties of a range of plain-weave fabrics made by using ST² yarns in both warp and weft.

Table III
Properties of Fabrics from ST² Yarns

Property	Resultant Yarn Linear Density (tex)		50	60	80
Threads/cm	Warp		19	17	15
	Weft		16	15·5	14·5
Weight (g/m²)			197	211	272
Strength, 50-mm strip (kgf)	Warp		35	35	43
	Weft		29	31	41
(N)	Warp		343	343	422
	Weft		284	304	402
Extension at break (%)	Warp		40	44	44
	Weft		49	37	42
Abrasion-resistance, Martindale (10^3 rubs)			26	30	50
Relaxation shrinkage (%)	Warp		6·1	−0·3	−0·5
	Weft		1·2	2·0	2·2

The results in Table III are typical of the wider range of fabrics actually produced and show that the properties of ST² fabrics are very similar to those of fabrics from ring-spun yarns. Other fabric properties, such as stiffness, hygral expansion, and crimp extension, were also similar.

3.7.5 Future Prospects for ST² Spinning

Because of the linear-density limitations of the four-strand structure and the subsequent development of later structures to achieve the same ends, further work on the process was discontinued in 1967. However, it should be remembered that the process would be a cheap method for producing weavable yarns at very high speeds without the need for subsequent twisting. If suitable end-products can be defined, the method may find a niche in the range of spinning techniques available.

3.8 (ST)m Yarns

These three-strand yarns are made by 'self-twisting' an ordinary in-phase self-twist yarn with one continuous filament. Strength–phase curves similar to those in Fig. 4 showed that the two twisting units should be phased at

110° to give maximum yarn strength. The most striking property of the yarn is its even appearance throughout the cycle compared with some of the structures considered above. This applies particularly to heavier yarns, and thus it is the most likely structure to be used for carpets. An example of yarn strength for a 600-tex (ST)m yarn made from a New Zealand carpet-wool blend with one 2·2-tex nylon filament is a mean breaking load of 20 N and an extension at break of 6%. This yarn has been successfully tufted and appears to have adequate strength for this purpose.

Carpets made from the yarn have uniform appearance and have satisfactory performance properties, though much remains to be done before the process can be recommended for commercial use.

3.9   STmm Yarns

3.9.1   Introduction

These yarns, formed by self-twisting an STm structure with another filament suitably phased, are perhaps the most important of the new yarns because they are ideally suited for fine-gauge knitting. STmm yarn is a completely balanced three-component yarn with a high (> 80%) staple-fibre content and is strong in fine linear densities, where strength is critical. Strength–phase curves similar to those of Fig. 4 showed that maximum strength is obtained at 110° phase. Because of its importance, considerable efforts were made to develop this spinning technique, the result being what is now called the SELFIL spinning system[6].

3.9.2   Spinning SELFIL Yarn

A production machine has been developed[7] and was shown to the Australian industry in July 1975. Similar machines were displayed at the Milan International Textile Machinery and Accessories Exhibition in October 1975. The production of the machine and filament content of the yarn are given in Table IV.

Table IV
Production of One Machine and Synthetic-fibre Content of the Yarn

Yarn Linear Density (tex)	English Cotton Count of Yarn	Percentage Filament		Yarn Production	
		2·2-tex Filament	1·7-tex Filament	(kg/ machine–hr)	(kg/week*)
150	5·5	2·9	2·3	16·2	1800
70	12·5	6·3	4·9	7·6	840
35	25	12·6	9·7	3·8	420
31	28·5	14·2	11·0	3·4	380
26	34	16·9	13·1	2·8	310
22	40	20·0	15·4	2·4	270

*Based on a 123-hour week at 90% efficiency.

The yarn package produced on the machine is a 1·5-kg cheese suitable for package-dyeing[8], and the preferred sequence is: spin, dye, clear and wax, knit.

3.9.3   SELFIL-yarn Properties

SELFIL yarns[9] are completely torque-balanced and hence do not need steaming before further processing. They have a slightly lower CV of

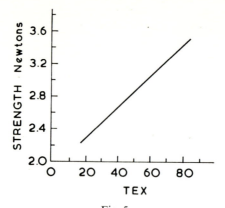

Fig. 5

SELFIL yarn strength as a function of yarn linear density

evenness and fewer over-all yarn imperfections than ring-spun yarns and are much stronger in fine linear densities, as is shown in Fig. 5 for a series of yarns made from 19·5-μm wool and 2·2-tex nylon filaments.

The spinning limit is finer than that for most other structures, as is shown in Table V for 1·7-tex filaments.

Table V

Wool diameter (μm)	19	20	21	22	23	24
Limit (tex)	19	20	22	23	25	27

The package size is usually such that clearer-winding and waxing are one to one, which thus minimizes creeling and knots and lowers winding costs. The fault rate is usually 10–12 per kg for fine yarns, and after waxing the yarn friction is substantially the same as for ring-spun yarns.

3.9.4   Knitting SELFIL Yarns

Fabrics produced satisfactorily from these yarns include 18- and 22-gauge double jersey, 22-, 24-, and 28-gauge single jersey, 15- and 21-gauge fully fashioned socks, and 40-gauge raschel. In addition, over 25,000 kg of yarn were knitted commercially before the process was first released in July 1975. By the time of this Conference, commercial production should be many times this figure.

3.9.5   Properties of SELFIL-yarn Knitted Fabrics

The fault rate is lower than that for ring-spun yarns, and mending is reduced by about 60%. Skewing of single-jersey fabrics is completely eliminated. Fabrics have better dimensional stability, higher abrasion-resistance, clearer stitch, and more even appearance and are stronger and cheaper. Properties of typical double-jersey fabrics are given in Table VI, the filaments used being 2·2-tex nylon.

Table VI
Properties of SELFIL-yarn Knitted Fabrics

	Punto-di-Roma		Single Jersey 24-gauge
	18-gauge	22-gauge	
Weight (g/m²)	350	299	193
Yarn linear density (tex)	31·6	23·4	26·6
Thickness (mm)	1·3	1·2	0·55
Needle damage	0	0	0
Abrasion-resistance, Martindale (10^3 rubs)	34	38	20
Pilling	0	0	0
Stretch (%) at 400 gf (3·92 N) Length	26·8	34·0	
Width	87·6	97·8	

3.9.6   Weaving SELFIL Yarns

SELFIL yarns are designed primarily for knitting, where they have undoubted over-all advantages[10] over ring-spun yarns. However, they can also be used as weft in weaving. So far, their use as singles warp yarn has not been successful. They can be used as warp in weaving when two-folded at low twist levels (from one-half to one-third of normal), as with (2STm)T yarns (see Section 3.6), and also when sized.

3.10   (STm)² Yarns

3.10.1   The Structure of (STm)² Yarns

These yarns are made by self-twisting two STm yarns together and are intended primarily as weaving yarns. Although they are a four-strand structure, the use of fine filaments enables the linear-density limit to be reduced to about 30 tex for wool.

3.10.2   Spinning (STm)² Yarns

Maximum strength is obtained by twisting units to $\pi/2$ as for ST^2 (Fig. 4), though (STm)² yarns are considerably stronger.

3.10.3   Properties of (STm)² Yarns

The yarns are torque-balanced. Table VII gives details of the properties and weaving performance of a range of (STm)² yarns made by using 1-tex nylon filament and 20-μm wool of 60-mm Hauteur.

Table VII
Properties of (STm)² Yarns

Property Linear Density (tex)	25	30	50	100
Wrap turns/half-cycle	35	33	29	27
Self-twist/half-cycle	47	43	32	22
Tenacity (mN/tex)	82	78	68	51
Extension at break (%)	12	11	9	6
Weaving breaks* (per 10^4 ends × 10^4 picks)	16	5	0	0

*Woven to 0·9 compactness[5]; 50 m warp except 25-tex yarn, which was 10 m.

The table shows that the yarns are quite strong and give good weaving performance. A linear density of 25 tex is the limit for spinning this wool.

3.10.4 Properties of Fabrics Made from (STm)² Yarns

Table VIII gives the physical properties of two typical plain-weave fabrics made by using (STm)² yarns in both warp and weft. The wool used was of 21-μm diameter and 65-mm Hauteur, and the filaments were 1-tex nylon 6·6. The finishing routine used was: blow, scour, dye, stenter.

Table VIII
Properties of Fabrics from (STm)² Yarns

Property / Linear Density of Resultant Yarn (tex)		30	50
Threads/cm	Warp	22	19
	Weft	22	18
Weight (g/m²)		145	205
Nylon (%)		6·7	4
Strength, 50-mm strip (kgf)	Warp	25	49
	Weft	24	44
(N)	Warp	245	481
	Weft	235	431
Extension at break (%)	Warp	31	51
	Weft	26	52
Abrasion-resistance, Martindale (10³ rubs)		20	54

(STm)² fabrics have a higher strength and abrasion-resistance than similar fabrics made from ring-spun yarns, the differences being greater if coarser nylon filaments are used, e.g., 1·7 tex or 2·2 tex. Apart from this and a difference in appearance, the fabrics have very similar properties. Again, as with ST² yarns, with adequate weft-mixing, the fabrics have a slight over-all streaky appearance when viewed under critical lighting conditions.

3.10.5 Future Prospects for (STm)² Spinning

This process should be the cheapest method known for producing what is effectively a two-ply weaving yarn, since no twisting is required and the yarn can be beamed directly from the spinner (after clearing). The success of the process therefore depends on the acceptance of slight streakiness and the inclusion of a small percentage of a continuous filament. These percentages would be the same as those given in Table IV for SELFIL yarns. There is no reason why production rates of 300 m/min should not be achieved for spinning this yarn as has been achieved for SELFIL yarns. As envisaged, the production per machine would be as in Table IX, where the yarns are designated, e.g., R31/2 tex, which is a better description than R31/4.

Table IX
Yarn Production for (STm)² Yarns

Linear Density (tex)	Production	
	(kg/machine–hr)	(kg/machine–week*)
R150/2	13·5	1500
R70/2	6·3	700
R50/2	4·5	500
R35/2	3·2	350
R31/2	2·8	315

*Based on 90% efficiency, 123 hr.

Table X

Summary of the Yarn Structures and Their Applications

Yarn	End-use	Whether in Commercial Use	Potential	Disadvantages	Advantages
ST	Intermediate to STT	Yes	—	Weak	Low cost
	Some knitting	Yes	—	Rotation under tension	Large dyeable package
	Weaving sized	No	Yes		Small lots
STT	Weaving	Yes	—	Torque-lively	Low cost
(2ST)T	Weaving	Some	—	Torque-lively	Low cost when four-strand yarn needed. Excellent appearance
				Linear-density limit 60 tex	
STm	Weaving	No	No	Weak. Low transverse stability	
(STm)T	Weaving	No	Yes, but unlikely	Cost	Linear-density limit 15 tex
(2STm)T	Weaving	No	Yes	Union dyeing or white filament shows in dark colours	Low folding twist. High strength and abrasion-resistance. Large dyeable package
ST²	Weaving	No	Yes, but unlikely	Linear-density limit 60 tex	No subsequent twisting. Torque-balanced
				Fabric appearance	
(ST)m	Production of carpets and tufted fabrics	No	Yes		Low cost. Torque-balanced
	Knitting	No	Unknown		Large dyeable package
STmm (SELFIL)	Knitting	Yes	—	Filament content	Low cost. Torque-balanced. Large dyeable package. High strength and abrasion-resistance. Linear-density minimum 17 tex
	Weaving	Yes	—	Union dyeing or white filament shows in dark colours	
(STm)²	Weaving	No	Considerable	Filament content. Union dyeing or white filament shows in dark colours. Fabric appearance	Low cost. Torque-balanced. Large dyeable package. High strength and abrasion-resistance. Linear-density minimum R35 tex/2

In each case, the machine is spinning two singles yarns and then twisting them together, in one operation, to produce a torque-balanced yarn. Other advantages of the process are expected to be similar to those of SELFIL: a large dyeable package from the spinner, more even yarns with fewer faults, stronger yarns, better performance in winding and weaving, and stronger and more abrasion-resistant fabrics. The process has considerable potential.

4. SUMMARY

Ten different yarn structures have been described (see Fig. 2) and the present applications and properties of these yarns and their resulting fabrics outlined (for a summary, see Table X). Of the ten yarn structures, two, ST and STT, have been in fairly widespread use for about four years and have been accepted commercially. One, STmm or SELFIL for knitting, has been in commercial use in Australia for nearly a year and elsewhere for a few months. It seems certain to achieve widespread acceptance in the industry. Two other yarn structures have considerable potential as weaving yarns; one, (2STm)T, could be developed fairly quickly by adding a filament creel to a standard self-twist spinner; the other, (STm)^2, would be more difficult to produce, since a two-stage machine is needed, and this would probably be developed from the SELFIL machine. Thus, for this development, there would need to be some assurance of the acceptability of the fabrics, though the yarn would be the cheapest available weaving yarn. A third structure with some potential is (ST)m for carpets and tufted fabrics, but evaluation of this is still in the early stages, and considerable development time would be needed.

REFERENCES

[1] C.S.I.R.O. B.P. 1,144,614 (Australia, 9 Aug., 1966).
[2] W. V. Morgan in Shirley International Seminar, Shirley Institute, Manchester, 1971.
[3] B. C. Ellis and G. W. Walls. *J. Text. Inst.*, 1970, **61**, 279.
[4] G. W. Walls. *J. Text. Inst.*, 1970, **61**, 245.
[5] L. Love. *Text. Res. J.*, 1954, **24**, 1073.
[6] G. W. Walls. *Proc. Int. Wool Text. Res. Conf. Aachen*, 1975, to be published.
[7] G. W. Walls. *Text. J. Aust.*, 1975, **50**, No. 8, 9.
[8] V. A. Williams. *Text. J. Aust.*, 1975, **50**, No. 9, 16.
[9] B. C. Ellis. *Text. J. Aust.*, 1975, **50**, No. 8, 11.
[10] P. Hendry. *Text. J. Aust.*, 1975, **50**, No. 9, 19.

Division of Textile Industry,
C.S.I.R.O.,
Geelong,
Victoria,
Australia.

16—THE DEVELOPMENT OF NOVEL YARNS AND FABRICS FROM NEW ZEALAND CROSSBRED WOOL

By K. Jowsey

The wool produced in New Zealand is mainly of Romney-crossbred (Romcross) type, with a mean fibre diameter of more than 30 μm. Some 60% of this wool is used in carpets. In order to increase and spread the demand for New Zealand wool, the development of new products and the processing of crossbred wool on new spinning systems have been investigated at the Wool Research Organisation of New Zealand. Details are given in this paper of the experimental work carried out on the self-twist-spinning system and of the development of crossbred knitwear, woven worsted fabrics, and some new styles of blankets.

1. NEW ZEALAND WOOL TYPES AND THEIR USES

The New Zealand wool clip is mainly composed of crossbred wool from dual-purpose sheep, i.e., those producing both meat and wool.

A breakdown of the clip by quality number is given in Table I[1]. In New Zealand, 'crossbred' wool is mainly of Romney or Romcross origin and has a mean fibre diameter of more than about 30 μm (52s quality number). In many other countries, the term crossbred relates to any wool not derived from merino sheep and coarser than about 24μm (60s). The New Zealand wools from about 24 to 30 μm are called 'halfbred' and are derived mainly from merino–strong-wool crosses such as Corriedale; they are chiefly used in apparel and blankets. The fine and medium types of crossbred wool are virtually free from medullation, but the coarser types, which are chiefly used in carpet manufacture, are partly medullated.

From Table I, it can be seen that the major proportion of New Zealand wool is crossbred. New Zealand is also the world's largest producer and exporter of crossbred wool: in 1970–71, the country was responsible for about 40% of the world production of crossbred wool of 46/50s quality number and coarser[1]. The total annual production of greasy wool in New Zealand is about 300,000 tonnes.

It is evident that crossbred wool is of considerable importance to the country's economy. However, its value per kg is lower than that of finer wools because of limitations on its current use and potential usefulness. About 60% of the wool produced in New Zealand is used in carpet manufacture locally and overseas, and the remainder is used in relatively few textile products, such as blankets, woven apparel fabrics, knitting yarns, upholstery fabrics, and drapes[2].

Table I
Composition of the New Zealand Wool Clip

Wool	Quality No.	Percentage of Clip
Merino	60s and finer	2
Halfbred	56s–60s	8
Fine crossbred	50s–56s	11
Medium crossbred	46s–50s	59
Strong crossbred	46s and coarser	20

In the last 25 years, there has been a changing pattern in fibre usage in relation to end-products. New fibres and new methods of manufacturing textile products have been evolved. Life styles and values have also changed and often require lighter, less durable, and lower-cost products, for example, knitted polyester-fibre suits and needle-punched blankets. Many of these changes have resulted in the decline of crossbred-wool products and the erosion of their traditional markets.

The reasons behind the loss of crossbred-wool markets are complex, despite the suitability of the fibre for manufacturing first-class products. They include such factors as fluctuating wool prices, weak selling, and changes of policy of manufacturing companies.

Methods of carpet manufacture have largely changed from Axminster- and Wilton-weaving to tufting and needle-punching. The growth of tufted-carpet production has been spectacular, particularly in the U.S.A., where about 95% of all carpets are now manufactured by this technique.

Similar changes in methods of manufacture have also occurred with other products. Blankets are now made by needle-punching and tufting as well as by weaving, and other forms of bed covers, such as continental quilts, have become of increasing importance. The ladies'-apparel market has swung rapidly away from woven woollen-spun products to warp- and weft-knitted fabrics and in particular to double-jersey fabric.

It is in these areas of new technology that crossbred wool has lost ground. Thus, in the U.S.A., the use of wool in carpets has declined from 95,000 tonnes per annum to 9,000 tonnes per annum during the last 25 years.

It is worthy of note that in New Zealand practically all carpets, both tufted and woven, are manufactured from crossbred wool, together with speciality carpet wools. This is due to a desire to use a locally produced raw material and thus save overseas exchange and to a Government policy that controls imports of synthetic fibres. The carpet section of the textile industry, however, has developed a great deal of expertise, particularly in tufting crossbred wool, and it now exports 30% of its production, mainly to Australia and the Far East.

The amount of wool tufted carpet produced in New Zealand in 1974 was 6 million m² (70% of the total), against 17 million m² for the rest of the world. The total world tufted-carpet production was 1300 million m². It can therefore be seen that there is a large potential for increasing the use of New Zealand crossbred wool in this product overseas.

It is evident from the above remarks that it is desirable both to develop new end-uses for New Zealand crossbred wool and to extend its use on all processing systems.

2.   PRODUCTION OF SELF-TWIST (REPCO) CROSSBRED YARNS

2.1   Introduction

The self-twist system of spinning, developed by the Division of Textile Industry of the C.S.I.R.O., Australia, is a comparatively new technique for directly producing two-fold yarns. It was considered for some time that coarse wool fibres, such as New Zealand crossbred, would not process satisfactorily on this spinning system because the long strong fibres would bridge across the two strands and thus cause end-breakages. The system was therefore recommended for use only with wool qualities of 58s (i.e., of diameter 26 μm) and finer.

The potential of this spinning system led the Wool Research Organisation of New Zealand (W.R.O.N.Z.) to investigate the problems of spinning crossbred wool on the self-twist-spinning machine[3]. The investigation centred firstly on basic spinning problems and secondly on the application of crossbred-wool self-twist (ST) yarns for knitwear and uptwisted self-twist (STT) yarns for woven (worsted) fabrics.

2.2 Spinning Trials

The initial trial was carried out on three wools with mean fibre diameters of 26, 28, and 30 μm. The problem of bridging fibres causing end-breakages was not generally encountered, and few difficulties were experienced in spinning. It was noticed that, in general, end-breakages and machine stoppages increased as the linear density of the yarn being spun from a given wool quality was decreased, as would be expected.

Noble-combed rovings were used in two weights from each wool quality. The rovings were spun to a range of linear densities, and, although the spun yarns were relatively unlevel, the end-breakage rate was within accepted tolerances until the number of fibres in the single-strand cross-section was reduced to about 40. It was observed that the spinning efficiency was slightly improved when lighter rovings and lower drafts were used. To determine whether more level yarns could be produced, series of stepwise adjustments were made to variables in the drafting zone for the 30-μm wool and a commercial 64s-quality roving that was spun for comparison. The yarn levelness was improved and was similar to what could be expected from ring-spinning[3].

In view of these encouraging results, further samples of crossbred wools were spun with mean fibre diameters of 32, 34, and 36 μm. Problems were encountered in spinning the 36-μm wool because of soft package build. This appeared to be caused by drafting of the threads during take-up. The other wools spun reasonably well provided that the mean take-up tension remained between 12 and 35 gf (118 and 343 mN). It was found necessary to increase the roller-loading when the fibre diameter was increased in order to obtain the desired twist level.

This work showed that wools coarser than 26 μm could be spun commercially on the Repco self-twist-spinning machine up to a limit of approximately 34 μm. In consequence, the machine manufacturer has withdrawn the recommendation that the machine is unsuitable for such wools.

2.3 Self-twist (ST) Knitwear Yarns

2.3.1 Scope and Limitations

The initial success in spinning New Zealand crossbred wools on the Repco machine led to examination of the suitability of these yarns for knitwear. Experiments indicated that, when ST yarns were used for single-jersey fabrics, considerable stitch distortion resulted[4]. A study of the nature of these effects indicated that stitch distortion occurred when the input tension of the yarn caused it to be trapped in the fabric with net torsional energy. This suggested that ST yarn could be used successfully on circular machines at a low tension but not on fully fashioned machines, where it is necessary to maintain yarn tension to control the yarn during knitting, particularly during stitch transfer.

Several garments with patterned structures were made on Spenser Purl circular machines and flat-bed machines of relatively coarse gauges. The yarn linear densities used ranged from R110/2 tex to R150/2 tex. With the exception of single-jersey fabrics, it was shown that products with an acceptable appearance could be manufactured from ST yarns.

2.3.2 *Uncombed ST Knitwear Yarns*

In order to reduce the cost of production, it was decided to eliminate combing and some gilling operations in the manufacture of ST crossbred yarn: in effect, to manufacture a semi-worsted yarn but with the ringframe replaced by a Repco spinner. The production route was carding, three passages of gilling, cone-roving, and Repco spinning to R110/2 tex from a 33-μm fleece wool. The yarns were package-dyed and commercially knitted without difficulty on flat-bed and circular machines. Garments produced in this way are currently being wear-tested, good results having been obtained so far.

The cost-savings achieved by using this route appear very attractive when a conventional two-fold worsted ring-spun knitting yarn is replaced. The trial undertaken was of necessity relatively small but suggested that there are commercial opportunities in the production of uncombed ST yarns for knitwear.

2.4 ST Fancy Yarns

If a coloured woollen slubbing is introduced into the drafting zone of a Repco machine, it is drafted into short clumps of fibres, which are randomly dispersed as slubs and trapped in the two-fold structure of the base yarn. Up to 20% of effect slubbing has been introduced successfully, apart from some difficulty in feeding the slubbing owing to its low tenacity. Since the commercial production of small quantities of coloured woollen slubbing would also pose problems, the system has been modified to use worsted roving and low-twist woollen yarns as effect materials, these being fed intermittently. The machine is ideal for making small lots of fancy yarns.

2.5 ST Carpet Yarns

Samples of carpet in both cut-pile and loop-pile constructions have been produced from self-twist yarns. The yarns were produced on a modified Repco spinner as ordinary ST yarn and also as ST yarn further self-twisted with a multifilament synthetic-fibre strand. The continuous-filament strand was caused to wrap preferentially around the twist-changeover zones, which thereby improved yarn appearance and increased yarn strength and twist stability. The yarns were spun to a maximum linear density of 680 tex.

The ST yarn had a low tenacity but tufted with reasonable efficiency, particularly in loop-pile structures. The loop-pile carpets had a different appearance from those manufactured from ring-spun-yarns in that, because of the varying twist angle, the loops tended to lie at different angles on the surface. This appearance has been considered unacceptable by some observers but desirable by others.

The ST yarn in a cut-pile construction produced carpet with good cover but poor tuft definition; an improvement was obtained by twisting the ST yarn with a synthetic-fibre strand, which also increased its strength and tufting efficiency. There was a problem of loop-'spearing' with both yarns in cut-pile structures; this was no doubt influenced by the low twist in the yarns and the twist reversals.

The present Repco and SELFIL machines, the latter of which will be discussed in Section 2.6 below, are not suitable for the manufacture of heavy carpet yarns because of the take-up-package size, guide sizes, roller-groove depths, etc., since the machines were designed for the production of relatively fine yarns. The laboratory experiments carried out at W.R.O.N.Z. have been made to assess the performance of yarns processed on the self-twist system and the appearance of carpets made from them. The feasibility of economically manufacturing carpet yarns by this system will no doubt be examined by textile-machinery manufacturers.

2.6   SELFIL (STmm) Crossbred-wool Yarns

The self-twist principle has recently been further developed by the Division of Textile Industry of C.S.I.R.O. to produce a finer 'single' yarn, suitable for fine-gauge knitting, which has been discussed in the preceding paper[5]. The new product, called 'SELFIL', consists of a single strand of staple fibre, self-twisted with two separate very fine continuous-filament synthetic-fibre yarns on its periphery. Depending on the yarn linear density, the filaments contribute up to 20% of the weight of the composite yarn, and they make it strong and torque-free so that it knits without producing spirality in the fabric.

Trials have been carried out on a SELFIL machine with rovings from 31- and 34-μm crossbred wool and from blends of 33- and 36-μm wool with 3-den (3·3-dtex) nylon. The results indicated that there were no major difficulties in processing the crossbred rovings. Socks and other knitted products have been made from the yarns. It is considered that the yarn may be particularly suitable for socks, since the synthetic-fibre filaments will improve its abrasion-resistance, and the replacement of two-fold yarns with a singles SELFIL yarn has commercial advantages.

3.   CROSSBRED SUITING FABRICS

A 50/52s-quality wool (of diameter 31 μm) has been used for some time by a New Zealand manufacturer for suiting fabrics with considerable commercial success. Yarn is spun from combed top-dyed material on the shortened Bradford–ASD system to R110/2 tex and woven in both plain weave and 2/2 twill into fabrics of 300 and 340 g/m², respectively. The finishing process, which included flat-setting with sodium bisulphite, was designed to provide an acceptable handle, and this, together with the attractive appearance of the fabrics, has resulted in their widespread acceptance for suits and jackets.

A recent trial has been carried out in which one half of a batch of 31-μm tops was processed on the shortened Bradford–ASD system and the other half on the Repco system followed by uptwisting (STT). The yarns were manufactured into identical cloths and finished in the same manner.

The yarns produced on the two systems showed little difference in physical properties, and no real problems were encountered in processing the crossbred roving on the Repco machine. The two fabrics were practically identical in their physical properties, though it was felt by some observers that the STT fabric had a slightly crisper handle and cleaner appearance. However, any difference between the two fabrics was marginal.

4.   SEMI-WORSTED CROSSBRED YARNS

In earlier work, W.R.O.N.Z. set out to determine whether it was possible to make attractive salable knitwear from New Zealand crossbred wools.

Two wool qualities were selected with mean fibre diameters of 33 and 37 μm and processed into yarns on the semi-worsted and woollen systems in a range of linear densities and twists. The yarns were test-knitted into plain-web and 1 × 1-rib fabrics on a 5-gauge V-bed machine.

The knitted panels were evaluated for handle and appearance. The 33-μm (48/50s) semi-worsted yarns gave an appreciably better handle than the 37-μm (44/46s), and, in the opinion of most of the observers, the handle of fabrics knitted from the former was acceptable for men's knitwear. The handle of the woollen knitted samples was considered to be inferior and unacceptable.

The appearance of the fabrics immediately after knitting was quite satisfactory. However, after wet relaxation, some stitch distortion became apparent, particularly in the 37-μm semi-worsted plain-web fabric. All the relaxed semi-worsted 1 × 1-rib samples showed a zigzag configuration of the wales, which was found to be peculiar to 1 × 1-rib fabrics knitted on flat-bed machines. Other common structures, such as plain-web, half-cardigan, full-cardigan, and 2 × 2-rib constructions, were free from the defect. Steam relaxation by open-steaming the fabric on a Hoffman press immediately after knitting largely reduced the incidence of both stitch distortion and the zigzag distortion in a 1 × 1-rib fabric.

A range of garments was made from semi-worsted-spun yarn of 33-μm mean fibre diameter. The yarn was spun and twisted to R150/2 tex with twists of 240 turns/m single and 130 turns/m folding. It had a tenacity of 6·1 gf/tex (59·8 mN/tex) and a value of $U\%$ of 12·0. The garments were knitted on coarse-gauge flat and circular machines (4–6½ gauge). The garments have been worn and have performed reasonably well, apart from some pilling on those with half-cardigan stitch (this could probably be overcome by the use of higher twist factors).

5. SEMI-WORSTED CROSSBRED TUFTED BLANKETS

Although practically all blankets manufactured in New Zealand are woven from woollen-spun yarn, an increasing number are being made on fine-gauge tufters in Australia, often from acrylic-fibre yarn. The acrylic-fibre tufted blankets are generally piece-dyed and raised to a high curly pile known as 'Sherpa finish'.

A New Zealand manufacturer made tufted blankets from woollen yarn for some years, and W.R.O.N.Z.[6] has recently carried out some extensive experiments on the use of semi-worsted-spun yarns, which are stronger and have a higher tufting efficiency.

A sound New Zealand crossbred full-fleece wool with a mean fibre diameter of 33 μm was selected for the trial. The linear density of one of the four yarns used was 130 tex, two yarns were of 150 tex with different twist factors, and the fourth yarn was of 180 tex. The yarns were tufted on a 5/64-gauge machine at stitch rates of 37, 45, and 53 stitches/10 cm and to two pile heights of 3·2 and 6·4 mm. A plain-weave cotton cloth of 150 g/m² was used as the substrate. The tufted material was piece-dyed in a winch, and various raising techniques, involving wet and dry wire-raising, teazling, and tumbling were carried out. A curly finish could be obtained in the high-pile samples by wet tumbling followed by tumble-drying, the fabric having previously been treated with 4% o.w.f. DCCA before piece-dyeing: the appearance of the finished fabric somewhat resembled that of a curly lambskin.

Large variations in dimensional stability to washing were evident. All samples were within the New Zealand Woolmark care category of 'Hand-wash or Dry-clean' (relaxation shrinkage), and some samples, especially high-pile blankets, were within the stability requirements of the Woolmark 'Machine-washable' category. However, under harsh washing conditions, pile-felting was apparent, and the resulting appearance was poor.

The blankets had good thermal-insulating properties compared with those of conventional woven blankets, mainly because of the higher degree of raising. Thus the average thermal resistance of the nine lightest tufted blankets was nearly double that of a range of blankets of comparable weight recently examined by the Consumers' Institute of New Zealand[7].

It was concluded that New Zealand crossbred fleece wool with a mean fibre diameter of 33 μm and processed on the semi-worsted system provided sufficient yarn strength for tufting and produced blankets with resilient pile and acceptable handle.

6. VARIEGATED WOOLLEN-SPUN YARNS

W.R.O.N.Z. has developed a process for the production of a woollen yarn that varies in colour along its length in a controlled and reproducible manner[8]. This system has been designed to enable a greater colour variety to be obtained in products manufactured from woollen-spun yarns.

In this process, stock-dyed wools for making variegated yarn (V-yarn) are first scribbled separately on a woollen card to produce slivers, which are stored in cans. The different-coloured slivers are then fed in a controlled manner through a sliver-selector feed mechanism onto the feed sheet of the carder section of the card, so that slubbing is produced which varies in colour along its length.

The sliver-feed mechanism is controlled electronically from a programmed punched-tape control unit. A complete change in colour can be made in as little as 20 m, or it can be made very gradually over a period of some 2000 m or more of yarn.

V-yarns are at present being manufactured commercially by one firm in New Zealand for use in weft-faced blankets. The relatively long period of the colour change, a minimum of 20 m, suggests that V-yarns will more readily find outlets in weft-predominant fabrics. These include weft-knitted products, weft-faced woven fabrics, and warp-knitted materials with weft-insertion.

7. CONCLUSIONS

In this paper, an attempt has been made both to outline the need to develop more outlets for New Zealand crossbred wool with the aim of increasing the demand for it and to describe some of the developments that have taken place at W.R.O.N.Z. in the last few years.

The use of crossbred suiting fabrics in both plain and twill weave is already well established in New Zealand. Large quantities of crossbred ST yarns have been knitted into half-hose, and ranges of variegated blankets are just going on sale. It is expected that other manufacturers in New Zealand and overseas will be manufacturing these products in the near future.

ACKNOWLEDGEMENTS

Most of the work reviewed in this paper was done by members of the Textile Technology section at W.R.O.N.Z. Commercial trials have been made with the assistance of Alliance Textiles (N.Z.) Ltd, Lane Walker Rudkin Ltd, and Mosgiel Ltd.

REFERENCES

1 'Guidelines for Wool Production in New Zealand', Editorial Services, Wellington, 1974.
2 International Wool Secretariat. 'End-uses of Crossbred Wool', Market Investigation Report, 1970.
3 G. A. Carnaby. *Text. Inst. Industr.,* 1974, **12,** 269.
4 G. A. Carnaby. *J. Text. Inst.,* 1973, **64,** 738.
5 G. W. Walls in 'The Yarn Revolution' (edited by P. W. Harrison), the Textile Institute, Manchester, 1976, p. 142.
6 B. W. Baudinet. 'Tufted Wool Blankets', W.R.O.N.Z. Confidential Report No. 22C, 1975.
7 Consumers' Institute of New Zealand. *Consumer,* 1975, No. 116, 74.
8 D. A. Ross and I. D. McFarlane. *Proc. Int. Wool Text. Res. Conf. Aachen,* 1975, to be published.

Wool Research Organisation of New Zealand Inc.,
Christchurch,
New Zealand.

THE YARN REVOLUTION

New Developments in the
Production of Spun and
Textured Yarns and their
Exploitation in Fabric Form

Papers of the 60th

Annual Conference
of the
Textile Institute
1976

Held at Harrogate

The Textile Institute,
10 Blackfriars Street,
Manchester M3 5DR

ISBN 0 900739 23 1

D
677·0286'2
TEX

Printed by Derry and Sons Limited   Canal Street   Nottingham